Science,

Community,

and the

Transformation

of American

Philosophy,

1860–1930

Daniel J. Wilson

Science, Community, and the Transformation of American Philosophy, 1860–1930

The University
of Chicago Press
Chicago and London

DANIEL J. WILSON, associate professor of history at
Muhlenberg College, is the author of *Arthur O.
Lovejoy and the Quest for Intelligibility* and coeditor
of *The Cause of the South: Selections from DeBow's
Review, 1846–67.*

The University of Chicago Press, Chicago 60637
The University of Chicago Press, Ltd., London
© 1990 by The University of Chicago
All rights reserved. Published 1990
Printed in the United States of America
99 98 97 96 95 94 93 92 91 90   5 4 3 2 1

∞ The paper used in this publication meets
the minimum requirements of the American National
Standard for Information Sciences—Permanence of
Paper for Printed Library Materials, ANSI Z39.48–
1984.

Library of Congress Cataloging-in-Publication Data

Wilson, Daniel J., 1949–
    Science, community , and the transformation of
American philosophy, 1860–1930 / Daniel J.
Wilson
        p.   cm.
    Includes bibliographical references.
    ISBN 0-226-90143-2
    1.   Philosophy, American—19th century.
    2.   Philosophy, American—20th century.
    3.   Philosophy and science. I. Title.
B895.W55   1990
    191—dc20   89–35929
                                                        CIP

For Carol

Contents

Acknowledgments

The research and writing of this book have stretched back more than ten years. In that time I have accumulated a number of debts to institutions and to individuals, which I would like to acknowledge in gratitude. Without their assistance, I could not have completed the project.

I would first like to thank those institutions that supported this project with financial resources and with time away from teaching. The initial work was undertaken as part of a feasibility study for a proposed history of the American Philosophical Association funded by the American Academy of Arts and Sciences. Although that project did not materialize, I want to thank Maurice Mandelbaum, Lewis White Beck, the American Philosophical Association, and the American Academy of Arts and Sciences for the opportunity to survey a number of manuscript holdings and to begin the research for the manuscript that I did write. Much of the research for the book was undertaken in 1981–82 when I was the recipient of an American Council of Learned Societies fellowship. I am especially grateful to the American Council of Learned Societies because the fellowship gave me an extended block of time when I was not yet eligible for a sabbatical.

Muhlenberg College has been extremely supportive, as have two of its presidents, John H. Morey and Jonathan C. Messerli, several of its deans, including Harold L. Stenger, Walter E. Loy, and Nelvin L. Vos, and two department heads, Katherine S. Van Eerde and Edwin R. Baldrige. In addition to granting the leave of absence in 1981–82, Muhlenberg appointed me the first Class of 1932 Research Professor in 1986–87. This appointment enabled me to write the first draft of the manuscript, and I am grateful to the College, to the Class of 1932, and to Dean Robert C. Williams, who was instrumental in the appointment. Bob Williams not only lent institutional support to the book, he also shared a keen interest in the subject and before his untimely death stimulated my thinking on Peirce, James, and Dewey. The College has also supported several summers of work through its faculty summer research program. Two Muhlenberg librarians, Christine Fiedler and Scherelene Schatz, patiently answered my questions and found obscure sources. Finally, I want to thank Elaine Bailey Petkus and Marcia Teeno of the college word-processing center and John Malsberger of the history department, who introduced me to the mysteries and joys of the computer. I am very grateful to Muhlenberg for all its support.

I want to thank two journals for permission to reprint in chapter seven parts of essays that originally appeared in their pages: *The Journal of the History of Philosophy,* for permission to use parts of "Professionalization and Organized Discussion in the American Philosophical Association, 1900–1922"; and *The Transactions of the Charles S. Peirce Society,* for permission to use parts of "Science and the Crisis of Confidence in American Philosophy, 1870–1930."

This book is about the community of philosophers, and it is only appropriate that I have benefited from the contemporary community of scholars. Over the years several colleagues have read all or part of the manuscript. I would especially like to thank James Hoopes, James Kloppenberg, Bruce Kuklick, Theodore Schick, Ludwig Schlecht, and Larry Shiner. All have made valuable suggestions, even if I have not always followed their advice.

The support of friends and family has made the rather lonely work of scholarship easier to enjoy. At Muhlenberg, John Malsberger, Joanne and Charles Mortimer, Ludwig Schlecht, and Ann Wonsiewicz have been especially supportive. Paul Paskoff and Roger Ekirch have continued the support and encouragement that began in our days as graduate students. My family, especially my sister, brother, mother, and mother-in-law, have always been warmly encouraging. Finally, I owe the greatest thanks to Carol, who has known this book as long as she has known me. Carol has become a good editor, a fine friend, and a wonderful companion. For all that, and more, this book is dedicated to her with love.

ONE

Introduction

In 1901 William James rejected an invitation to join the newly established American Philosophical Association with the observation that "the philosopher is a lone beast dwelling in his individual burrow." James later relented and joined the association, but his hesitancy reflected his conviction that individual vision was the central feature of anyone's philosophy. His friend Charles Sanders Peirce, on the other hand, wanted to bring philosophers out of their burrows and to encourage cooperative inquiry with other philosophers and scientists. Peirce, in spite of his personal isolation, envisioned bringing philosophy into the ranks of science, "where investigators, instead of contemning each the work of most of the others as misdirected from beginning to end, coöperate, stand upon one another's shoulders, and multiply incontestable results."[1] Peirce urged the creation of a community of inquiry dedicated to the pursuit of truth through scientific methods. James's and Peirce's conceptions of the philosopher represented the extremes—the individual man of vision versus the cooperative man of science—as philosophers between 1860 and 1930 tried to come to terms with the rising power and prestige of the sciences, with the tendencies toward professionalization and specialization gaining wide acceptance within the universities and academic disciplines, and with their own feelings of inadequacy engendered by these changes. The comments of James and Peirce suggest the range of the philosophers' responses as they sought to adjust their modes of inquiry, their conceptions of truth and knowledge, and their sense of what it meant to be a philosopher and to do philosophy to the emerging academic consensus that put a premium on science, specialization, and professionalization.

1

   This study explores the American philosophers' responses to the rise of the natural, physical, and social sciences at the end of the nineteenth century and to the emphasis which academic culture placed on scientific values and methodology, specialization, and professionalization. Beginning with three philosopher-scientists—Chauncey Wright, Charles S. Peirce, and William James— it traces philosophers' evolving ideas on the proper relationship between the values and the methods of science and the influence these ideas had on their conception and practice of philosophy. In addition, I will examine the creation of a professional academic discipline of philosophy by the early twentieth century. How philosophers conceived their tasks and the philosophical positions they adopted, and how these conceptions were affected by the social and cultural contexts in which philosophers lived and worked, are both crucial to tracing the evolution from theologically tinged moral philosophy to scientifically oriented, professional philosophy between 1860 and 1930.

   The turn-of-the-century philosophers' responses to the prevailing scientism of the period and to the professionalization of higher education had important consequences for the practice of philosophy in America in the twentieth century. By attempting, in diverse ways, to accommodate philosophy to the power and success of science and the scientific method, they set the stage for the rise of technical, professional philosophy later embodied in logical positivism and analytic philosophy. In taking this course, they unintentionally created the basis for philosophy's growing marginalization in twentieth-century American culture, as the community of philosophic discourse contracted to a relatively small professional circle. Yet, at the same time, the work of the three great pragmatists—Charles Peirce, William James, and John Dewey—laid important groundwork for the late twentieth-century reaction against a narrow analytic philosophy. James's and Dewey's critiques of a dogmatic scientism and Peirce's and Dewey's arguments for a communal notion of truth have received renewed emphasis in the work of such diverse philosophers as Richard Rorty, Hilary Putnam, Richard Bernstein, and Karl-Otto Apel. These are the themes which I will explore, but the context of emergent scientism and professionalism in the late nineteenth century first needs to be established.

   At the beginning of this period moral philosophy prevailed in philosophical instruction at the nation's colleges and universities. Moral philosophy embraced the humanities and much of what is now regarded as social science. Usually taught by one professor, often the college president, moral philosophy mixed metaphysics, social science, and religion in an amalgam that was both descriptive and prescriptive. The appeal of moral philosophy to antebellum America lay in its ability to "supplement religious sanctions with natural bases for value" and to perform "the integrative, synthesizing function theology" had once undertaken. Moral philosophy's central role in the curriculum was soon to be diminished.[2]

American science in 1860 stood ready to be launched upon its modern career. Scientists in the early-national and antebellum periods had begun the transition from gentleman amateurs to trained specialists. By midcentury a community of professional scientists had clearly emerged. They were increasingly specialized in their education and in the subject matter of their inquiries and characteristically found employment in the colleges of the period. Modern American science, in the view of Robert Bruce, was launched between 1846 and 1876. Science became even more specialized; its growing complexity demanded "formal scientific education and full-time professional work." The requirements of higher education, of close communication among active researchers, or "reliable evaluation" of results, and of the institutions, laboratories, and funding to support experimentation meant that "the pursuit of science had to become a collective enterprise." More and more, "science came to see itself, and society came to see it, as an established profession."[3] Because the education of scientists and so much of the research was centered in the colleges and universities, the rise of modern science transformed higher education, the academic professions, the criteria of truth and knowledge, and, inevitably, philosophy.

The development of university-based science altered significantly the structure and curriculum of the antebellum college and gave rise to the modern research university by the end of the nineteenth century. Roger Geiger has recently argued that natural science gained "a foothold in American higher education around the 1850s," that colleges institutionalized "utilitarian objectives" in the 1860s, and that they established "research-based graduate training" in the 1870s. Combined, these three trends reshaped the intellectual and academic landscape. Academically, they meant the creation of new departments, disciplines, and schools, the development of new courses of study, and the establishment of new procedures for the education, hiring, and retention of scholars. Intellectually, these developments fostered the triumph of the "general principle of cognitive rationality—knowing through the exercise of reason" that was quickly becoming "a paramount intellectual value in strategically important institutions." This "advancing scientism," as Laurence Veysey recognized, was not universally applauded or accepted within the academic world. Nonetheless, it shaped the institutional and intellectual matrix within which philosophy and the other developing academic disciplines operated.[4]

The professional academic disciplines developed in tandem with the rise of the research university. The pattern of the early nineteenth century had been scholars who were broadly educated in science or the humanities and professors who taught a wide range of subjects under the umbrella of natural history or moral philosophy. More than one professor observed that his chair was really a "settee." By midcentury, especially in the sciences, specialists were coming to be more highly valued than generalists. The growth of knowledge and the higher level of education necessary to understand the new sciences, to teach them, and to perform research, fostered specialization. Specialization in turn encouraged the creation of distinct academic disciplines and professions.[5]

The emergence of the academic disciplines in the last quarter of the nineteenth century was a manifestation of the "culture of professionalism" characteristic of the period. Several features of intellectual life and of higher education encouraged the creation of distinct academic specialties organized as separate disciplines and professions. The growth of specialized and often esoteric bodies of knowledge required specialization in scholarship. Such scholarship necessitated extended and narrowly focused training which became available with the development of doctoral programs in the last quarter of the century. That higher level of education and the awarding of specialized degrees gave scholars grounds for claiming authority over particular bodies of knowledge. Once a field had begun to be differentiated, its practitioners formed a community in order to secure recognition of their authority and legitimacy. Professional associations, annual meetings, specialized journals, and separate university departments characteristically marked the creation of a new discipline. In addition, academic professionalization usually meant some degree of commitment to the idea of scientific rigor and empirical investigation and, not infrequently, a belief that real progress in the discipline was possible through scientific cooperation. An established profession had the power to determine the criteria for admission to its membership, to establish the boundaries of legitimate inquiry and professional practice, to resist external standards of evaluation, and to win recognition of its professional status and autonomy from other professions and from the society at large.[6]

Professionalization involves more than the establishment of journals, associations, and departments. In addition to these institutional features, there is also a substantive component. The substantive dimension embraces the broad intellectual consensus and the methodological framework within which recognized professionals work. The achievement of substantive consensus is more elusive but no less important than the institutional aspects in shaping the future of a profession. The degree of substantive coherence with regard to legitimate questions, values, and methodologies strongly influences the institutional coherence and vigor of a profession, at least in its formative years. Although philosophers had established the institutional features of an academic profession by 1900, they failed throughout this period to create a firm substantive consensus. The result was repeated defections from the traditional preserve of philosophy and a crisis of confidence in the ability of philosophy to withstand the challenge of science to its values and methodologies.

The philosophers' success in emulating the institutional features of the academic professions, combined with their failure to achieve substantive consensus, had some benefits. It enabled philosophers to transform their study from an all-embracing humanistic inquiry into a recognized and accepted academic discipline without entirely discarding the heritage of moral philosophy. The process of professionalization within philosophy was at odds with the typical pattern of the other disciplines. The disciplines characteristically coalesced around a newly specialized body of knowledge. Scholars sought to have their knowledge and authority in a particular area legitimized and recognized, and so they cooperated in the establishment of associations, journals, and departments. The process often meant separation from more general associations and departments and the creation of more narrowly specialized journals. The result, especially in the sciences, was the creation of a more exclusive community centered on a newly defined consensus of competent investigators.[7] The pattern of philosophy, however, was significantly different. It was from the Middle Ages to the nineteenth century the "queen of the sciences" from which such specialized studies as economics, sociology, political science, and psychology emerged. When the philosophers organized at the turn of the century it was a defensive move, an effort to prevent further defections by taking on the characteristics of the already professionalized disciplines. The philosophers wanted to restore the authority and legitimacy philosophy had once enjoyed and to partake of the strength and prestige that seemed to accrue to the more highly organized disciplines. Theirs was not so much an effort to create a new exclusivity as to gather up the remnant of the old moral philosophy, rejuvenate it with the values and methods of science, and restore philosophy to its rightful place at the center of human inquiry and the university curriculum.

Ironically, the new trends toward professionalization and specialization encouraged in philosophy an acceptance of subspecialties that worked against any effort to reshape the discipline on the model of the sciences. While some of the younger men and women fought to establish scientific values and methods as the touchstone of professional philosophy, other philosophers struggled to preserve for their study the broader, humanistic characteristics. While the science-minded emphasized those inquiries they thought most susceptible to a scientific treatment, such as logic or epistemology, the more traditional scholars pursued metaphysical and ethical studies. The scientific philosophers never proved strong enough in this period to define philosophy solely in their own image, and the tendency toward specialization helped preserve the older methods, as a kind of pluralism was accepted. By the 1920s, philosophers found themselves specializing in one or more fields, such as logic, epistemology, ethics, or metaphysics. The logicians and epistemologists might regard their study as more scientific and thus in some sense better than that of the metaphysicians, but they could all find a place as specialists under the umbrella of the professional discipline of philosophy. The failure of the scientific philosophers to enforce substantive coherence upon the discipline prevented the defections that surely would have taken place had a scientific standard been imposed. If the resulting profession was less coherent and less "scientific" than its disciplinary competitors, it nonetheless won grudging recognition from the other academic professions, an established position in the new universities, and the benefits of an intellectual community for its practitioners.

Science was the model for these professionalizing philosophers, but science's precise lineaments were often in dispute or ambivalently regarded. The philosophers of this period were not consistent in their understanding of what science was, either as a set of values or as a methodological system.[8] Many philosophers thought their own inquiries were scientific so long as that meant only that they were careful, logical, and rigorous. Others went further in advocating the adoption of more specific scientific methods and values taken over from the special sciences like chemistry or physics. Those like John Dewey, Charles Sanders Peirce, and Arthur O. Lovejoy argued that where and when philosophers sought truth it could be achieved only through scientific methods. Still more restrictive were philosophers like Christine Ladd-Franklin who proposed to limit philosophy to those inquiries most amenable to scientific treatment. There was, however, considerable variation within these broad categories. Most philosophers developed a distinct standpoint vis-à-vis science, and some, such as Dewey and Peirce, saw their ideas change as their philosophies matured.

Much of what the philosophers responded to between 1860 and 1930 was not science, but rather the prevailing scientism of the period. The emergence of modern science early in the period, the scientists' continued success in providing physical explanations of natural phenomena, the translation of abstract science into practical technology, and the rise of scientific study and research in the emerging universities fostered a high regard for scientists and scientific values and methods among scholars and ordinary citizens alike.[9] Ironically, the first generation of philosophers—Wright, Peirce, and James—was more solidly trained in science than its students and successors. The second generation of professional philosophers was educated in the scientific ideal, not in science, and was less scientific and more scientistic. Many in the second generation felt the appeal of an ostensibly more certain means to truth that had won wide approbation both within the university and within the larger community, and they grew anxious for the fate of philosophy if it was thought to be unscientific.

The seductiveness of the prevailing scientism and the anxiety over philosophy's ability to conform to an emerging intellectual and academic consensus gave rise to a crisis of confidence among American philosophers. What was the proper relationship between philosophy and science? What was the proper role for philosophers in the new universities? Could, or should, philosophy become a specialized science or must it retain its broad synthesizing role and emphasis on values? The failure to answer these questions definitively undermined the philosophers' confidence in the centrality of their work to the academic and intellectual life of the nation.

The challenge of the sciences in this period came on three levels: the metaphysical, the methodological, and the sociological. All three will be discussed in the pages that follow, but the emphasis will be upon the methodological and sociological challenges. Metaphysically, science seemed to undermine the older, value-oriented world view which had recourse to providence, final causes, and absolutes, and which had provided a basis for understanding the nature and destiny of humans. The success of scientific methodologies in establishing solid knowledge of the physical world challenged philosophers to explore the extent and ways in which philosophical inquiry could or should be modeled upon them. Sociologically speaking, the philosophers were forced to confront the increasing prestige of science and scientists within the university and the larger scholarly community. Philosophers thus struggled to define a new role for themselves consistent both with the new scientific disciplines and with the more traditional conceptions of philosophy. By the 1920s the crisis of confidence was resolved in favor of scientific rigor and philosophical specialization, but earlier that outcome was by no means certain, as philosophers sought ways to incorporate the benefits of science without losing the traditional strengths of philosophy.

In studying the transformation of philosophy between 1860 and 1930, my approach has been shaped by the concept of communities. The idea of community has been a particularly fruitful one in twentieth-century thought. Several of the philosophers discussed here developed sophisticated and important theories of community, particularly Charles Peirce, John Dewey, and Josiah Royce. More recently, historians such as David Hollinger, Thomas

Bender, and Thomas Haskell, philosophers including Richard Rorty, Hilary Putnam, and Karl-Otto Apel, sociologists such as Magali Sarfatti Larson, and literary critics including Stanley Fish, have placed the notion of community near the center of their analyses of intellectual activity.[10] The idea of community is thus both the subject of much of this study and a concept useful to understand the development and transformation of American philosophy. Consequently, community as understood by the philosophers and community as an organizing principle of this book need to be clarified before proceeding.

David Hollinger's idea of "communities of discourse" provides a basis from which to begin to analyze the philosophical communities of the turn of the century. Hollinger has described discourse in this context as "a social as well as an intellectual activity; it entails interaction between minds, and it revolves around something possessed in common." Participants share "certain values, beliefs, perceptions and concepts," but especially they share "*questions.*" A particular community of discourse establishes boundaries within which ideas and questions are held in common and regarded as important. The community may be informal or formal, intimate or dispersed, but membership originally established on intellectual or social criteria is ultimately recognized by both those within and those outside the community. In philosophy at least, professionalization and specialization involved community formation, as small numbers of like-minded scholars recognized their affinities and shared values, entered into frequent and stimulating conversation, sought to establish criteria for participation in the more exclusive discourse of the community, and ultimately struggled to secure public and academic recognition of the new profession and discipline.[11]

Shared discourse entails a shared vocabulary, shared methodology, and shared ideals or goals for the conversation. Hollinger's notion of discourse enables us to define the broad contours of the community, but it needs to be supplemented by some basis for determining the means by which the participants recognize their discursive colleagues. Vocabulary, methodology, rhetoric, and the uses of institutional power redefined the philosophical community in this period. For example, the vocabulary of philosophical debate shifted at the turn of the century toward the use of scientific terms; to participate in the debate meant accepting new terms and new meanings for old ones. A sensitivity to the vocabulary of the debates and to the shifting meanings provides an entry into the shifting contours of more specialized discourse within the larger philosophic community. As Richard Rorty has noted, the choice of a vocabulary is determined largely by perception of one's relationship to the "history of philosophy," by which he means contemporary debates as well as historical ones.[12] Similarly, rhetorical devices can not only shape the debate, but can help determine who is qualified to participate and can serve to exclude those who are not. David Leary, for example, has recently argued that certain rhetorical strategies, particularly well-chosen analogies, helped ensure the triumph of the New Psychology between 1880 and 1920.[13] The metaphors and analogies of philosophical discussion in this period helped to create the ideal of the new, more scientific philosophy which attracted many philosophers. Methodological considerations can also be used to include or exclude particular participants in the debate. The way one responded to the call for establishing a more scientific philosophical method, modeled on that of the natural and physical sciences, served to place one within the debate. Finally, as Magali Sarfatti Larson has recognized, the institutional aspects of a discipline can be employed to determine who has the "right to speak in the name of Science."[14] The struggle to organize discussion within the American Philosophical Association is one example of the uses of institutional power to reshape the community. These concepts, then, provide a means to discern the shifting boundaries of the subcommunities within the broader community of philosophical discourse.

The idea of community and of discourse as understood by Hollinger and others thus serves as a method of analysis in the pages that follow. Several of the philosophers central to the course of philosophy in this period developed important notions of community and communal notions of truth and knowledge. For Peirce, the community of inquiry was central to his conception of the scientific method, both in science and in philosophy. His community of inquiry was the most narrowly and scientifically conceived. He envisioned a community of inquirers dedicated to the pursuit of truth in some indefinite future, whose best collective judgment provided warranted belief for the present. Josiah Royce built upon Peirce's ideas to develop his own idea of a community of interpretation. Royce's community of interpretation was more broadly conceived, although it contains within it a conception of the scientific community. For Royce late in his career, reality became a process of interpreting the world, a process infinitely extended, with spiritual unity the ultimate but unattainable goal. John Dewey's instrumentalism also had a strong communal component, for truth was socially validated as part of the communal process of inquiry, leading eventually to community action ensuring social reconstruction. More clearly than Peirce or Royce, Dewey focused his democratic community on reconstructing the lived-in context of the members of the community, through a process involving all members of the community. Finally, although James was the most individualistic of the pragmatists, his pragmatic test of truth, as James Kloppenberg has argued, had a social dimension. Truth could not be pragmatically validated in the long run unless it was ultimately consistent with the experiences of others.[15]

These different and contemporary conceptions of community provide an important way to understand the transformation of philosophy at the turn of the century. Peirce's austere notion of a community of inquirers dedicated to a pursuit of truth based on his view of scientific process provided a model to philosophers seeking to turn philosophy into a science. But, as we will see, many philosophers in the period were uncomfortable with such a restricted conception of philosophy. Royce and others also wanted to view philosophy as a community, but a community with a wider basis than science and with a wider range of methodologies consistent with the long history of philosophical thought. Dewey and his followers were willing to accept the contributions of science to knowledge and to adhere in some measure to a scientifically based method of inquiry. However, unlike Peirce, they thought inquiry should focus on the practical problems of social reconstruction.

These rival conceptions of community helped shape the debate about how philosophy and philosophers should respond to the challenge of science and scientific method between 1860 and 1930. By the 1920s, however, something approaching Peirce's narrower conception of inquiry was becoming ascendent. Broader metaphysical and ethical studies began to give way to technical studies addressed primarily to a more restricted audience of professional colleagues. Although rival conceptions by no means disappeared, the more technical study, represented by the work of C. I. Lewis, was coming to be seen by many of the younger philosophers as the proper style of philosophical inquiry. The narrowing of philosophical inquiry and philosophical discourse was accentuated after 1930 by the rise of logical positivism and analytic philosophy, which dominated much of post-World War II American philosophy.

In the past fifteen years, the pragmatic notions of community and of the communal conceptions of truth and knowledge have received new attention from philosophers. In reacting against analytic philosophy, some philosophers have moved away from the idea that scientific inquiry can, if properly conducted, provide a certain basis for truth or can provide a foundation for our inquiries. Richard Rorty, for example, has built upon Dewey's ideas to criticize representational theories of knowledge and to support his idea of conversation.[16] Hilary Putnam and Karl-Otto Apel have found support in Peirce as they have developed their ideas of warranted belief.[17] Finally, Richard Bernstein has drawn upon both Peirce and Dewey to support the communal aspects of praxis.[18] These contemporary debates lend a new relevance to the debates of the turn of the century over the impact of science and the development of a philosophical community. Although most of the following chapters will focus on the historical debates, I will explore some of the contemporary ramifications in the conclusion.

Many of the disputes about the role of science in philosophy and about the rival conceptions of community which are traced in the following chapters reveal philosophers struggling to define the new boundaries of their discipline. What, exactly, was to be the role of scientific values and methodology in determining who was to be considered a philosopher? Which criteria were to be used in determining whether scholarship was philosophical, scientific, or mystical? Just what kind of community should the philosophers constitute? Much of the anxiety expressed by both the more scientific and the traditional philosophers turned on this question of who was a participant in a particular community of discourse. The scientific-tending philosophers tried to remold philosophy into a science to overcome their worries about recognition from the scientific communities. The traditional philosophers worried that the drive to make philosophy more scientific would exclude them from the community of recognized philosophical discourse. Although the boundaries of philosophical discourse contracted from the broader claims of the moral philosophers, they ultimately proved sufficiently elastic to harbor a wide range of philosophical subspecialties in the academic discipline of the early twentieth century.

T W O

The Scientist

as Philosopher:

Wright, Peirce,

and James

The publication of *The Origin of Species* in 1859 has long been considered a landmark in the shift of modern thought from a religious and theological basis to a more secular and scientific foundation. Chauncey Wright testified for many young men when he wrote a friend in early 1860, "I have just finished reading [*The Origin of Species*], and . . . I have become a convert."[1] The publication of Darwin's book came at an opportune time. The broader issue of the role and place of science had for some time been growing in importance and had prepared fertile ground for the appearance of new theories and explanations. Had the groundwork not been laid in the scientific, philosophical, and even theological writings of the century, the conversion of young men like Wright would not have come so easily. Darwin's writings, however, along with significant progress in the physical and practical sciences, set off a wave of reflection on the relationship of the sciences and their methods to the more traditional pursuits of philosophy and theology.

The writings of Darwin and the discoveries in the sciences encouraged a new mode of philosophizing more informed by the values and methods of the natural and physical sciences. Throughout much of the nineteenth century, American scientists had been held in the grip of a Baconian image of science closely allied to the common-sense philosophy of the Scottish Realists. The Baconian thrust of American science was often vaguely conceived, but generally embraced empiricism (science is based on observation), an antitheoretical stance (the scientist avoids using hypotheses), and an emphasis on classification and taxonomy as the highest goals of science.[2] Baconian science and common-sense realism were allies in providing an explanation of the physical world based on the senses. It was an explanation which did not challenge the faith that there was some larger purpose to the universe, that there was a larger meaning to the material world. The developing sciences at midcentury were beginning to challenge this comfortable, even complacent, relationship of science and philosophy. While empiricism remained a cornerstone of the new science, it was now avowedly theoretical and hypothetical. Classification and taxonomy were no longer sufficient. The scientists increasingly developed theories to explain their evidence and offered hypotheses to guide future work. They relied on theories and hypotheses even when all the evidence was not yet in. The explanatory power of these new theories quickly reduced the need and inclination to refer to and to rely upon divine power; now, workable explanations could be offered solely within the material realm. This new science not only reshaped understanding of the physical world, but forced as well a redirection and reconstruction of philosophy.

Three young men trained as scientists—Chauncey Wright, Charles Sanders Peirce, and William James—led the shift toward a philosophy significantly influenced by the new science, if not entirely grounded in it. These men brought to their philosophizing a thorough training in the methodology and values of science and a conviction that scientific methodology provided a sure path to knowledge about the physical world. They were not, however, without their differences on the value of science or on the proper relationship of science and philosophy. Though science undoubtedly would have had a significant impact on American philosophy had Wright, Peirce, and James not bridged the two disciplines in the 1860s and 1870s, their experiences and ideas are important to the scientific turn in American philosophy at the end of the century.

The ideas of Wright, Peirce, and James are crucial to the transformation of philosophic thought in America, but these men also represent a transition in the practice of philosophy. Philosophy had traditionally been the preserve of theologically orthodox moral philosophers who had used their positions, often as college presidents, to bolster the moral and religious fiber of their students. The task of the moral philosophers was not to uncover new truth, but to defend the old. Although the best of the moral philosophers, such as James McCosh, were well aware of the scientific controversies of the early nineteenth century and tried to keep abreast of new developments, the scientific training of Wright, Peirce, and James clearly represented a departure.[3] Their scientific education had prepared them to ask new questions, to expect that philosophy would be compatible with the new sciences and not ignorant of nor hostile to them, and to be open to inculcating philosophy with the values and methods of the physical sciences.

The education and careers of these three men represent a crucial transition from the moral philosophers of the denominational colleges to the professional academic philosophers of the emerging universities. At midcentury most collegiate philosophers still came from theological or religious backgrounds, and religious orthodoxy was still a key test for appointments in philosophy. For example, Princeton University trustees seeking a new president in 1868 found James McCosh appealing, in part because he was "a solid religious thinker in an age of waxing scepticism." McCosh was a more subtle philosopher than many of the collegiate philosophers; he had made genuine contributions to the development of Scottish Realism and to the history of philosophy. More typical, perhaps, were Mark Hopkins of Williams and Francis Wayland of Brown, whose texts on moral science enjoyed wide readership at midcentury. These texts and the philosopher-presidents who taught from them "rationalized man's duties and exhorted the students to carry them out." The moral philosophers emphasized understanding human nature and its varied products as manifestations of God's will. Moral philosophy at most antebellum colleges, thus, "performed the integrative, synthesizing function theology had performed at medieval universities."[4] However sophisticated, the moral philosopher's writing and teaching was firmly rooted in religious tradition.

By the turn of the century most academic philosophers were products of graduate schools in philosophy or psychology. The scientific training of Wright, Peirce, and James thus distinguished them from both their predecessors and successors. Their difficulties in obtaining academic posts in the late 1860s and the 1870s, and, excepting James, in keeping the appointments they received, reflect both their temperaments and their incompatibility with the emerging professional culture. The personal characteristics of Wright and Peirce might have made an academic career difficult at any time, but their discomfort was increased because they did not fit the traditional patterns of philosophy, and a new pattern had yet to be established. James, after a protracted struggle, eventually found a position at Harvard. Once there, he helped lay the foundation for the creation of a specialized and professional academic discipline, even while remaining aloof from its more restrictive aspects.[5]

Two aspects of this transition in philosophy warrant careful scrutiny: the social, cultural, and intellectual milieu in which Wright, Peirce, and James came of age, were educated, and began to philosophize; and their initial efforts to reconcile the apparently competing claims of science and philosophy. What was common to and distinctive about their formative experiences which impinged on their philosophical development? What were the social and intellectual imperatives that led them to a new mode of philosophizing more cognizant of the values and methods of science? How did these influences, intellectual and otherwise, come together for them as a philosophical stance toward science in the two decades after *The Origin of Species?* What were they proposing, and how different were their conceptions of the relationship of science and philosophy? These questions must be addressed if we are to understand the part played by Wright, Peirce, and James in the alteration of American philosophical thought and practice in the third quarter of the nineteenth century.

The three young intellectuals came together in Cambridge, Massachusetts, in the 1860s and 1870s. Wright, the oldest, was born in Northampton, Massachusetts in 1830; Peirce, in Cambridge in 1839; and James, in New York City in 1842. In the early 1870s Wright served as the philosophical mentor to the younger men, especially Peirce, although Wright's intellectual background was the least impressive. Wright's father was a deputy sheriff and merchant in western Massachusetts, whereas Henry James, Sr., and Benjamin Peirce were both significant intellectual figures. The senior James, freed from the necessity to earn a living by a substantial inheritance, was a well-connected philosophical theologian and a prime exponent in the United States of the ideas of Emmanuel Swedenborg. Benjamin Peirce was a prominent mathematician and scientist and a long-time professor of mathematics and astronomy at Harvard. In contrast to the relative isolation of the Wright household in Northampton, both the James and Peirce homes were centers of intellectual activity.[6]

While both the elder James and Peirce played host to the diverse intellectual figures of antebellum America, a more eclectic and less scientific group seems to have passed through the James residence. Henry James was particularly close to Ralph Waldo Emerson and the circle around him. Furthermore, James frequently moved his family, often in search of better or different educational experiences for William and Henry, Jr. The peripatetic family took up residence in New York, Newport, Albany, and Boston, as well as in various European cities. Once the James family settled in Cambridge in 1866, their circle of intimates intersected significantly with that of the Peirces.[7] The Peirce home in Cambridge was similarly a center of intellectual activity, though scientists dominated. Charles recalled that because of his father's prominent position as a leading mathematician and scientist, "all the leading men of science, particularly astronomers and physicists, resorted to our house; so that I was brought up in an atmosphere of science. But my father was a broad man and we were intimate with literary people too." As Murray Murphey has noted, "the Peirce children thus grew up in an atmosphere which was at once scientific and cultured—in the best Boston sense."[8] Peirce and James had the advantage in growing up of wide exposure to the leading intellectuals. For them, intellectual activity was not pursued in isolation, but in a community of scholars and inquirers.

Wright's entry into this intellectual and scientific milieu came later, following his graduation from Harvard in 1852. At Harvard, he had been a student of Benjamin Peirce excelling in mathematics. Following his graduation he took a position with the *Nautical Almanac,* where he again came in contact with the senior Peirce. Wright had his own circle of intimates in Cambridge, which included James Thayer, who would edit his letters, Ephraim Gurney, later to become Dean of Harvard, and Charles Eliot Norton and his sisters Grace and Jane. After Henry James moved his family to Cambridge, Wright became a frequent visitor. By the mid-1860s, then, Wright had fully entered into the intellectual and social orbit of James and Peirce, and the close proximity of the three men facilitated intimacy and discussion.[9]

Though Wright was admitted to the intellectual community of Cambridge, he came as an outsider, albeit a brilliant and charming one, at a later stage in his development, and he never quite belonged. His hours were odd, his working habits unconventional, and his living arrangements solitary. The sense of intellectual community which James and Peirce imbibed from an early age would mark their philosophical views, just as Wright's isolation marked his. It is not merely coincidence that James was notoriously open and friendly to a diverse grab-bag of thinkers, while Peirce emphasized the community of inquiry, nor is it solely coincidence that Wright advocated scientific agnosticism with regard to broader theories, or upheld the suspension of judgment. Peirce and James had seen at an early age the benefit of communal inquiry, while Wright had had to pursue a more lonely course.

Their formal training in science set these three men apart from most of their contemporaries. Wright, Peirce, and James benefited from the growing presence of scientists in the colleges. By midcentury, the catchall natural philosopher had been replaced by several professors of mathematics, chemistry, geology, or botany. The increasing differentiation of the sciences reflected the growing complexity of scientific knowledge, but it also gave to the various disciplines a new credibility as each in turn gained a chair or professorship.[10] By the time Wright entered Harvard in 1848 he could receive a thorough grounding in the sciences. Benjamin Peirce, the Perkins Professor of Mathematics and Astronomy, made the greatest impression on the shy youth from western Massachusetts. Wright excelled in working proofs in Peirce's class and in tutoring his less-gifted classmates. Charles Peirce entered Harvard in

1855 after a rigorous intellectual upbringing supervised by his father. Peirce's college experience, however, was "notable chiefly for its utter lack of distinction." He studied mathematics under his father and his older brother, took a minimum of religion and as much science and philosophy as possible. The course work by and large failed to excite him, although his extracurricular studies in mathematics and in philosophy, particularly Kant, provided the excitement lacking in his classes.[11]

In 1847 Harvard had established the Lawrence Scientific School to give even greater credibility to and training in the sciences. Peirce, after a year surveying in Louisiana following his 1859 Harvard graduation, entered as a student in chemistry. Here his abilities were more fully engaged, and his talent began to reveal itself. After two years of study he received an M.A. in 1862, and the following year he received the first Harvard Sc.B. in chemistry granted summa cum laude.[12]

James studied chemistry at the Lawrence Scientific School, but with much less enthusiasm and success than Peirce. James came to Lawrence from Newport, where he had been studying art with William Morris Hunt. The shift from art to science was difficult for James and came, in part, out of deference to the wishes of his father. James initially studied chemistry with Charles W. Eliot and then anatomy and physiology with Jeffries Wyman. Eliot later recalled that "James was a very interesting and agreeable pupil, but was not wholly devoted to the study of chemistry." In addition to Eliot and Wyman, Louis Agassiz played a major role in James's scientific education. James first heard him at the Lowell Institute. Then, in 1865–66, he worked with Agassiz on a scientific and exploring expedition to Brazil. When he left for Brazil, James had already shifted his studies from the Lawrence Scientific School to the Harvard Medical School. The shift was also not an entirely happy one, as James's wayward course to a medical degree would indicate. His formal education as a whole was marked by repeated trips to Europe to escape tensions at home and at school, to take cures for various physical and neurasthenic ailments, and to further his studies, especially in psychology. In spite of the interruptions, James completed his M.D. in 1869, though he never practiced medicine and seems never to have had any real intention of doing so.[13]

Wright, Peirce, and James thus had the benefit of perhaps the best scientific education to be had in America. By later standards, it was somewhat haphazard and unfocused. There were, for example, no formal entrance requirements to the Lawrence Scientific School and no prescribed curriculum; the degree was conferred by examination when the professor determined the student was sufficiently prepared.[14] Still, it was an education in which the methods and values of science, not of theology or philosophy, dominated.

While Wright and Peirce were clearly more committed to the study of science than James ever was, all three men had received training that was unusual for the time and unheard of for a philosopher.

Wright, Peirce, and James shared more than an education in Cambridge; they also shared ideas. The intimacy of the Cambridge setting encouraged interchange among intellectuals who had been educated together and who now found themselves seeking an outlet for their speculations. Before ideas ever saw print, they were presented, discussed, and criticized in the clubs, drawing rooms, and studies of Cambridge and Boston. Wright's strongest talents, by all accounts, lay in philosophical conversation and Socratic dialogue. In the late 1850s, Wright was part of a group, composed largely of Harvard friends, which called itself the Club, or the Septem. They met informally but regularly, for the reading of papers and ensuing discussion.[15] Later, in the early 1870s, Wright, Peirce, and James were core members of a group which Peirce called the Metaphysical Club. Here Wright became the philosophical mentor to the younger scientist-philosophers. Peirce, in fact, described Wright "as our boxing-master whom we—I particularly—used to face to be severely pummelled." Less a formal club than a regular opportunity for sustained philosophical conversation, it gave the members the chance to test their ideas against the sharpened intellects of their peers.[16] However much they looked to Wright for intellectual leadership, Peirce, James, and their colleagues possessed that self-confidence which enabled them to work toward their own philosophical positions. Wright influenced their thought, sometimes negatively—particularly with James—but his was a liberating rather than a stifling influence.

Their education completed, Wright, Peirce, and James each found it difficult to settle into a career. Although they were more highly trained in science than most of their peers, their philosophical speculations best suited them for appointments in philosophy. Yet in the 1860s and 1870s appointments in philosophy were still reserved for the religiously orthodox, which this trio most decidedly was not. What James wrote Henry Bowditch in 1869 regarding the professional options facing Peirce applied equally to all three: "The poor cuss sees no chance of getting a professorship anywhere. . . . It seems a great pity that as original a man as he is, who is willing and able to devote the powers of his life to logic and metaphysics, should be starved out of a career, when there are lots of professorships of the sort to be given in the country, to 'safe', orthodox men."[17]

Wright's habits of indolence and indifference to institutional demands would have made any career difficult. After graduating from Harvard in 1852, Wright took a position as a mathematical computer with the *Nautical*

Almanac. The work suited his mathematical skills, even though he found the requirements of the position distasteful. He quickly discovered shortcuts which enabled him to perform the necessary calculations in three months, leaving the rest of the year for his philosophical and scientific speculations. Still, he disliked working so intensely that he would postpone his tasks to the last possible moment, when he would stay up all night for days on end to finish the computations. When his father died in 1872 and left him a small inheritance, Wright left the *Nautical Almanac.* He seems to have viewed his work as a mathematician more as a burden than as a career.[18]

Wright had two opportunities to teach at Harvard, but his students and colleagues soon discovered that his skill at Socratic dialogue when surrounded by friends did not carry over into the classroom. Wright was brought to Harvard by two friends who respected his intellect and ideas, President Charles W. Eliot and Dean Ephraim Gurney, both former members of the Septem. In 1870 Wright delivered a course of lectures on psychology and in 1874 he took over in the middle of a course on theoretical physics, for a professor who had found the work too burdensome. Even his friend Gurney admitted that the lectures in psychology "were not very successful," and that in physics Wright's students were lost, because "his heavy artillery was mostly directed over their heads." Gurney concluded that in spite of the soundness of Wright's views on education, "he had no adaptability in practice." As an informal tutor, however, Wright's skills were outstanding. Henry W. Holland recalled that his lessons in physical and mental science with Wright were "one of the most important and fortunate events of my life. He was an extraordinary teacher for any one who really wanted to study,—always ready with explanations and illustrations of difficult points, always patient and interested."[19]

It is significant that neither of Wright's two forays into teaching were in philosophy. Though his philosophical skills were widely admired in Cambridge, they were still too unorthodox to be put before a class of Harvard men. Wright's agnosticism was also well known in Cambridge and at Harvard. As one local minister put it, "He is, is he not, the one who led Charles Norton astray?"[20] The community was willing to tolerate and even to encourage Wright's scholarship by publishing him in the *Nation* and in the *North American Review* and by giving him private forums through his tutoring and clubs, but even liberalizing Harvard in the 1870s still clung to a more conservative role for philosophy. Wright might be safe and acceptable on science, but not on philosophy. He was thus the first of the three to encounter the prevailing orthodoxy in the teaching of philosophy.

Peirce's early career as a scientist and philosopher revealed far more promise, but it too ended in early failure. Peirce had entered upon a career as a scientist even before graduating from the Lawrence Scientific School. Upon his return from Louisiana in 1860 he accepted a position with the United States Coast and Geodetic Survey. His father had long been associated with the Coast Survey and would serve as its director from 1867 to 1874. Though Benjamin Peirce's influence secured the appointment, Charles was well suited for the position. He served in a number of capacities with the Coast Survey, but in the early 1870s gained an international reputation in photometric research of stars with a view to determining the shape of our galaxy, and in pendulum-swinging experiments designed to fix more accurately the shape of the earth. His work with the Coast Survey over the thirty-one years he was employed with them involved mathematics, chemistry, astronomy, geodesy, and metrology. Through it all, Peirce considered himself to be primarily a chemist.[21]

The importance of Peirce's work with the Coast Survey was not limited to his contributions to astronomy and geodesy. It tended to confirm his conviction that scientific inquiry was fundamentally communal in nature. Though his observations of his father's scientific community had laid the groundwork for Peirce's own experiences, it was his research in the late 1860s and early 1870s in the United States and in Europe that gave him direct knowledge of shared inquiry. His participation in expeditions to observe eclipses of the sun, his presentations at international geodetic conferences, and his pendulum-swinging experiments in Europe and the United States gave him entry into the scientific community. Peirce was well aware that his contributions, however significant, were only a part of the puzzle. Only cooperative effort could move the sciences closer to real knowledge of the material world.[22] Although Peirce's initial formulations of his community of inquiry came before his extensive scientific activity of the early 1870s, his convictions were no doubt strengthened by his work as a scientist.

Peirce early showed promise in philosophy, as well as in science. In spite of James's gloomy assessment of Peirce's chances for an permanent appointment, Peirce did have several early opportunities to present his ideas to Harvard and Boston audiences. In 1864–65 he lectured at Harvard on the philosophy of science, and in 1866–67 he gave a series of Lowell lectures on the logic of science and induction. He was also beginning to write and publish on a variety of topics in logic, mathematics, and the philosophy of science.[23] If he had not yet received an academic appointment, he had by the late 1860s "established himself as one of Harvard's most promising young men." There was, however, a disquieting aspect to Peirce's early success at Harvard and at the Coast Survey. Most of his achievements to this point had come through the sponsorship of his father. The younger Peirce had not yet escaped the reach of Benjamin Peirce's influence. Murray Murphey rightly concludes that "no one ever questioned Charles Peirce's brilliance—he earned his recognition by his own ability: but because he was his father's son he was not held to account as others were. The indulgence was to bear bitter fruit."[24]

As for a permanent academic appointment for Peirce, James's 1869 assessment proved accurate, in spite of James's own considerable efforts on Peirce's behalf. In 1875 James recommended Peirce to Daniel Coit Gilman, who was recruiting faculty for the soon-to-be-opened Johns Hopkins University. James noted that Peirce was trained in mathematics and "what is rarer in mental philosophers, thoroughly trained in physical science." James thought that no one in Cambridge rated higher "in general power and originality," except perhaps Wright, and "*effectively* Peirce will always rank higher than Wright." In any case, Wright had recently died. Peirce was not, however, immediately chosen. Gilman pursued G. Stanley Hall, George Sylvester Morris, and James himself. Finally, in 1879 Gilman offered Peirce a lectureship in logic for 1879–80. Though no appointment to a professorship was forthcoming, Gilman reappointed Peirce on a yearly basis through 1883–84.[25]

While at Johns Hopkins Peirce seems to have been a successful teacher. He taught primarily logic to graduate students, many of them from mathematics. In addition to his course work, he formed a Metaphysical Club, which, like the earlier Cambridge incarnation, met for the discussion of papers. During the club's first three years, under Peirce's influence logical topics dominated the discussions. His courses were reasonably popular, given their abstract and difficult character. Peirce's students and other graduate fellows with whom he had contact in these years included Josiah Royce, John Dewey, Thorstein Veblen, Joseph Jastrow, and Christine Ladd-Franklin, who later recalled that Peirce did not possess an "inspiring personality," but achieved results "by creating the impression that we had before us a profound, original, dispassionate and impassioned seeker of truth." Peirce seems to have viewed Johns Hopkins as an embodiment of the community of scholars. The small faculty was distinguished, he had outstanding students, and faculty and students alike could and did contribute to the process of inquiry. Joseph Jastrow remembered "the terms of equality" upon which Peirce met his students. Jastrow and his colleagues were "members of his 'scientific' fraternity" and "this type of cooperation and delegation of responsibility came as near to a pedagogical device as any method that he used." Peirce was putting into practice at Johns Hopkins the cooperative pursuit of truth he was advocating in his essays.[26]

Peirce may have seen the Johns Hopkins community as united in the pursuit of truth, but his own stay in that community was sometimes controversial. To begin with, Peirce was apparently unwilling to commit himself fully to the academic profession because of his continuing responsibilities with the Coast Survey. In addition, his relations with James J. Sylvester, professor of mathematics, were difficult and stormy. Both men had a reputation for being difficult to work with, and they clashed over the priority of reaching certain conclusions in algebra. Peirce's own apparent reluctance to commit himself to Johns Hopkins, in spite of repeated professions of interest in obtaining a professorship, and his prickly temperament may have weighed in Gilman's decision to appoint G. Stanley Hall to a professorship in psychology in 1884. The exact circumstances of Peirce's dismissal, however, remain a mystery. He was notified in January 1884 that his appointment would expire at the end of the academic year. Peirce was never told the real reasons for his dismissal, and he denounced the university for handling it in such a manner as "to injure me as much as possible." Whatever the reason, the injury was done, and Peirce would never again hold another academic post. He continued his work with the Coast Survey, though his relations with his superiors became increasingly strained. Inheriting a small sum of money, in 1887 he retired to Milford, Pennsylvania, and left the Coast Survey permanently in 1891. In his exile he grew increasingly embittered and isolated. Peirce and his second wife lived in poverty, sustained only by occasional lecture fees and funds contributed primarily through the efforts of James.[27]

Without knowing the real reasons for Peirce's dismissal or whether he was effectively blacklisted by Gilman and others, it is difficult to assess the causes of Peirce's failure to achieve a professorship in logic or philosophy. Still, part of Peirce's failure to secure a permanent position can be laid to that continuing preference, which James had identified, for safe, orthodox men. Peirce's training was in mathematics and science, and he was a working scientist. Though logic had close affinities with mathematics, it was still considered within the realm of philosophy. If Peirce did not fit the traditional pattern of a philosopher, neither did he fit the emerging professional pattern. He had not taken advanced study in Europe and had not received the Ph.D.; he was no narrow specialist. In addition, his irascible temperament, his chafing at institutional restraints, and his divorce and remarriage in 1883 raised questions about his suitability as a colleague, at a time when professors were still expected to be gentlemen.

It is ironic, however, that the philosopher who so forcefully argued for the communal nature of scholarship should by the age of forty-five have been almost totally excluded from the scientific and academic communities of his time. Peirce seems to have recognized that his personal traits had been one factor in his isolation. Writing in 1902, he bitterly condemned a situation in which a scientist's "acquisition of books, instruments, laboratory, etc., depends upon qualifications in which the man of science is usually rather wanting—as wealth, diplomacy, popularity as a teacher—so that he is less likely to be provided with them than men less qualified to use them for the advancement of science."[28] The result of Peirce's exclusion was unfortunate for Peirce and for philosophy. Peirce lived out his last years in poverty and exile, isolated from new developments in philosophy and logic, and seeking, unsuccessfully, to complete his philosophical projects. American philosophers caught only occasional glimpses of Peirce's genius in his irregular lectures and publications, in James's frequent references to him, and in the recollections of his former students. But without a Metaphysical Club to sharpen his thinking, without a university post to support his research, and without colleagues and students to criticize his ideas and make suggestions, the bulk of Peirce's philosophical thought remained fragmented and unpublished in his lifetime. Peirce was perhaps temperamentally unsuited for the academic community, though his early success with the Coast Survey would suggest otherwise. It is quite clear, however, that the secularizing and professionalizing universities, or perhaps their presidents, were sufficiently discomfited by Peirce to deny him a permanent place in their community.

In contrast to the mysteries which still surround Peirce's career, there has been massive documentation of James's struggle to find a vocation and to secure an appointment. Howard Feinstein's study *Becoming William James* focuses on James's protracted struggle with his father to establish his own identity. Feinstein argues that the complex psychological dynamics in the James family and between father and son hindered and ultimately shaped William's choice of a career. Attracted first to art, then to science and medicine, out of deference to paternal desires, James only slowly and painfully moved toward a career more in accord with his own interests and inclinations, as a psychologist and philosopher. Although James's struggle to free himself from the coils of parental influence were important, his difficulties were compounded by the transitional character of the philosophical profession in the 1860s and 1870s.[29]

As early as 1865, in a letter to his parents from Brazil, James declared his intention "to study philosophy all my days." But forming that resolution was easier than achieving it. He spent the next four years intermittently studying medicine, traveling, studying, and taking cures in Europe to relieve the tensions at home, finally receiving his degree in 1869. James drifted for the next four years, living at home, reading widely in philosophy, psychology, science, and literature, and attending meetings of the Metaphysical Club after its founding. It was in this period that James experienced the depression he so vividly described in *The Varieties of Religious Experience*. Finally, in 1872 Charles W. Eliot offered James the kind of opportunity he was seeking, an appointment as instructor in physiology. The subject lay outside James's major intellectual interests at the time, but he welcomed the chance to teach as "a perfect God-send." Though concerned that an appointment in physiology might preclude a more desired post in psychology or philosophy, James in February 1873 resolved to make the most of his academic status: "I decide today to stick to biology for a profession in case I am not called to a chair of philosophy. . . . Philosophy I will nevertheless regard as my vocation and never let slip a chance to do a stroke at it."[30] Here lies a clue to James's academic success, in contrast to Peirce's failure: he was willing to make the best of a less than desirable position, in the expectation that it might lead to something better. Fortunately for James, his own interests coincided with the changing needs of Harvard under Charles Eliot. With Eliot's support and encouragement, James was able gradually by 1880 to shift his responsibilities to psychology and then to philosophy. Thus, despite his pessimism concerning the prospects for someone of his training and outlook, James was the only one of the three scientist-philosophers to have a distinguished academic career.

The reasons for James's success where Wright and Peirce failed can only be suggested here. Part of the answer lies in the temperaments of the three men. Wright's indifference and indolence and Peirce's irascibility unsuited them for what was still a gentleman's profession, whereas James's openness and amiability made him an ideal colleague. All three men were somewhat unorthodox in their religious beliefs, but Wright had the strongest reputation as an agnostic and that undoubtedly worked against him. His early death at forty-five in 1875 deprived him of any later opportunity to take advantage of the liberalizing tendencies in higher education. Those tendencies had proceeded far enough to permit James's appointment in physiology and Peirce's in logic, but only James was able to convert his appointment into a permanent position in philosophy. By the end of the 1870s, places like Harvard and Johns Hopkins were at least open to the possibility of appointing a scientist-philosopher, but it appears that the personal characteristics and habits of the instructor had as much to do with whether the appointment was made permanent as his qualifications and skill as a philosopher. James obviously passed the test and became a member of the club; Peirce, for whatever reason, did not.

In their writings of this period, Wright, Peirce, and James explored the methods and values of the physical and natural sciences and considered their applicability to metaphysics and to philosophy. All three men shared an appreciation of the achievements of the special sciences, especially of the success of the various sciences in offering explanations of the material world. The question remained, however, whether the sciences were complete in themselves. Was there any longer a role for metaphysics and philosophy? Could or should philosophy be turned into a science, and what would be the costs and benefits of such a development? As Wright, Peirce, and James addressed these questions in the 1860s and 1870s, they developed their own perspectives within a general agreement on the validity of scientific methods and the significance of scientific values. Each of them, however, retained distinct ideas about science and the extent to which scientific methods and values were appropriate for the philosophic enterprise. A shared intellectual milieu and close personal contact did not blunt their differences on these issues.

Chauncey Wright's metier seems to have been philosophic dialogue: "I confess to the heartiest sympathy with Plato's preference for a *man* who can question and answer, rather than for a book."[31] Fortunately, he set down his ideas in a series of essays published in the *Nation* and in the *North American Review* and in long letters to his friends. Here Wright developed his ideas on the history of science, on the method and motives of modern science, and on the relationship between philosophy and science. They reveal Wright to have been a committed positivist who saw science as the chief method of attaining knowledge in the real world, an individual capable of suspending judgment where knowledge was not possible, and a scientist who conceded to philosophy a broad role, but who wished to distinguish sharply the separate realms of science and philosophy.

Wright argued that what separated the old science from the new was less a method than a motive. The science of the ancients was not, he claimed, particularly deficient in method or in its approaches to truth. What distinguished the modern sciences was not "the employment of a new method of research, but . . . the exercise of greater virtue in the use of old methods." The "motive" to scientific inquiry characterized modern science. If the methods had been there all along, why then did the motive to modern scientific virtue develop only in the wake of the scientific revolutions of the sixteenth and seventeenth centuries? Francis Bacon, the scientific model for many nineteenth-century American philosophers, had contributed little in the way of method, according to Wright. Bacon's real contribution had been to sever "physical science from scholastic philosophy."[32] Wright believed that the work of men like Galileo and Kepler provided workable explanations for natural phenomena and that as the decades passed these explanations began to accumulate into a body of particularly useful knowledge. The new scientific motive arose, in part, out of the momentum of scientific research and discovery: "We find, then, the explanation of the modern development of science in the accumulation of a body of certified knowledge, sufficiently extensive to engage and discipline rational scientific curiosity, and stimulate it to act independently of other motives."[33]

Wright distinguished two motives to inquiry: the subjective and the objective. The subjective motive had "its origin in natural universal human interests and emotions." The objective motive "had an empirical origin, arising in the course of an inquiry, springing from interests which are defined by what we already know, and not by what we have always felt,—interests which depend on acquired knowledge, and not on natural desires and emotions." Wright acknowledged the power of felt human needs and desires and conceded that the objective motive was the weaker one. Still, "a body of systematic, well-digested, and well-ascertained scientific truth" in itself served as a spur to the objective motive and to further inquiry.[34] By the middle of the nineteenth century, the momentum of science and the objective motive was almost irresistible, at least to someone like Wright.

For Wright, truly scientific inquiry was marked by three characteristics which set it apart from other modes of explanation: (1) a neutrality with regard to competing philosophical and theological systems; (2) the suspension of judgment by its practitioners until the facts were in and the truth determined; and (3) a clear, well-articulated, and successful method for the testing and verification of hypotheses. Wright traced the attitude of scientific neutrality to Francis Bacon. He argued that Bacon had developed no system, but had been instead an opponent of systems, who aimed to establish for "science a position of neutrality, and at the same time of independent respectability" among the systematizers of his own day. Bacon's achievement, Wright believed, "secured the true status for the advancement of experimental science, or of experimental philosophy, as it came to be called." Wright argued that Bacon's principles led to a flowering of the sciences in Great Britain, whereas the penchant for system building in Germany retarded the sciences there until the beginning of the nineteenth century. The difference in attitude had been most recently demonstrated by Darwin. Writing in the Baconian tradition, according to Wright, Darwin took no stand on the theological questions of the origin of life—they were simply irrelevant to his purposes as a scientist. The Germans, however, still wanted to build Darwin's discoveries and theories into a system of Darwin*ism*, which for Wright violated the scientific neutrality he prized.[35]

If science, as a discipline, required neutrality with regard to competing systems, Wright expected an analogous requirement of the would-be scientist, suspension of judgment until hypotheses were tested and verified. Wright realized that the ability to suspend judgment was difficult for many, especially if vital human or practical interests were at stake. He went so far as to describe "a suspended judgment" as "that commonly painful mental attitude." Even Wright found it difficult to suspend judgment on every point. Writing to F. E. Abbot, he acknowledged that his "interest in philosophical and disputed matters is . . . almost entirely speculative. It is not quite so, because clear, scientific knowledge has important practical consequences." Still, as he noted, "so long as there is room for dispute and enlightened doubt, there are no practical applications which can rightly prejudge theory."[36]

For Wright, a suspended judgment was necessary so as to avoid any tampering with the facts or creating of bias in the drawing up of theories. "True science," he wrote to Abbot, "deals with nothing but questions of facts,—and in terms, if possible, which shall not determine beforehand how we ought to feel about the facts." To bring practical interest or "moral bias" to the facts is "one of the most certain and fatal means of corrupting evidence." Once the facts were freely determined, then Wright found that "practical science comes in to determine what, in view of the facts, our feelings and rules of conduct ought to be."[37] Wright shared with Peirce this attitude regarding the deleterious effects of practical concerns on true science.

Wright's friends and colleagues found his agnosticism to be one of the most striking and difficult aspects of his character, personality, and philosophy. His friend E. W. Gurney, who knew Wright from their days as students at Harvard, admitted that "Chauncey was so purely intellectual and his intellect so predominantly scientific, with most precise canons of evidence rigidly applied, that it was hardly possible that he should do full justice to natures of a different type, into whose judgments the feelings are always filtering." William James admired Wright's knowledge of scientific aims and methods and saw in him "the ideal scientific temper—restrained, impersonal, and scrupulous." But Wright's positivism and agnosticism were ultimately too much for the younger philosopher. Wright's rigorous standards for belief seemed to James to be "nihilism," to make the universe into a "nulliverse."[38] Part of James's own philosophical struggle of these years was to establish grounds for belief in religion, in metaphysics, and in common sense, as well as in science. Wright's standards were too limiting for James, who gradually worked his way to establishing grounds for the right to believe in his 1896 essay "The Will to Believe."[39] Whatever his friend's reservations, Wright remained convinced that scientific neutrality and a suspended judgment were essential to the scientific method and to progress.

Neutrality and suspended judgment were necessary to the process of testing and verification that lay at the core of the scientific method. Wright argued that the origin of ideas made little difference. The key to their verification lay in tests of "sensible experience": "Science asks no questions about the ontological pedigree or *a priori* character of a theory, but is content to judge it by its performance." Scientific knowledge "maintains a strict neutrality toward all philosophical systems and concerns itself not at all with the genesis or *a priori* grounds of ideas."[40] This was not to say there were no a priori assumptions in science; in fact, Wright argued that one a priori "presumption" was crucial to the "expectation of constructing the sciences into a true philosophy of nature." Wright assumed that "physical causation is universal; that the constitution of nature is written in its actual manifestations, and needs only to be deciphered by experimental and inductive research." For him, the necessary postulate to a scientific method was to presume that "the order of nature is decipherable, or that causation is everywhere either manifest or hidden, but never absent." This presumption undergirded Wright's confidence in the "objective method" of "verification by sensuous tests, by tests of sensible experience."[41]

The task of science was to provide "knowledge of things and events either as effects of general causes, or as instances of general classes, rules, or laws." Wright defined science as that inquiry which investigates those phenomena which can be observed and which can be presumed to have an ultimately observable cause: "Scientific doctrines and investigations are exclusively concerned with connections in phenomena which are susceptible of demonstration by inductive observation, and independent of diversities or resemblances in their hidden natures, or of any question about their metaphysical derivation or dependence." The scientist observes the facts and attempts to derive more general explanations of the phenomena in terms of "general classes, rules, or laws." Once laws have been developed and verified by the inductive method, the scientist can attempt to develop laws of increasing generality which unite particular facts and specific rules and laws. Ultimately for Wright the "scientific character" of any knowledge consists of "the conscious purpose of arriving at general facts and at an adequate statement of them in language, or of bringing particular facts under explicit general ones."[42]

Wright argued that scientific research is not pursuit of the bare facts alone, but, rather, "that the proper objects of scientific research are all of them processes and the result of processes." The scientist seeks not isolated facts, however important, but "the permanent relations of co-existences and sequences, which are hidden in the confusions of complex phenomena." In a world of constant change even these processes change: "Nothing shows a trace of an original, immutable nature, except the unchangeable laws of change." But if there are no eternal constants, at least the pursuit of verifiable facts, rules, and laws leads the scientist to "the discovery of the real truths of nature" then operative. "The physical laws of nature," Wright wrote to a friend, "are thus to my mind the only real types of general order in the universe." Provisionally, at least, these laws establish knowledge of what can be known, even if they are "far from illustrating the general results of the interactions of natural forces."[43]

Though Wright had been trained as a scientist, his most important writings were philosophical. The bulk of his scientific work after college was the drudgery of performing calculations for the *Nautical Almanac*. In evolutionary theory, where he was an early and able defender of Darwin, Wright's contribution lay not in original research, but in defending the methods and conclusions of the English scientist. Broadly speaking, he helped provide a philosophy of science which undergirded the rigorous inquiry and findings of Darwin and which questioned and condemned the looser speculations of Spencer and the critics of natural selection. Wright did not hold that every investigator must verify for himself the laws of nature, so long as he had "good reason" to accept them as verifiable and as verified. More important was his confidence in the method of verification. The would-be authority, whatever his contribution to science as researcher or expositor, must exemplify "true scientific virtue," which Wright characterized as the ability "to balance evidences, and to bring doubts to civil terms; to resist the enthusiasm of these aggressive axioms, and not to be contented with the beliefs which are only the most probable, or most authentic on strictly inductive grounds."[44]

The difference between science and philosophy lay both in the method of inquiry and the motive to it. "Philosophy," Wright argued, "passes like a judge upon its questions, as if, in practical matters, decision were quite as important as truth." Science, however, takes up problems "as matters of curiosity or of possible future utility, and looks, at its leisure into them. It acknowledges no burden of proof in its judgments, and is content to wait." In spite of this difference in method, Wright asserted that the fundamental difference between science and philosophy was traceable to "original *motives* rather than to differences of *method* in research."[45] Method thus determined whether a particular inquiry was scientific, but only investigation into the motives for inquiry could reveal why one investigator relied on scientific method and why another did not.

Though clearly an advocate of scientific motives and methods, Wright did not entirely dismiss philosophy and metaphysics. He recognized, however, that metaphysics had been little "affected by the speculative interests and methods of modern science." Wright postulated "a sort of resemblance between philosophy and poetry." What mattered most to philosophers and poets was not the object of thought, but the new angle of vision which they brought to their work. "To throw a new light on old objects" was the aim of philosophy, which was merely "poetry in the abstract." Wright denied that he was so much a positivist that he was unable to see any value in "mystical and poetical philosophies," but he demanded that "they must be the works of real genius,—of a Plato, a Hegel, or an Emerson."[46]

These works of "real genius" could contribute to our understanding of the broader world, even if they failed to increase our knowledge of it. In discussing the work of Berkeley, Wright defended faith and philosophy's connection with it: "Science, as such, has nothing to do with faith, but philosophy, which aims to embrace the whole man, can never ignore faith and its data and phenomena." Even the most determined effort to focus on "sense perceptions" alone is bound to fail, because metaphysical and spiritual "phenomena remain, and the human mind is certain to revert to them and seek their solution." While acknowledging the separate claims of philosophy and science, Wright also wanted to differentiate clearly between the two modes of thought: "A conflict between them arises, however, only where either disposition invades the proper province of the other." Positivists, Wright felt, ought not to oppose metaphysics so much as to ignore it. The older philosophies ought to be left to compete as best they could with the sciences whose "methods, hypotheses, and principles" promised "actual knowledge."[47] The realm of philosophy and metaphysics, however valuable to some, was in Wright's mind clearly inferior as a method to obtain "actual knowledge" and a relic from older, more traditional modes of thought. Though he granted metaphysics a place because it met felt human needs and dealt with certain phenomena, the place of honor in the pursuit of knowledge was clearly reserved for science.

Wright did not directly address the question which would dominate so many philosophical debates in the coming decades: Could philosophy become a science? To the extent that the motive for inquiry distinguished the sciences, a philosopher, as much as any scholar, could be actuated by the scientific motive. Wright once described the scientific mind as one which is "held rigidly to the truth of things, . . . and [which] is *narrowed* to the closest, most uncompromising study of facts, and to a training which enables it to render in imagination the truest account of nature as it actually exists." There is no a priori reason why at least some philosophers could not be so described. For some of the younger men and women at the turn of the century, something very much like Wright's formulation became central to their drive to make philosophy more scientific. However, for any philosophy to become a science in Wright's terms its practitioners would have to adopt a strict neutrality with regard to competing systems, to suspend judgment until facts and theories were verified, and to adopt a rigorous method for the testing and verification of hypotheses. Wright remained skeptical that the philosophic mind, with its "habit of viewing and interpreting nature according to its own dispositions," was really open to and suited for scientific inquiry.[48] He certainly displayed none of the confidence of the later philosophers that the discipline could and should be turned into a science.

Throughout Chauncey Wright's brief career as a philosopher, Darwinian evolution remained a vital touchstone for him. The same can not be said for Charles Peirce, who did not share his friend's enthusiasm for the theories of Darwin. Peirce was surveying in Louisiana when *The Origin of Species* reached the United States in late 1859, but he was aware of the controversy and excitement it generated. He did not, however, become a committed Darwinian upon his return to Cambridge. Philip Wiener, in his study *Evolution and the Founders of Pragmatism,* argues that Peirce was skeptical about the scientific validity of the hypothesis of natural selection. Peirce conceded that Darwin's method was empirical, but he also came to the conclusion that Darwin's theories "themselves would barely command scientific respect." Peirce seems to have preferred Lamarckian and cataclysmic views of evolution because they were more consistent with his own developing evolutionism.[49]

Peirce disagreed with Wright not only on the scientific validity of Darwin's theories, but on the question of scientific neutrality as well. Peirce believed that Darwinism had triumphed as an explanation because it was consistent with the climate of the times—an argument Wright would have regarded as irrelevant. More importantly, Peirce sought to extend the idea of evolution to embrace a generalized philosophical position well beyond what was scientifically verifiable. As Wiener has observed, Peirce ultimately transmuted "evolution into a cosmology of 'evolutionary love', which for sheer speculative audacity was a worthy rival of the absolutism of Schelling and Hegel."[50] Thus it seems that evolutionism in its broader meaning, which embraced Lamarck and the cataclysmic advocates as well as Darwin, provided the intellectual backdrop to Peirce's evolutionism. He did not hold to the stricter scientific views of Wright, but sought to expand the reach of evolution as a fundamental cosmic phenomenon.

Regardless of his differences with Wright over Darwin and evolution, Peirce considered himself very much the scientist. His model of science was the physical sciences, particularly physics and chemistry. Near the end of the century he recalled that he had been "thoroughly grounded not only in all that was then known of physics and chemistry, but also in the way in which those who were successfully advancing knowledge proceeded." He had continued to pay "the most attention to the methods of the most exact sciences" and took pride in his own contributions in "mathematics, gravitation, optics, chemistry, [and] astronomy." With reason, Peirce concluded: "I am saturated through and through, with the spirit of the physical sciences."[51]

Peirce, however, rejected the idea that scientific training and outlook resulted in a narrow positivism. Influenced by his study of Kant and Whewell, Peirce argued that "progress in science depends upon the observation of the right facts by minds *furnished with appropriate ideas.*"[52] Here again, Peirce diverged from the insistence on scientific neutrality and suspended judgment that rendered Wright's conception of scientific method more positivistic. But even Wright had argued that rules and laws could become working hypotheses for further inquiry, and in that sense at least, he had created a role for ideas in the scientist's confrontation with the facts. Still, Peirce gave more weight to the role of theory and ideas in the scientist's approach to research and experimentation than did Wright.

Although trained in science and saturated with its spirit, Peirce believed in the basic compatibility of science and philosophy. Science and philosophy were, in his view, dependent upon each other: "Just as Science cannot advance without Philosophy—because (to use Kant's expression) Induction pure is Blind—so Philosophy cannot exist without science—because Deduction pure is Void. Science and Philosophy must advance together." At this point in his thinking Peirce argued that "philosophy is a condition of all science, that it deals with what we immediately know, and that it progresses from the elements." Peirce equated philosophy with metaphysics and defined metaphysics as "the philosophy of primal truths." These truths, he asserted, "should be the primary conditions of all science." Thus metaphysics, though called a science, did not employ the method of the sciences and in fact provided the primal truths which underlay proper science.[53]

Peirce was convinced that philosophy lay behind all theorizing and inquiry, even in the sciences. "Philosophy," he wrote in his Lowell lectures of 1866, "is the attempt to form a general informed conception of the *All.*" We can not escape the need to philosophize, even as scientists: "Those who neglect philosophy have metaphysical theories as much as others—only they are rude, false, and wordy theories." Contrary to the arguments of the positivists, metaphysics did not stand in unalterable opposition to science. The conclusions of metaphysics were at the time less certain than those of science, and the differences among metaphysicians were greater than among many scientists, but that was cause for neither alarm nor condemnation. That condition of uncertainty was neither unusual nor permanent: "Every great branch of science has once been in the state in which metaphysics is now, that is when its fundamental conceptions were vague and consequently its doctrines utterly unsettled: and there is no reason whatever to despair of metaphysics eventually becoming a real science like the rest."[54]

Peirce rejected Chauncey Wright's argument that agnosticism and a suspended judgment were essential to a scientific method. "We cannot begin with complete doubt. We must begin with all the prejudices which we actually have when we enter upon the study of philosophy." To pretend to doubt all, to hold all judgments in suspense, "must be mere pretense." Any philosopher or scientist has doubts, of course, especially with regard to "almost all psychological or very general propositions," but that does not deny a firm foundation to science and philosophy. All science and philosophy ought to rest, according to Peirce, upon "those ordinary facts which (in a general way) we are actually assured and therefore *cannot,* if we would, mistrust."[55]

In what appears to be a direct reference to Wright's personal habits and ideas, Peirce condemned a "fruitless and indolent scepticism" which prevented any scientific progress. Like Wright, however, he argued that the physical sciences gained in credibility as evidence accumulated through the testing of theories. But to begin the train of experiments that leads to such accumulation requires that some scientist cast aside "caution" and begin with unsupported and untested theories. Metaphysics, like the physical sciences, "must be content to rest upon tangible external facts and to begin with theories not supported by any great multitude of different considerations or held with absolute confidence." Galileo's initial hypothesis, for example, was more than "a shrewd guess"; it was "a regular and deliberate inference, but not supported on all sides."[56]

Peirce's formulations here share some similarities with those of Wright, but they arrive at their conclusions from very different points. Wright thought the origin of theses was irrelevant, whether from legitimate inference or from inspired revelation. The scientist must suspend judgment on the validity of any untested thesis. Peirce disagreed fundamentally. No scientist or philosopher came to inquiry as a blank slate; all were burdened or endowed with prejudices and provisional theories. Both men held that the new and successful lines of scientific inquiry were the result of the actions of a genius who formulated a thesis which could be tested and verified through the accumulation of data. Wright, however, held to scientific neutrality with regard to the origin of the thesis, whereas Peirce suggested that ultimately provable theories were more likely to be the result of "a regular and deliberate inference." Both men allowed for the work of genius to take science in new directions, but Peirce argued that genius, even when discarding caution, worked within a framework of established and a priori ideas, while Wright described a theoretical nihilism in which ideas appeared de novo, to be sustained or discussed through subsequent research.

Like Wright, Peirce in his early writings distinguished between the motive to scientific inquiry and the methods of it. Peirce described scientific motivation as "a craving to know how things really were and an interest in finding out whether or not general propositions actually held good—which has over-balanced all prejudice, all vanity, and all passion." The man motivated by the scientific spirit spends his day in "laboratories and in the field . . . *observing*— that is perceiving by the aid of analysis,—and testing suggestions of theories." This method of observation was not limited solely to "natural objects." Mathe-maticians, in particular, had no natural objects to observe yet were intensely interested in "testing general propositions and particular cases."[57] Not the object of observation, but the motive to and the method of observation deter-mined whether a particular discipline was a science. By this criterion, there was no a priori reason to bar philosophy and metaphysics from the realm of science.

Given Peirce's formative experiences in the scientific community of his fa-ther and his experiences as a working scientist with the Coast Survey, it is not surprising that the community of inquiry was central to his conception of sci-ence. Science, in his view, was not conducted by individuals working in isolation, but by communities working together. Science was conducted in an atmosphere of openness and its results belonged not to the individual scientist but to the community of science: "Scientific progress is to a large extent public and belongs to the community of scientific men of the same department, its conclusions are unanimous, its interpretations of nature are no private in-terpretations, and so much must always be published to the world as will suffice to enable the world to adopt the individual investigator's conclu-sions."[58]

The goal of the scientist was truth, but the achievement of truth was collec-tive: "To make single individuals absolute judges of truth is most pernicious." In science, truth resides in the solution which the community of science de-vises: "The followers of science are fully persuaded that the processes of investigation, if only pushed far enough, will give one certain solution to every question to which they can be applied." The perfection of method, whatever the initial results, will lead scientists investigating the same question inexora-bly "toward a destined centre . . . to one and the same conclusion." The method of science brings about the cessation of doubt among those compe-tent to judge the question: "In science a question is not regarded as settled or its solution as certain until all intelligent and informed doubt has ceased and all competent persons have come to a catholic agreement."[59]

This conception of science raises significant problems regarding the nature of reality. Superficially, Peirce seemed to be arguing that reality is what the competent scientists agree upon; their agreement, based on scientific method, establishes truths about reality. But Peirce was not a relativist in this regard. He held that real things exist and can be known through the communal exercise of scientific method: "The real, then, is that which, sooner or later, information and reasoning would finally result in, and which is therefore independent of the vagaries of me and you. Thus, the very origin of the conception of reality shows that this conception essentially involves the notion of a COMMUNITY, without definite limits, and capable of an indefinite increase of knowledge." The problem, of course, with this conception of reality is that the ultimately real seems unattainable, in spite of the best efforts of the community of scientists. The real seems to exist in some indefinite future, to be found only after some "indefinite increase of knowledge." The best that can be done in the present is to use the scientific method to fix beliefs and to settle opinion, at least provisionally.[60]

Peirce did not restrict the applicability of scientific method nor his conception of truth to the hard sciences. Metaphysicians, it was true, were prone to rely far too heavily upon their own judgment and conclusions for metaphysics to be considered a true science. They needed, in Peirce's view, to give up their pretensions to individual insight and to participate in communal inquiry: "We individually cannot reasonably hope to attain the ultimate philosophy which we pursue; we can only seek it, therefore, for the *community* of philosophers." Peirce, in fact, argued that "philosophy ought to imitate the successful sciences in its methods, so far as to proceed only from tangible premises which can be subjected to careful scrutiny, and to trust rather to the multitude and variety of its arguments than to the conclusiveness of any one."[61]

Because Peirce had the most experience as a working scientist, his early conceptions of the communal nature of truth and its implications for both science and philosophy bore the closest relationship to the way science actually worked. Peirce was trying to generalize on his experiences in his father's household and on his own knowledge of the scientific community gained in the Coast Survey. Peirce's ideas, when applied to the discipline of philosophy, had great appeal for the next generation of philosophers. These men and women sought to meet the intellectual and professional challenge of the sciences in colleges and universities by making philosophy itself over into a science. The community of inquiry, the consensus of the competent, and the imitation of the sciences in their methods characterized the demands of the young scientizing philosophers like Christine Ladd-Franklin and Arthur O. Lovejoy. Not all philosophers agreed with Peirce on the applicability of these methods and values for philosophy. One who remained skeptical of the more extreme claims for science and of those who would turn philosophy into a science was Peirce's close friend William James.

James was sufficiently grounded in science to be aware of the power of scientific methods. The "great authority" which "physical science" enjoyed rested, according to James, upon its "solidity of premises and certainty of conclusion." Physical science had earned that authority through "the excellence of her method." Keys to the scientific method were the ability to hold "all conclusions as provisional and subject to future correction" and to subject all theories and all facts to rigorous tests of verification.[62] Despite the successes the physical sciences had experienced with these methods, James remained skeptical that they could totally supplant faith and belief outside of fairly narrowly conceived scientific disciplines.

James, sensitive to the intellectual currents of the third quarter of the century, recognized the appeal of science as a method of obtaining knowledge and practical progress. As he noted in discussing the state of philosophy in American colleges, "physical science is becoming so speculative and audacious in its constructions, and at the same time so authoritative, that all doctrines find themselves, willy-nilly, compelled to settle their accounts and make new treaties with it." It was reaching the point where only a properly trained scientist could criticize the new developments in philosophy.[63] This pervading scientism, which all too often shaded into the harder forms of materialism and positivism, distressed James because it denigrated the nonscientific aspects of thought and life. Furthermore, the more extreme materialists and positivists were claiming more for their philosophy than a strict scientific method permitted. Conclusions about the physical basis of all life could not then be supported by the available evidence. James attacked the extreme advocates of science in characteristic language:

> Many persons nowadays seem to think that any conclusion
> must be very scientific if the arguments in favor of it are all
> derived from twitching of frogs' legs—especially if the frogs
> are decapitated—and that, on the other hand, any doctrine
> chiefly vouched for by the feelings of human beings—with
> heads on their shoulders—must be benighted and super-
> stitious. They seem to think too, that any vagary or whim,
> however unverified, of a scientific man must needs form an
> integral part of science itself. . . . The lecturer knows
> nothing more deplorable than this indiscriminating gulping
> down of every thing materialistic as peculiarly scientific.
> Nothing is scientific but what is clearly formulated,
> reasoned, and verified.[64]

Without denying the very real authority of the sciences within their proper realms, James sought to preserve room for faith and belief, to preserve a broader conception of philosophy. He saw in philosophical study the best opportunity "to give young men a wide openness of mind and a more flexible way of thinking than special technical training can generate." Like Peirce, James held that some metaphysics was inevitable, in spite of the fact that his own day prided itself "particularly on its love of Science and Facts and its contempt for all metaphysics." There was no denying that "Metaphysics of some sort there must be. The only alternative is between the good Metaphysics of clear-headed Philosophy and the trashy Metaphysics of vulgar Positivism." Metaphysics was, for James in this connection, "the quest of the last clear elements of things."[65]

In developing a "clear-headed Philosophy," a man's entire being came into play: "Intellect, will, taste, and passion co-operate just as they do in practical affairs." For James, no neutrality or suspended judgment was possible in the development of a philosophy: "It is almost incredible that men who are themselves working philosophers should pretend that any philosophy can be, or ever has been, constructed without the help of personal preference, belief, or divination." The philosopher and the "man of science" alike must at crucial points take "his stand on a sort of dumb conviction that the truth must lie in one direction rather than another."[66]

The scientist, philosopher, or ordinary citizen regularly posits a "working hypothesis," which for James was synonymous with "faith." James, in fact, argued that "we cannot live or think at all without some degree of faith." Each of us in our various capacities attempts to confirm and verify our working hypotheses. "The only difference is that while some hypotheses can be refuted in five minutes, others may defy ages." Science enters here with its command "to believe nothing not yet verified by the senses." This, James felt, was "a prudential rule intended to maximize our right thinking and minimize our errors in *the long run*." If the long run increases the probability of certainty, much as Peirce's community of inquiry did, we nonetheless cannot always wait. James recognized that in matters of deep human significance, in those areas under the sway of religious faith, we cannot afford to wait as the scientist might for verification and confirmation in the long run. If we choose to play by "the rules of the scientific game," they are binding upon us, but in deeply personal matters we can not always delay, "for the long run which exists indeed for humanity," does not exist for us individually.[67]

James's early views on the relationship of science and philosophy thus share elements with those of his older friends and yet are marked by crucial departures. James, on the whole, was more skeptical of the claims of science, especially of the more extreme claims being put forth by certain materialists and positivists. He rejected, as we have seen, Wright's agnosticism and suspension of judgment, especially where matters of religious faith were at stake. James was willing to play by Wright's rules in certain carefully delimited scientific studies, but he decisively rejected those rules as a method for the conduct of life in any broader sense. With Peirce, James was more cognizant of the role of personal preference and belief in the drawing up of theories and inferences. But whereas Peirce established a rigorous set of rules for the verification of working hypotheses, James wanted to play by the rules only in certain limited areas—the physical and natural sciences. In the fundamentally more important areas James refused to dismiss faith and belief. Finally, one sees in James, as in Peirce, the notion that truth, or at least scientific truth, will be established only in the long run. But whereas Peirce emphasized the community of scholars in its collective and long-sustained pursuit of truth, James deferred to the individual's need to decide in the here-and-now. Humanity in general and science as a mode of inquiry may have long runs, but we as individuals must make our vitally important decisions in our own much shorter allotted time. James, characteristically, sided with the individual.

The two decades from 1860 to 1880 were important in the transition of philosophical practice and thought. Chauncey Wright, Charles Peirce, and William James, in their efforts to become philosophers and to set down their ideas on science and its relationship to philosophy, played vital roles in the process of creating new patterns in American philosophy. They began giving new direction to thought and practice even when unable themselves to find a permanent place in institutions of higher learning.

The careers of these three men were representative of the shift from theologically oriented moral philosophy to professional academic philosophy. By the end of the nineteenth century academic philosophy was detached from theology. Though the process had begun earlier, by the 1870s and early 1880s positions in philosophy had opened sufficiently at places like Johns Hopkins and Harvard to permit the appointment of men like James and Peirce. Scientific training had begun to supersede religious orthodoxy as a criterion for appointment. It was still the case, however, that the profession of college teaching was a small club which restricted departures from the norm. All three ran afoul of this sense of propriety; only James was able to surmount the obstacles to membership and to make for himself a career in philosophy. In so doing, he helped open the door wider to those who would follow.

Wright, Peirce, and James were among the first in America to bring to philosophy thorough training in science and scientific methods. Each, however, reflected differently upon his training, and the result was three quite distinctive, though related, philosophies. They all attempted in some measure to outline a scientific method and approach appropriate to both science and philosophy. Peirce in these decades developed the fullest philosophy of science, in his conception of the community of inquiry and the communal nature of truth. Wright's conceptions were more narrowly positivistic. James, though respectful of the achievements of science, sought to limit the more imperialistic claims of the scientists.

In the early 1880s, when Peirce was lecturing in logic at Johns Hopkins and James was shifting more and more of his teaching responsibilities at Harvard to philosophy, a decided change began to steal over American philosophy. To be sure, most of the positions, especially in the small denominational colleges, were still in the possession of the safe, orthodox men. But now, at a few places the student of philosophy could be taught by men steeped in a scientific tradition. James in particular, through his advocacy of Peirce and younger men of diverse views, was helping to create an academic climate hospitable to more secular, scientifically oriented philosophers. These decades, too, saw the passing of the Baconian tradition in American science and philosophy. The newer approaches of Darwin and the physical scientists were becoming the models for emulation. That is not to say that the traditional concerns and patterns had been swept away by 1880, for they had not, even in the thought of James and Peirce. Nonetheless, the early careers of these three scientist-philosophers represent a significant scientific turn in American philosophy.

THREE

The Appearance of the Professional Academic Philosopher: Hall, Royce, and Dewey

G. Stanley Hall, a young graduate student at Harvard, wrote the *Nation* in 1876 suggesting the need to assess the state of philosophy in American colleges. Hall's visits to various classrooms had convinced him that few branches of learning were "so inadequately taught as those generally roughly classed as philosophy." New developments in science, in the history of philosophy, and in English and German thought were being almost totally ignored, in favor of continued reliance on familiar treatises of "moral science." Hall lamented that "this whole field of study is generally given into the hands of one of the older and 'safer' members of the faculty, under the erroneous belief that it should be the aim of the professors of this department to indoctrinate rather than to instruct—to tell *what* to think, than to teach *how* to think."[1] Hall's gloomy assessment reflects his own failure to secure a position in that centennial year, but contains little hint of the changes that would come over philosophy in the next two decades, as younger, more scientifically oriented philosophers like William James, John Dewey, and Hall himself moved into positions formerly held by the older and safer men.

American philosophy in the quarter-century from the centennial to 1900 underwent a major shift in both personnel and focus. The older, more traditional generation began to be replaced in these decades by younger men, many of them educated in the new Ph.D.-granting institutions of the United States, instead of in Germany. These men, trained in the post-Darwinian era, were more open to science and scientific method, cognizant of the newest developments in European thought, and convinced that at least some part of philosophy—if not philosophy itself—could take on the attributes of science. The old-time college was being replaced by the university, and the moral philosopher by the professional academic philosopher. The transition was difficult for those seeking positions in philosophy in the late 1870s and the 1880s. There were few positions to be had, religious orthodoxy was still often a criterion for appointment, and new avenues to appointment, retention, and permanence were not yet clearly established. Those who received their doctorates between 1875 and 1885, aided by their slightly older mentors, began to establish new criteria for education and hiring, which became the characteristics of an academic discipline by the end of the century. The younger philosophers, however, first had to struggle to obtain Ph.D.s, to secure permanent academic posts, and to define their role in a world increasingly dominated by science.

Such concerns were reflected in Hall's letter to the *Nation* and in William James's unsigned reply in the same issue. James agreed that the overall quality of philosophical instruction was deplorable and pointed to many of the same conditions: the "safeness" of the instructor (usually the college president), the tendency toward edification rather than enlightenment, and the conformity to religious orthodoxy. James's broader conception of philosophy envisioned its giving "young men a wider openness of mind and a more flexible way of thinking than special technical training can generate." Philosophical study should open alternatives, encourage skepticism of received knowledge, and foster freer thought; "in a word, it means the possession of mental perspective." James was little concerned about which specific doctrines were taught. More important was inculcating "the living, philosophic attitude of mind, the independent, personal look at all the data of life, and the eagerness to harmonize them."[2]

Although James agreed with Hall in assessing the sorry state of philosophy, he was more optimistic regarding the imminence of change. The impetus to change, he thought, lay in the progress and the appeal of science. New developments in the physical sciences, physiology, and psychology, especially in England and Germany, had sufficient "prestige," regardless of their ultimate truth, to awaken even the "sleepiest doctor-of-divinity-like repose." These scientific developments were forcing the philosophers themselves to become thoroughly grounded in science if they wished to remain current and to retain their traditional critical role. Philosophy, James wrote, would now find its subject in "physics and natural history." Sounding more confident than perhaps he was, James assured his readers that "young men who aspire to professorships" and who were as well trained in the sciences as in philosophy would "before many years find a number of vacant places calling for their peculiar capacity."[3]

Three years after this brief exchange, Hall, having finished his philosophy

Ph.D. on a psychological topic under James at Harvard, returned to the problem of philosophy in America in a longer essay published in the English
journal *Mind*. Hall claimed to have surveyed the offerings of some three hundred colleges; he found the situation little improved. Religious interests still
dominated, even in schools claiming to be nonsectarian, and philosophical
instruction typically attempted to "inoculate the mind with insidious ortho-
doxies." More pessimistic than his former professor, Hall concluded that
there was only a "very small chance that a well-equipped student of philosophy in any of its departments will secure a position as a teacher of the subject."
Despite these depressing conclusions, Hall found some small comfort in the
realization that the situation was "in a much better condition" at the larger
and the more Eastern schools. Hall singled out for praise Williams College
and Mark Hopkins, Union College and L. P. Hickok, and Yale College and
Noah Porter. He also praised Harvard as the place where a student could find
"the most extended course of philosophic study" then offered in the United
States.[4]

Hall found grounds for encouragement regarding American philosophy
even beyond the schools he praised. He cited the publication of the *Journal of
Speculative Philosophy* under the editorship of William T. Harris as a particularly hopeful sign, and he urged Harris to open his journal to psychological
studies, such as Hall's, as well as to metaphysical and aesthetic essays. In addition, he called particular attention to Charles S. Peirce's series on the logic of
science, then appearing in *Popular Science Monthly*. This series, which included "How to Make Our Ideas Clear" and "The Fixation of Belief,"
contained some of Peirce's most influential early essays. Hall judged them to
be among "the most important of American contributions to philosophy."
These diverse productions were evidence for Hall of America's "hetero-
geneity." The diversity, though generally positive, resulted in an inevitable
diffusion of philosophical energy; there were simply too many distractions to
be able to sustain much "original work." Nonetheless, Hall took some comfort in believing that despite the distractions and despite the temptations of
business, foundations were being laid for a "maturity of philosophical insight
deep enough at some time to intellectualise and thus harmonise all the diverse
strands in our national life."[5]

If the members of the younger generation experienced many of the same
career frustrations as James and Peirce, their grounding in science and, consequently, their approaches to philosophy were quite different. Whereas Wright,
Peirce, and James were trained scientists before they become philosophers, the
next generation typically came to philosophy from a background and training
outside of science. In most cases, their prior training had been sufficiently lib-

eral so that they were open to the values and methods of the sciences. Still, when it came to understanding, interpreting, and criticizing the methods and results of science or of adapting scientific modes to philosophic purposes, they spoke as outsiders in a way that Wright, Peirce, and James did not. The science of the younger generation of philosophers was imported from without, as they sought to capture some of the success and prestige of science for their own studies by adopting, in some measure, the values and methods of the apparently more successful fields.

It would be almost impossible to identify one individual as the typical philosopher of the generation who received doctorates between 1875 and 1885, but three men illustrate well the frustrations of beginning a career in philosophy in the last quarter of the nineteenth century: G. Stanley Hall, Josiah Royce, and John Dewey. All three came to advanced philosophical study from backgrounds stronger in theology, ethics, and metaphysics than in science. All three also experienced varying degrees of anxiety and difficulty in securing permanent academic posts. A brief review of their early careers will reveal the vicissitudes of becoming a professional academic philosopher in Gilded Age America.[6]

G. Stanley Hall received in 1878 the first Ph.D. in philosophy that Harvard granted for a dissertation in psychology. His route to that degree and to a permanent academic position was circuitous. Born into a strict Congregational family in Ashfield, Massachusetts, in 1844, Hall early saw education as an avenue of escape. Following a year at a local academy, Hall attended Williams College beginning in 1863. Early literary and artistic interests were supplanted by philosophy when Hall came under the influence of Mark Hopkins and John Bascom. As president and professor of moral philosophy, Hopkins was a good example of philosophical instruction at a small college. Widely respected as a teacher, Hopkins emphasized moral philosophy while developing an elaborate scheme that linked the inorganic, the organic, and mind in the service of God's purpose. Bascom, professor of rhetoric and later president of the University of Wisconsin, introduced Hall to more empirical thinkers such as John Stuart Mill and to a more "romantic, rationalistic, and individualistic strain" of thought. Hopkins and especially Bascom seem to have turned Hall in the direction of philosophy. When he graduated in 1867 Hall wanted to pursue his studies in Germany, but lacking the resources, he reluctantly settled for theological study at Union Theological Seminary in New York.[7]

Hall's work at Union only increased his desire to study philosophy in Germany, then the goal for most aspiring young scholars. Inspired by the example of George Sylvester Morris, who had recently returned from Germany, Hall found funding and traveled to Germany in 1869. In Germany he came under the influence of F. A. Trendelenberg, who emphasized an empirical approach to philosophical problems. Running short of money, Hall was forced to return to the United States without his Ph.D. He completed his divinity studies and began to search for a position in philosophy, hoping his study in Germany would lend credibility to his applications. In at least one case, however, his German studies apparently cost Hall a position. A midwestern university president turned Hall down with the comment that his ideas would "unsettle men and teach them to hold no opinions." For two years he served as a tutor to a wealthy New York family, and then in 1872, he received an appointment at Antioch College.[8] Hall's first academic post reflected the eclecticism then expected of most college instructors. Initially he taught French, German, rhetoric, English literature, and Anglo-Saxon. In his second year, following the resignation of the president, Hall became professor of moral philosophy and English literature. He gladly gave up Anglo-Saxon and took on the senior course in philosophy. As Hall recalled, his chair was a "whole settee." Hall expanded his participation into other college activities and into the community. In spite of his best efforts to ingratiate himself into the life of the college and the community, Hall's position proved to be temporary. The college entered a period of financial difficulty and declining enrollments which left Hall with too few students to justify continuing his appointment. By 1876 he was again seeking a position in philosophy.[9]

In spite of his upbringing and his divinity studies, Hall found himself running afoul of the religious test for appointments in philosophy. By the mid-1870s, he began to see psychology, with its emphasis on scientific methods, as a safer route to a permanent appointment. Germany was then the center of psychological research and education, but Hall still lacked the funds to study at a German university. In 1876, Hall began graduate work in philosophy and psychology under James in Cambridge. While studying for his doctorate, Hall, as we have seen, complained publicly in the *Nation* about the lack of suitable positions for a man of his training. In 1878 Hall completed his doctorate in philosophy with a psychological emphasis and with a dissertation entitled "The Muscular Perception of Space." With no job in the offing, Hall secured funds to return to Germany for advanced study, in hopes of strengthening his credentials, especially in the psychological laboratory.[10]

Hall conducted a long campaign to secure a post in either philosophy or psychology at the newly opened Johns Hopkins University. Between 1876 and 1881 he repeatedly offered his services to President Daniel Coit Gilman. Gilman, however, was still uncertain as to the direction philosophical instruction should take at the university and initially sought someone with more stature than Hall. Others in the running included William James, Charles S. Peirce, and George Sylvester Morris. James, after long negotiations with both Gilman and President Charles W. Eliot of Harvard, finally in 1881 decided to stay in Cambridge. Peirce, as we have seen, was eventually offered a lectureship in logic, but his ties to the Coast Survey and his personal problems precluded a permanent appointment. Morris gave several sets of lectures at Hopkins in the late seventies and early eighties, but he held a concurrent appointment at the University of Michigan and had no laboratory experience. It was not simply a matter of elimination, however, that led to Hall's first appointment to lecture at Hopkins in 1881. Hall's laboratory training appealed to Gilman, especially his most recent work in Wilhelm Wundt's German laboratory. He came highly recommended by James, and his new interest in educational psychology allowed Gilman to argue more convincingly that thee was indeed a practical side to science at the new university. Hall brought the right scientific qualifications, and his background and divinity degree offered some assurance to the community that the new science of psychology was not wholly at odds with religion. That was an important consideration in a city shocked by the materialism of Thomas H. Huxley's address at the opening of the university and concerned about the scientific emphasis of the first faculty. Thus, after observing Hall for several semesters as lecturer in psychology, Gilman appointed him professor of psychology and pedagogics in November 1884. Even though it was in psychology rather than in philosophy, Hall finally had the position he had been seeking for more than a decade. He later recalled that his appointment at Johns Hopkins "ended what might be called my long apprenticeship of fourteen years since graduation, during much of which I had been very uncertain of my future."[11]

Josiah Royce's path to a Harvard professorship was nearly as circuitous as Hall's was to Johns Hopkins. In the end, it was the efforts of William James as much as Royce's own considerable skills in philosophy that won him an appointment from Eliot. But the path from Grass Valley, California, to Cambridge was long and hard. Royce was born in 1855 in one of the mining camps of California's Sierra Nevada mountains. After receiving his early education in San Francisco, where the family had moved, Royce entered the recently opened University of California in 1871. Though he initially registered in the College of Civil Engineering, Royce ultimately completed the classical course in the College of Letters. His course work was traditional and broadly based in mathematics, science, languages, and literature. Though he had twenty courses in physics, chemistry, geology, and astronomy, he excelled only in his geology courses with Joseph LeConte. These courses did not make him into a scientist, as his real interest lay in philosophy. By the time of Royce's graduation in 1875 at the age of nineteen, his talents were widely recognized both within the university and in the community.[12]

Following graduation, Royce sailed to Germany to continue his studies. The money for the trip had been contributed by local citizens at the urging of Daniel Coit Gilman, then president of the University of California. Royce went initially to the University of Leipzig where he studied, among other subjects, logic and anthropology with Wilhelm Wundt and the history of philosophy with Wilhelm Windelband. In the spring of 1876 he moved to Göttingen to study metaphysics and practical philosophy with Rudolf H. Lotze. Though he could have remained in Germany, he returned to the United States in the summer of 1876. His primary motivation in returning was to take one of the first fellowships at Johns Hopkins, offered him by Gilman, who was now president. Royce thoroughly enjoyed his two years in the small academic community of Hopkins and in the diverse culture of Baltimore. In addition to pursuing his own studies, he offered courses in a variety of areas ranging from Schopenhauer to Spinoza to German Romanticism. Since Hopkins at the time had no permanent professor in philosophy, Royce in many ways taught himself. He did, however, attend the lectures offered in 1878 by George Sylvester Morris and William James. In June of that year he received his Ph.D. with his dissertation, "Interdependence of the Principles of Knowledge," being approved by Morris and Noah Porter, president of Yale. That behind him, Royce faced the far more difficult task of finding a position.[13]

Royce wanted to stay in Baltimore, or at least on the East Coast, but no appointment was forthcoming from Gilman or anyone else. In July 1878 he received an offer of an instructorship in English at the University of California to teach beginning courses in composition and literature. Though he was reluctant to be exiled from philosophy and from the East, the absence of any alternative led Royce to accept the position. The familiar surroundings and friends did not lessen Royce's sense of isolation, and to compensate he threw himself into his work. His initial assessment of his new position was hardly enthusiastic; he wrote Gilman early in his first term that "my new work is not, so far, very uncongenial."[14]

Royce did not slacken in his determination to return east to a position in a more intellectually congenial institution. He repeatedly declared his desire to move to James, Gilman, and other correspondents. He wrote James, for example, that "nobody really studies philosophy here. Metaphysically I am lonely." In part, his loneliness stemmed from a realization that he was not sufficiently orthodox for an appointment in philosophy. Describing to James a gift to the University of California to establish a chair of moral and intellectual philosophy and civil polity, Royce concluded that the appointment would likely go to "some aged Methodist preacher" rather than to "anybody under forty and [under] suspicion of heterodoxy." Not that Royce wanted the professorship permanently, but it might have served as a vehicle to hasten his escape.[15]

James eventually provided the means by which Royce could return from exile. Royce had met James in 1877 and had studied under him briefly when James had lectured at Johns Hopkins in 1878; the two men quickly became friends and philosophical correspondents. Throughout Royce's sojourn in Berkeley, James remained alert for more promising opportunities. In 1880 he recommended his younger colleague for a position at the University of Minnesota. A year later, James thought that there might be a position available at Harvard, but in the end, both men were disappointed. James's decision to take a leave of absence in 1882–83 provided the opportunity Royce was seeking. James persuaded Eliot to appoint Royce for the year at $1250, half of James's salary, to teach psychology, a course on Locke, Berkeley, and Hume, and a graduate course in advanced psychology. James warned Royce of the risks of leaving his more secure position in California, since there were no guarantees that Eliot would continue the appointment beyond the first year. James confided to his friend that he could not "imagine why you should *not* succeed as a teacher here, and that I should suppose your coming for the next year would be practically tantamount to perpetuity. . . . But the *risks,* such as they are, are yours."[16]

In spite of the risks and his family responsibilities to a wife and infant son, Royce's desire to escape California for more hospitable intellectual climates overrode any hesitation. Royce resigned his position at the University of California and in September 1882 boarded a train with his small family for the long transcontinental journey. James's warning about the risks attendant on the move proved to be overstated, but Royce's first three years at Harvard were nonetheless precarious. While no permanent position was immediately forthcoming, he received a second one-year appointment to replace George Herbert Palmer, who had taken a leave. In the third year, he held on only by working part of the time in English. His teaching load in these years ranged from psychology to logic, ethics, metaphysics, and the supervision of advanced composition. Finally, in 1885, Eliot appointed him to a five-year term as assistant professor of philosophy. Not until 1892 was Royce's tenure secure, when he was appointed professor of the history of philosophy.[17]

James's assistance went beyond the practical matters of recommending Royce and pushing Eliot to act on his appointment. Equally important, James provided the moral and emotional support that the lonely and discouraged young philosopher and aspiring professor needed. Royce later testified to James's pervasive influence on him:

My real acquaintance with our host [James] began one
summer day in 1877, when I first visited him in the house
on Quincy Street, and was permitted to pour out my soul to
somebody who really seemed to believe that a young man
might rightfully devote his life to philosophy if he chose. I
was then a student at the Johns Hopkins University. The
opportunities for a life work in philosophy in this country
were few. Most of my friends and advisors had long been
telling me to let the subject alone. Perhaps, so far as I was
concerned, their advice was sound; but in any case I was so
far incapable of accepting that advice. Yet if somebody had
not been ready to tell me that I had a right to work for truth
in my own way, I should ere long have been quite discouraged. I do not know what I then could have done.
James found me at once—made out what my essential
interests were at our first interview, accepted me, with all
my imperfections, as one of those many souls who ought to
be able to find themselves in their own way, gave a patient
and willing ear to just my variety of philosophical experience, and used his influence from that time on, not to win
me as a follower, but to give me my chance. It was upon his
responsibility that I was later led to get my first opportunities here at Harvard. Whatever I am is in that sense
due to him.[18]

William James's role as mentor was central to the academic success of both
Hall and Royce. James's actions on behalf of his students, as well as for friends
like Charles Peirce, illustrates the development of a philosophical profession
in the new universities of the early 1880s. In order for philosophy to develop
into an academic profession, two elements had to be in place. First, the establishment of positions was needed, to which young, newly trained scholars
could be appointed. This was beginning to occur in the early eighties, though
more slowly than the younger men would have liked. For some of these positions at least, the test of religious orthodoxy was less stringently applied,
though applicants still worried, and rightly so, whether their views would pass
muster. A second factor in securing a position in this time of transition was the
flexibility of the candidate. Aspiring philosophers had to be willing and able
to adapt their skills and interests to the needs of a college or university. They
might be required, as were Hall and Royce, to forego their primary interests in
order to secure teaching posts of some description. The needs of a school and
the desires of its president clearly took precedence over the special interests or
skills of the candidate. In many cases, the applicant had to endure a period of

"apprenticeship." A lectureship or a series of one-year appointments enabled the president to observe close at hand the ability and personal qualities of the potential professor. Full club membership, in the form of a professorship, came only when the aspirant had proven himself to be a skilled teacher, a publishing scholar, and a relative conformist on religious and personal grounds. It was not so much that particular religious views were prescribed, but that certain heterodox ones (materialism, atheism) were proscribed. Personally, an element of eccentricity was tolerated, but successful applicants were still expected to conduct their affairs as gentlemen.

Given these constraints for appointment and retention, the role of mentor can be clarified. James was successful in guiding and assisting Hall and Royce to secure and retain permanent positions because these two men were willing to play by the rules. They obtained their doctorates, they served their apprenticeships in exile, they adapted their skills to the needs of the school and the demands of the president, they moderated their heterodox views, and they proved to be congenial colleagues. They persisted, they held on in whatever position would move them closer to the goal, they published and gained a reputation. Finally, their ability and effort, combined with the efforts of mentors like James, secured them appropriate positions. The case of Charles Peirce provides an instructive counterexample. Though Peirce is today recognized as perhaps America's greatest philosopher, his exile was more thorough-going than anything endured by Hall or Royce; by the mid-1880s it was permanent. All of James's best efforts to secure for Peirce a post commensurate with his intellectual gifts were for naught. The reasons for Peirce's failure, as we have seen, are complex and still partly obscured. However, part of the problem lay in Peirce's unwillingness to play the game by the rules then in force. He failed to obtain a doctorate. At Johns Hopkins, he was unwilling to take the risk of severing his ties to the Coast Survey to devote all his energies to his academic responsibilities. His personal characteristics and behavior barred him from full membership in the club of the professoriate. James, or any mentor, could succeed in advancing the career of a protege or friend only with the cooperation of the candidate. A potential professor had to be willing to take advice, to bend and adapt to the situation, and to wait for the appropriate vacancy. Hall and Royce were willing, if somewhat restive, apprentices; Peirce was not.[19]

The case of John Dewey, the youngest of the three philosophers to enter into a career between 1875 and 1885, reveals how quickly the profession of philosophy was developing. When Dewey received his Ph.D. from Johns Hopkins in 1884 he was able to step immediately into a position at the University of Michigan. There was an element of luck here, for his graduate advisor, George Sylvester Morris, was also professor of philosophy at Michigan and thus knew

Dewey and his work intimately. Dewey's early career nonetheless will serve as a good example of the way in which the steps to a professorship of philosophy were becoming more regular, if not yet commonplace.

Dewey was born in Burlington, Vermont, in 1859. He was raised under the evangelical influence of his mother, though beginning in adolescence he rebelled against her strict limitations. In church and college he was exposed to a more liberal evangelicalism, which had a significant influence upon him. Following his high-school education in Burlington, he stayed on to attend the University of Vermont. Though a state institution, the university still had the flavor of the old-time college, with a liberal Protestant bias in most of the instruction. A small school (enrollment never exceeded one hundred while Dewey attended), the university provided close contact between faculty and students. The intimacy of the place facilitated the molding of character as well as of minds.[20]

Dewey pursued a traditional course of study, enrolling in the classical curriculum. Many of his courses barely held his interest, though apparently the sciences, with their exciting new discoveries, appealed to him. Dewey read widely outside the classroom, largely in areas of economics, politics, social problems, ethics, and religious and philosophical issues. Dewey's last year of study, however, proved most fruitful. Here the emphasis was on moral and mental philosophy, history, and law. H. A. P. Torrey, the professor of mental and moral philosophy, left an especially deep impression on the young scholar. An intuitionist and a Kantian, Torrey held that innate ideas were a necessary precondition for knowledge. Fortunately for Dewey, Torrey's broader philosophical views were eclectic and he was unwilling to impose his personal beliefs upon his students. Torrey introduced Dewey to idealism, something that would be an important element of the younger man's early philosophy. Despite his growing interest in philosophy, stimulated by Torrey, Dewey's initial plans upon graduation in 1879 were to take up high-school teaching.[21]

Dewey's career as a high-school teacher lasted only three years, during which he pursued his growing interest in philosophy while instructing his students in Latin, algebra, and science. He taught for two years in Oil City, Pennsylvania, where a cousin was principal. Then in 1881–82 he taught the winter term at Lake View Seminary, south of Burlington, Vermont. Throughout these years Dewey pursued his philosophical reading and began to set down some of his own ideas on paper. W. T. Harris published two of Dewey's early essays in the *Journal of Speculative Philosophy* in 1882. When he returned to Vermont in 1881, Dewey renewed his relationship with H. A. P. Torrey. During the months when Dewey was not teaching, he and Torrey were frequently together discussing the philosophy Dewey had been reading. Dewey later recalled that he owed Torrey "a double debt, that of turning my thoughts definitely to the study of philosophy as a life-pursuit, and of a generous gift of time to me during a year devoted privately under his direction to a reading of classics in the history of philosophy and learning to read philosophic German." It was during this year that Dewey, encouraged by Torrey, decided to begin graduate work in philosophy.[22]

Dewey applied to Johns Hopkins. Since his finances were limited, he hoped to receive one of the five-hundred-dollar fellowships the university offered. Despite Torrey's high praise Dewey received neither a fellowship nor one of the lower-paying scholarships. Still, his desire for advanced study was so strong that he borrowed five hundred dollars from an aunt and entered Johns Hopkins in 1882. Dewey knew full well the uncertainties surrounding his decision. Writing more than forty years later, he recalled that "to enter upon that new thing, 'graduate work' . . . was something of a risk; the work offered there [at Johns Hopkins] was almost the only indication that there were likely to be any self-supporting jobs in the field of philosophy for others than clergymen."[23]

At Johns Hopkins, George Sylvester Morris made the greatest impact on the aspiring philosopher. Morris was, as Dewey described him, a neo-Hegelian who "combined logical and idealist metaphysics with a realistic epistemology." Morris's philosophy appealed to Dewey not only because of the "enthusiastic and scholarly devotion" with which it was presented, but because "it supplied a demand for unification that was doubtless an intense emotional craving, and yet was a hunger that only an intellectualized subject-matter could satisfy." Unfortunately, in Dewey's time the department of philosophy was the weakest in the university. There was still no full professor; Morris lectured only for the half-year, and Peirce was only a lecturer in logic. Dewey eventually took Peirce's course in logic during his second year, but he was disappointed, for the lectures appealed "more strongly to the mathematical students than to the philosophical."[24] Dewey also took several courses in psychology with Hall, then newly appointed, and performed some laboratory experiments, but they seem to have made less of an immediate impression than his work with Morris. The limited opportunities to study philosophy at Johns Hopkins disturbed Dewey. Equally distressing was the empirical bias to much of the instruction throughout the university. Dewey hoped that philosophy could play a more important role in the future: "I hope that when the public mind is somewhat at rest on the subject of 'sciences' in education, there may be a humble agitation in favor of smuggling philosophy in somewhere; and that it will be found not altogether absurd to urge that our theology, our politics, and possibly even our science itself would be none the worse for thorough and scientific treatment of philosophy in our universities and colleges."[25]

Morris was important to Dewey not only as an intellectual mentor but also as a graduate advisor, who eased the young scholar's entry into a professional career. Morris quickly recognized Dewey's abilities, and in the spring of 1883 he secured Dewey an appointment to teach the history of philosophy to Hopkins undergraduates. Dewey described the experience as "enjoyable" and as giving him the opportunity to review the material. In 1883–84, Dewey, bolstered by recommendations from Morris, Torrey, and others, was finally awarded a fellowship. His own classes and his dissertation now took most of his time, though he still taught an occasional class in philosophy. His dissertation, "The Psychology of Kant," reflected a growing interest in psychology during his final year of study. Once Dewey completed the dissertation and the accompanying comprehensive examination, Morris again forwarded his career. George Holmes Howison had resigned as Morris's assistant at Michigan to take a post at the University of California, and Morris recommended Dewey as his replacement. In July 1884, President James B. Angell, who had known the Dewey family when he was president of the University of Vermont, offered Dewey an instructorship at nine hundred dollars a year.[26]

Dewey, unlike James, Peirce, Hall, or Royce, stepped immediately into a position in philosophy for which his education had prepared him. After a year on the Michigan faculty, Dewey was appointed to a permanent position when Morris became head of the department. Morris and Dewey reduced the theological bent of much of the instruction; they paid more attention to new developments in psychology and English philosophy. Still, their instruction was idealistic in these years. Between 1884 and 1888 Morris and Dewey revitalized philosophy at the university, and Dewey began to gain a national reputation through his growing list of publications. In 1888 his reputation as a scholar and teacher won him election as professor of mental and moral philosophy at the University of Minnesota. Only a year later he returned to Michigan to assume Morris's post following his teacher's sudden death.[27] His long academic career was now well launched.

Although Dewey worried about the risks of taking up a career in philosophy in the early 1880s, his path to a permanent position lacked the vicissitudes that had marked earlier careers. It was not simply a matter of Dewey's ability or luck. Rather, by the mid-1880s the growing emphasis on science, the presence of Ph.D.-granting institutions such as Johns Hopkins, the expansion of higher education, and the willingness of mentors and advisors like James and Morris to support their students facilitated the transition from graduate student to professor. Dewey, of course, possessed some advantages, in that his early idealism was compatible with Christian tradition, and at the same time he had some training in the newer psychological theories and methods. He was also a hard-working and congenial colleague. Notwithstanding Dewey's personal characteristics and the relative orthodoxy of his thought, the ease with which he moved from graduate student to full professor owed much to the growing professionalization of philosophy in the mideighties.

Professionalization was not confined solely to the academy, even if Hall and James in their assessments of American philosophy in the 1870s had focused primarily on the status of philosophy in the colleges and universities. That focus was appropriate, for if those like Hall and James were to have careers in philosophy, the best hope lay in a changed and revitalized university. Hall also pointed to another important aspect of an academic profession—appropriate outlets for the results of scholarly research. Writing, ironically, in an English journal, *Mind,* Hall commended W. T. Harris's *Journal of Speculative Philosophy,* which was established in 1867 and was perhaps the first philosophical journal in English. The journal was published under the auspices of the St. Louis Philosophical Society, a group which included among its members Harris, later United States commissioner of education, and George Holmes Howison, later professor of philosophy at the University of California. Despite the fact that it had no academic base, the *Journal of Speculative Philosophy* published many essays of the professionalizing academic philosophers. James, Royce, Peirce, and Dewey all published in Harris's journal. Hall was pleased to report in 1879 that the "quality of the original articles has steadily improved, and the influence of the *Journal* seems on the whole to be increasing in the country." Still, he urged Harris to do more to support the newer tendencies in philosophy and psychology: "There seems scarcely a doubt that, should Mr. Harris decide to open his *Journal* to psychological as well as to metaphysical discussions, and in preference to the aesthetical selections which have been so often weary and unprofitable, it would soon become not only self-supporting but remunerative." In addition to the *Journal of Speculative Philosophy,* Hall cited *Popular Science Monthly,* edited by E. L. Youmans as an outlet for the more scientifically oriented philosopher. *Popular Science Monthly* had recently published Peirce's "Illustrations of the Logic of Science," including the essays "How to Make Our Ideas Clear" and "The Fixation of Belief," which are often taken to be the founding statements of pragmatism.[28] Though Hall did not explicitly raise the issue, it is hard not to conclude that he wanted to encourage more avenues of publication and to ensure that they were open to the newer trends.

Hall's implicit call for new and better journals was only slowly taken up in the next two decades. Paul Carus, a German-born philosopher and editor who had emigrated to the United States, established two philosophical journals, *The Open Court* in 1887 and *The Monist* in 1888. *The Open Court* focused on ethical issues, while *The Monist* was more technical. Carus opened *The Monist* widely and invited submissions in the history of philosophy and the philosophy of science and of religion, from European as well as American philosophers. Though in part a vehicle for the advancement of Carus's own monistic views, *The Monist* published many significant essays by philosophers such as Dewey and Peirce.[29] Carus's journals reflected his idiosyncratic approach and, while providing outlets for publication, were not entirely suited to the publishing needs of the growing body of academic philosophers.

Not until the establishment of *Philosophical Review* at Cornell University in 1892 did the academic philosophers have a journal they could truly call their own. In his prefatory statement in the first issue of *Philosophical Review,* Jacob Gould Schurman, the journal's first editor, called attention to many of the developments discussed above to justify the establishment of the *Review.* Of particular concern to him was the absence of an "official organ" for the discipline, when competing disciplines such as mathematics, chemistry, biology, philology, and archaeology had all recently established professional journals. Philosophic progress, Schurman believed, rested on cooperation, and that was impossible with "neither an organ nor an organization of philosophical activity." Schurman pointed to "the establishment of new philosophical professorships and schools," to the growing number of graduate students in philosophy and psychology, and to the increase in the numbers and quality of philosophic authors as sufficient warrant to establish a new journal. The *Review,* he hoped, would not only publish the increasingly specialized researches of the philosophers, but would also foster increased cooperation in a discipline more and more divided by specialities.[30] The journal was thus conceived with a twofold purpose: to provide an outlet for the more specialized researches then coming into vogue in academic philosophy, and to counter the tendency of philosophy to splinter along specialized lines, by encouraging a spirit of cooperation. With *Philosophical Review* the academic philosophers had an "organ" of their own, but it was by no means an "official organ." The centrifugal tendency of specialization produced a proliferation of journals in the next decades, beginning with *Psychological Review* in 1894 and the *Journal of Philosophy, Psychology, and Scientific Methods* in 1904. When that happened, specialization began to win out over the broad-minded conception of cooperation envisioned by Schurman.

By the 1890s, then, the conditions for the creation of a professionalized academic philosophy were in place. The rise of the research university and the general expansion of higher education provided an increasing number of vacancies. The growth of graduate education and the acceptance of the Ph.D. in the wake of the founding of Johns Hopkins in 1876 established a means to educate and to certify potential professors. The willingness of men like James and Morris to become mentors and advisors to younger philosophers, and to use their influence to secure positions for their students, facilitated the appointment of these young scholars to appropriate posts. Specialization, though not yet commonplace, had begun to supplant the eclecticism demanded by the midcentury college, and more narrowly defined chairs replace "settees." At the same time, more technical and specialized journals such as *The Monist, Philosophical Review,* and *Psychological Review* were appearing to publish the results of the new research. The development of these facets of professional activity meant the emergence, by the early nineties, of academic philosophy as a self-replicating discipline. Membership in the profession was largely defined by those who were already members; new colleagues and successors were chosen almost exclusively from the profession's own students. The eclecticism of midcentury was disparaged, and even the relative openness of the 1870s, when James took up his academic post, was past. With few exceptions, subsequent generations of philosophers would follow the career path laid down by Hall, Royce, and Dewey in the last quarter of the nineteenth century.[31]

Certain continuities in the careers of James and the subsequent generation should not obscure the fact that Hall, Royce, and Dewey were not scientist-philosophers as were Wright, Peirce, and James. The younger men had indeed been exposed to the prevailing scientism of the period, had perhaps taken courses in the natural and physical sciences, and had perhaps even conducted experiments in the primitive psychological laboratories of the day. But they could not say, as Peirce had, that they were thoroughly saturated with science. Still, they were well aware of the power of scientific method and of the appeal and prestige of science, both in the university and in the broader culture. Even as they struggled to find and to secure permanent academic positions, these men tried to come to terms with the significance of the values and methods of science for the new philosophies they sought to create.

FOUR

Philosophy and the Challenge of Science at the End of the Nineteenth Century

The rise of specialization and professionalization in American higher education had provoked profound changes in the careers of philosophers during the 1870s and 1880s. Men as diverse as William James, G. Stanley Hall, Josiah Royce, and John Dewey had met that challenge by creating through their own careers the professional academic philosopher and psychologist. Their personal challenges were matched by an intellectual challenge that would shape philosophic dialogue in the coming decades. Science, in its values and methodology, posed fundamental challenges to traditional philosophy's assumptions, methods, and conclusions. Although Chauncey Wright, William James, and Charles Peirce had addressed some of these issues in the 1860s and 1870s, they were confronted anew in the 1880s and 1890s.

The question of whether philosophy was a science was the most basic question facing philosophers at the end of the century. Philosophy from the time of Plato and Aristotle had leaned heavily upon the science of the day, and certain philosophers, such as Leibniz and Descartes, had achieved renown in science as well as in philosophy. The pattern in America had been to coordinate scientific concerns with theological and moral issues. Science could provide basic descriptive and explanatory information about the natural world, but the philosopher's task was to interpret that information in a broad theological, moral, and philosophical context. It was in this sense that the Baconian science of the early nineteenth century was closely allied to the reigning Scottish Realism.[1] The publication of *The Origin of Species* in 1859, the growing number of discoveries and interpretive successes in the natural and physical sciences, and the obvious practical applications of science in the building of an urban and industrial America called into question the necessity and legitimacy of that intimate link between science, on the one hand, and philosophy and theology, on the other. Scientists had developed the ability to offer workable explanations and interpretations entirely within a scientific context; they no longer needed to rely upon philosophers and theologians to provide an intellectual or emotional context for understanding. In the last quarter of the nineteenth century, philosophers were forced to reassess their role and the relationship of their traditional discipline to the newly aggressive and assertive sciences.

The pervasive scientism of the late nineteenth century challenged the philosophers to rethink and perhaps to redefine the relationship of philosophy and science. Most fundamentally, Was philosophy itself a science? Philosophy's long heritage of intimate ties with science gave some philosophers grounds for believing that it was indeed a science, but one with a different subject matter or, perhaps a broader, more synoptic vision. Other philosophers acknowledged that their discipline was not yet a science, but exuded confidence that it might soon join the ranks of the sciences. A recurring question in these decades among philosophers of very different outlooks was whether philosophy should or could become a science. The appeal of scientific values and methodology was strong because of the apparent successes the scientists regularly unveiled and because of the esteem in which the academic community and the culture at large held the sciences and scientists. The effort to rethink and perhaps redefine philosophy was in part an effort to capture some of the glory and prestige that had recently accrued to science and to recapture some of the eminence that had once been philosophy's, when it had been the "queen of the sciences." But beyond this cultural anxiety there lay a serious intellectual issue: Did the methodology and values of modern science require the reconceptualization of philosophy as a science? If that was the case, then what were the implications for philosophy as a discipline, as a mode of inquiry, as a source of explanation and interpretation? If philosophy was not to be reconceived as a science of some description, then what was to be its role in a world increasingly given over to science? These were the issues that philosophers of all persuasions had to confront in the waning years of the century.

The same debates, in various forms, have persisted throughout much of this century. Subsequent to the period under study here, logical positivism and analytic philosophy at least implicitly addressed the issues by trying to develop a philosophical style and method analogous to that of the sciences. Although these approaches would dominate much post–World War II philosophy in America, there has also been a reaction against the more extreme claims of the scientizing philosophers. Philosophers as diverse as Richard Bernstein, Hilary Putnam, and Richard Rorty have taken up the question of whether philosophy is, can be, or ought to be a science. In answering with a qualified no, they have, significantly, returned to the work of the men under discussion here—Peirce, James, Dewey, and Royce—for inspiration and support.[2] The pragmatic turn in American philosophy can be fully appreciated only by understanding the debates on these issues as they took place some one hundred years ago.

William James, John Dewey, and Charles Sanders Peirce were the philosophers who most fully and most perceptively addressed the relationship of science and philosophy before 1900. James and Peirce, of course, had begun grappling with these issues more than a decade before Dewey, but all three responded to the rising challenges in the eighties and nineties. There were some areas of common concern, but each of these men developed a distinctive viewpoint regarding the proper ties between philosophy and science. All explored the characteristics of a science and the limits of scientific inquiry, though each established those limits differently. James tried to steer a middle road between the extremes of scientism and materialism on the one side, and the extremes of faith and spiritualism on the other. Dewey's concept of the relationship changed in these two decades, from viewing philosophy as the highest science, to conceiving of philosophy and science as two separate fields, with philosophy dependent upon science for knowledge of facts about the external world. Toward the end of the century, Dewey began to conceive of instrumentalism as reconciling the competing claims of science and philosophy in a concern for solving human problems. Of the three, Peirce was the most committed to making his philosophy, if not all philosophy, into a science based on logic. A scientific philosophy for Peirce was directed toward seeking truth for truth's sake, not toward any practical or humanitarian ends, but it also allowed room for the right to believe in the existence of God. Traditional philosophy had gloried in the development and elaboration of personal vision, but a science, however dependent upon the spark of genius for original insight, develops, as Peirce argued, through the consensus of the competent. Science ordinarily works within a consensual context in which there is broad agreement among practitioners upon crucial questions, basic interpretive structures, and proper methodologies. Peirce's ideas, in particular, have become the basis for a lively debate both in the United States and in Europe regarding the role of the community in establishing the possibilities of knowledge.[3]

The diversity of individual vision evident in the conceptions of James, Dewey, and Peirce suggest the difficulty of reconceptualizing philosophy as a science. Without a doubt, James, Dewey, and Peirce were among America's most competent philosophers, but, as we shall see, they shared no consensus on the precise relationship of philosophy and science, though there were some broad areas of agreement. The absence of a consensus continued to plague philosophers well into the twentieth century and eventually led some of the more extreme advocates of science to attempt to create a consensus by definition and by the exclusion from philosophy of those who could not or would not agree to the new conception. James, Dewey, and Peirce, then, not only helped to frame the debate on philosophy and science, but in their own failure to achieve consensus on key issues, they set a pattern for succeeding decades, when no single reconstruction of philosophy as a science would win the assent of those competent to judge the issue.

The scientist-philosopher William James remained forever divided between the two camps. Repelled by grand theorizing in the manner of his father, Henry James, Sr., he was yet unable to let go of the conviction that there is some larger order or meaning to things, and that by thinking clearly and obstinately we may gain some insight into the nature of that larger whole. Attracted by the very real achievements of scientific method, James was equally unwilling to go over completely to science and materialism. However valuable for understanding the world and ourselves, science and materialism are not wholly adequate explanations in themselves. In struggling to come to terms with the competing claims of science and philosophy, James set forth a definition of science as he understood it and pointed to the inherent limits of a scientific approach. Though James readily acknowledged the magnitude of scientific achievement, he was perhaps more interested in the fringes of scientific inquiry. It was in those fringes, which were not quite science and which might never become science, that James found the real creative impulse. Here boundary lines were questioned, accepted interpretations challenged, and human imagination given nearly free rein to explore the unknown. Though James could and did draw distinctions between science and philosophy, his real interest in this period lay in finding a middle path between the scientific extremists who would reduce all inquiry to science and all truth to that which could be discovered by scientific method, and the traditionalists and grand systematizers who subsumed all facts under an umbrella of faith and belief. James, like his mountain home with its "14 doors all opening outside," remained open to the possibility of truths developing according to the multifarious needs of individuals and groups. Thus, he would defend faith and belief against the rabid advocates of science and, conversely, urge his spiritualist friends to investigate their phenomena with a scientific temper. In pursuing this via media, James sought to reconcile not only his own competing impulses, but also those of his time and place.[4]

Despite the claims of its "votaries" who would create in science an "idol" for the modern tribe, James steadfastly held to his conviction that science was less than a religion. For him, the value of science lay primarily in its method. "The spirit and principles of science," he wrote, were "mere affairs of method." Since the "essence" of science was method, advocacy of scientific method did not commit one to any particular "fixed belief." James felt no compulsion to subscribe to materialism or to deny the personal and spiritual element of life when he accepted science as a particularly useful mode of inquiry into a wide range of problems. The methodology of science laid down certain "lines within which the rules of the art must fall," but individual creativity and genius shaped the final product within those guidelines.[5] The real power of science for James, then, lay in the success of its method in particular areas of inquiry, not in the validity of the scientific world view asserted by the more extreme materialists of the nineteenth century.

Though James found science most valuable for its methodology, he knew full well that science was more than a set of laboratory procedures or successful experiments. James acknowledged that an ideal science represented "a closed and completed system of truth." The "disciples" of the special sciences were, for James, all too easily convinced that their particular discipline approached the ideal. Skeptical that the ideal had often been achieved, James also recognized the appeal of a closed system, within which explanation and prediction are successful. Success comes in large part because scientific ways of thinking are "highly abstract." The scientist is highly selective in the problems he chooses to investigate, in the methods of his inquiry, and in the range of acceptable solutions. The scientist, through "selection and emphasis," breaks into the *"plenum"* of reality, into the "chaos" of the real world, to bring order to that confusion through "an abstract system of hypothetical data and laws." Since the whole can not be grasped and understood, we are forced to deal with fragments. Natural science "is a mere fragment of truth broken out from the whole mass of it for the sake of practical effectiveness exclusively. *Divide et impera.*" Science, thus, does violence to the fullness of reality, but in the service of some practical benefit for which its methods are particularly suited.[6]

Science and scientific method are valuable in part because they are "the greatest of labor-saving contrivances." James argued that "the best possible sort of system into which to weave an object, mentally, is a *rational* system, or what is called a 'science'." By classifying an object properly, by understanding causes and effects, and by seeing it as an instance of "natural law," we can know and manipulate that object much more successfully. Knowledge of a law, of the abstract formalization of individual detail, enables one to "discharge your memory of masses of particular instances." Science does not, in its formulations, reproduce the actual world, but it does provide shortcuts to understanding and to practical action.[7]

One difficulty in any scientific enterprise is ensuring the validity and truth of the results. Here James followed Peirce in arguing that the agreement of knowledgeable practitioners was the best guarantee of valid results, of scientific truth. Writing in *The Principles of Psychology*, James conceded that all observations are *"difficult and fallible"*: "Something is before us; we do our best to tell what it is, but in spite of our good will we may go astray." James argued that "the only safeguard is in the final *consensus* of our farther knowledge about the thing in question, later views correcting earlier ones, until at last the harmony of a consistent system is reached."[8] Science, then, for James was a practical method of inquiry, a useful abstraction from the chaos of reality which fostered understanding and successful application, and a process of verification based on securing the consensus of a jury of competent peers.

Any science, according to James, established certain limits to its inquiry and accepted certain basic assumptions without question, in order to ensure the verifiability of results and to prevent the scientist from becoming bogged down in illegitimate metaphysical quandaries. James surveyed the boundaries of science when he was trying to establish psychology as a science. In writing *The Principles of Psychology* he tried to keep "close to the point of view of natural science throughout the book. Every natural science assumes certain data uncritically, and declines to challenge the elements between which its own 'laws' obtain, and from which its own deductions are carried on." Psychology as a natural science, he argued, can go no farther than "the empirical correlation of the various sorts of thought or feeling with definite conditions of the brain . . . If she goes farther she becomes metaphysical."[9] Two years later, defending the scientific stance he had taken in his *Principles*, James wrote that "every special science, in order to get at its own particulars at all, must make a number of convenient assumptions and decline to be responsible for questions which the human mind will continue to ask about them." A scientific psychology, like the other natural sciences, must "renounce certain ultimate solutions," and "uncritically" beg "such data as the existence of a physical world, of states of mind, and of the fact that these latter take cognizance of other things." These metaphysical questions are the legitimate preserve of "general philosophy," not of natural science.[10]

But if James sought to limit science to empirical inquiry, he clearly found the problems which lay beyond the boundaries of natural science to be among the most interesting and challenging. James, in fact, believed that the fringe of science, the "irregular phenomena," provided both the greatest challenge to science and the greatest opportunity for scientists of genius. "Round about the accredited and orderly facts of every science," he wrote, "there ever floats a sort of dust-cloud of exceptional observations, of occurrences minute and irregular, and seldom met with, which it always proves less easy to attend to than to ignore." The advocates of ordinary science routinely ignore this "unclassified residuum" of their ideal science because unclassifiable phenomena are "paradoxical absurdities, and must be held untrue." But it is here in this fringe that genius and creativity flourish: "Only the born geniuses let themselves be worried and fascinated by these outstanding exceptions, and get no peace until they are brought within the fold. . . . *Anyone* will renovate his science who will steadily look after the irregular phenomena." James divided science into normal and anomalous science. He found the revolutionary and significant work of the scientist to lie in coming to terms with creating new paradigms out of the anomalous "*wild* facts." Temperamentally drawn to just those fringes in his own work in psychology, in psychical research, and in the study of religious belief, James defended those geniuses like himself who could not be confined by rigid disciplinary boundaries. Science, he believed, progressed not only by following the rules; when a "science is renewed, its new formulas often have more of the voice of the exceptions in them than of what were supposed to be the rules."[11]

Science is not some a priori system imposed upon human inquiry. For James, science was a very human activity the forms and methods of which reflect human needs and interests. The craving for rational understanding which lies behind science is also at the root of philosophy.[12] This individualistic component of science is best seen in those "flashes" of genius that give rise to new scientific interpretations. Similar intuitive leaps give rise to works of poetry and of metaphysical insight in other men. For both Wright and James, the difference between science and poetry or metaphysics lies in what happens after the moment of inspiration. Poetry and obsolete modes of science accept the insight as complete in itself, but modern "'scientific' conceptions must prove their worth by being 'verified.' This test, however, is the cause of their *preservation,* not that of their production."[13] Thus, whether a scientific formulation arises in the course of ordinary experimentation or in reflection on the "*wild* facts" of the fringe has little impact on its sustaining power and influence. Any scientific theory must be put to the test of being verified, of being submitted to the judgment of those competent to judge its viability.

Because the origin of ideas meant little to James, he was more willing than most of his scientific colleagues to take seriously psychical research. Most scientists, James acknowledged, dismissed psychical research with "contemptuous scientific disregard." But James could not so easily dismiss this fringe with its wild phenomena. He scored "academic and critical minds" for their slowness in recognizing unclassifiable facts and asserted that in the frequent debates between mystics and scientists, it was "the mystics who have usually proved to be right about the *facts*." But in granting the mystics the legitimacy of their facts, James still wanted those facts tested by scientific methods. The ultimate goal in psychical research was "to pass from mystical to scientific speculations," which James compared to passing from "lunacy to sanity." Rather than dismissing mystical "facts" outright, James attempted to bring them within the scientific fold, even if that meant risking his reputation as a scientist.[14]

James's advocacy of psychical research is a good example of his pursuit of a middle road in the scientific debates of the late nineteenth century. To the mystics and psychical researchers who were all too ready to accept unsubstantiated and untested phenomena as truth, James urged a strategy of scientific research to uncover, if possible, the real nature of psychic phenomena. As he wrote Thomas Davidson, "the urgent thing, to rescue us from the present disgraceful condition is to ascertain in a manner so thorough as to constitute *evidence* that will be accepted by outsiders, just what the *phenomenal conditions of certain* concrete phenomenal occurrences are. . . . '*Facts*' are what are wanted."[15]

Against this advocacy of science to a group not noted for scientific rigor must be set James's admonitions to scientists to limit their more extreme claims. James acknowledged that science had become "an idol of the tribe to the present generation." Science had achieved such exalted status because of its theoretical and practical achievements: "Science has made such glorious leaps in the last three hundred years, and extended our knowledge of nature so enormously both in general and in detail; men of science, moreover, have as a class displayed such admirable virtues—that it is no wonder if the worshipers of science lose their head." Despite their undeniable successes, the claims of the more imperialistic scientists overreached the existing state of knowledge. Modern science was too recent in its origin and still too imperfect in method to have triumphed totally over other modes of inquiry and other forms of knowledge: "Our science is a drop, our ignorance a sea." Though the achievements of science were great, James concluded that "the world of our present natural knowledge *is* enveloped in a larger world of *some* sort of whose residual properties we at present can frame no positive idea."[16]

As James sought to develop psychology as a natural science and to bring psychical research under the umbrella of science, he also sought to defend faith and belief against an aggressive and imperialist scientism. "Science," he wrote, "must be constantly reminded that her purposes are not the only purposes, and that the order of uniform causation which she has use for, and is therefore right in postulating, may be enveloped in a wider order, on which she has no claims at all." James wanted to shatter the complacent assumptions of both extremes. True believers needed to have their faiths "broken up and ventilated" by the "northwest wind of science." Academic and scientific audiences, however, needed to have a measure of faith restored, so that they might abandon their fruitless search for "scientific evidence" in their desire to "escape all danger of shipwreck in regard to truth." James tried to convince listeners on both sides that we all must sail in uncharted waters: "there is really no scientific or other method by which men can steer safely between the opposite dangers of believing too little or of believing too much. To face such dangers is apparently our duty, and to hit the right channel between them is the measure of our wisdom as men."[17]

In refining his views on science in the last decades of the nineteenth century, James sought to clarify his understanding of the essential characteristics of a science, to extend the boundaries of the ideal sciences into the unclassifiable fringe surrounding each, and to create an intellectual climate in which the legitimate claims and limitations of both science and faith would be respected. Each of us is, for James, master of his or her own fate. Our real challenge as we chart our own course in life is to escape both the hard rocks of scientific materialism and the misty swamps of belief.

John Dewey's formal training in the sciences was far less thorough and systematic than that of either James or Peirce, but no less than the older men, he felt the pull of science in the last decades of the nineteenth century. Dewey's early idealism and particularly his Hegelianism colored his initial approach to science. As a result, his early essays seem less scientific and more metaphysical than contemporaneous works of James and Peirce. Dewey began by merging science and philosophy in a Hegelian synthesis, without really appropriating either the values or the methods of the natural and physical sciences. Gradually, a firmer grasp of scientific method became evident, and Dewey began to acknowledge a distinction between science and philosophy. He still refused, as did James, to accept science as complete in itself; the task of philosophy was to give to the discoveries and theories of science the wider meaning they lacked in themselves. Finally, Dewey began to argue that in an instrumentalism directed toward human ends and goals we could reconcile the moral component of humanity with the factual component of science. Science remained independent, but under the direction of the instrumentalists scientific progress could be directed toward solving human problems and toward achieving human goals.

Dewey, like so many of his contemporaries, readily acknowledged the power of scientific method. It put into the hands of the investigator the method of experimentation, which permitted "exact measurement" and increased "power of analysis." By changing the variables in a particular case, the scientist could now "select the indispensable." These "advantages" of any science were so well known in the 1880s that Dewey felt they hardly needed comment. Beyond a useful methodology, scientists had contributed to society a string of interpretive and practical successes that had a pervasive influence on all activity, including philosophy. "Every important development in science," Dewey wrote, "contributes to the popular consciousness, and indeed to philosophy, some new conception which serves for a time as a most valuable category of classification and explanation."[18] For Dewey, however, this acknowledgment of the power and influence of science was only the first step toward placing science in its proper role in a larger sphere of knowledge and understanding.

In a brief statement published only two months after his essay on the new psychology celebrating the achievements of science, Dewey attacked the empty realism and materialism of much modern science. Never before had "the accumulation of facts" been "regarded so universally as an end in itself." Skepticism was rampant, and "thousands are spending their time and their strength in investigating the minutest facts of nature and of history." Dewey did not deny the potential value of such inquiries, but he argued that "these facts are not yet knowledge, until they have been brought into relation with the *whole nature of man*, or with his activities, social and moral." It is not enough to relate these facts to the nature of man. They ultimately must be brought into a relation with God: "That science or philosophy is worthless which does not ultimately bring every fact into guiding relation with the living activity of man, and the end of all his striving—approach to God."[19] Science by itself is thus devoid of meaning and essentially useless.

Dewey's most sustained effort in his early writings to bring science into a proper relationship with man and God was an essay entitled "Psychology as Philosophic Method." His purpose here was to develop a positive statement and defense of psychology as "the ultimate science of reality." Consciousness, Dewey held, is "the sole content, account and criterion of all reality." Psychology is "the science of this consciousness." It is the science of reality both in its totality and in its particulars. Because philosophy studies the totality, and because psychology is the method of philosophy, psychology becomes "in short, *philosophic method*." Dewey rejected any sharp dualism between universal consciousness and individual consciousness; psychology was the science of consciousness in both its universal and individualized aspects. Because we are human, we must begin our inquiry with the individual. The universal is only partially realized in humans, and, consequently, our science of consciousness can only be partial. But from these imperfect beginnings, Dewey argued, we might go on to philosophize about the universal.[20]

Dewey distinguished between philosophy and psychology as distinct sciences of absolute self-consciousness. Philosophy is the science of absolute self-consciousness, and psychology is the science of the manifestation of this absolute self-consciousness in "the knowing and acting of individual men." Dewey was not distinguishing between fundamentally different subject matters; it was simply "a distinction of treatment, of ways of looking at the same material." Just as he rejected a dualism in consciousness, Dewey argued for the essential unity of philosophy and psychology. The subject matter of philosophy is absolute self-consciousness, but the absolute can only be realized in and through man's "conscious experience." Thus, since psychology is the science of the absolute's realization in humans, "what else can philosophy in its fulness be but psychology, and psychology but philosophy."[21] Though Dewey here defines both philosophy and psychology as sciences, his definitions bear little resemblance to the more materialistic conceptions of most natural and physical scientists.

Dewey's conception of philosophy gives it the dominant role in its relation with science. Philosophy, he argued, stands "in a double relation to Science. In its first aspect it is *a* science—the highest of all sciences." The special scientists investigate their particular realms of reality, and their discoveries constitute the science. But the divisions of the special sciences are ultimately artificial. We are soon led to "broaden and deepen" our inquiry by connecting together the results of the individual sciences until "we ask after the nature of all reality, as one connected system. The answer to this question constitutes philosophy as one science amid the circle of sciences." But that is only one side of this double relation of science and philosophy: "At the same time that philosophy is seen as the completion of the sciences, it is seen as their basis." Philosophy is "no longer *a* science; it is Science." Because the special sciences contain only partial truth, none of them is "in strict truth science." The special sciences, restricted as they are to inquiries in their particular spheres, cannot legitimately investigate the relation of the particular to the whole of reality. But only "in this whole is categorical truth to be found . . . Philosophy as the science of this whole appears no longer therefore as *a* science, but as all Science taken in its organic systematic wholeness."[22] Philosophy then is both the science of the absolute self-consciousness and the unifying bond of the special sciences in their investigations of particular manifestations of the absolute.

The method of philosophy is psychology, which, like philosophy, stands in a dual relationship to its material. On the one hand, it is a special science like any other, based on "systematic observation, experiment, conclusion and verification." But it is also the science "in which every special science has its life, and from which it must abstract when it sets up for an independent existence of its own." The other special sciences deal with "some one phase of conscious experience," whereas psychology is the "manifestation and explication of this consciousness." Psychology thus appears "as Science itself, that is, as systematic account and comprehension of the nature of conscious experience."[23]

Dewey in his analysis of both philosophy and psychology as sciences clearly subordinated scientific values to an idealistic account of reality. The absolute self-consciousness is the basis of all reality and of all partial manifestations of self-consciousness in individuals. Scientific inquiry, in the physical, natural, or psychological sciences, cannot be complete in itself because it deals with only a partial reality. Only by using psychology as the method of philosophy are we able to universalize our individual experience and so gain some insight into the absolute. Dewey's scheme seems to allow for the special sciences to pursue their own investigations, but their discoveries are subordinate to the effort to gain a conception of the wider whole. As Bruce Kuklick has noted, the way in which Dewey united the sciences as Science and Philosophy "remains mysterious."[24] Still, in subsuming the sciences under philosophy as Science, Dewey enunciated one common strategy of philosophers to meet the challenge of science: science was successful within its own sphere, but it needed philosophy and philosophers to give it wholeness, to connect it with the deeper meanings of life.

This strategy of taking the special sciences into some greater philosophic unity differs significantly from the approach of James. James, of course, recognized that science was not complete in itself and that there were legitimate realms of faith and belief which were not subject to scientific analysis. Still, James was more willing to accept scientific inquiry and faith as distinct realms, and he felt little of Dewey's passion for unification under the umbrella of philosophy. The difference, I suspect, lies in James's scientific training and in Dewey's background in the Hegelianism of Torrey and Morris. For James, science as a mode of inquiry was complete in itself, even if we as humans have need of a broader range of faith and belief for our own well-being. But for Dewey in the mid-1880s, science could be understood only as a subordinate part of the effort to understand the absolute self-consciousness as manifested in the individual. James as philosopher retained the outlook of the scientist; Dewey revealed the imprint of Hegelian idealism.

Dewey, like James, sought to limit the reach of science as an all-embracing theory of the universe. Ethics was for Dewey one area in which the claims of the natural and physical sciences had little legitimate influence. He viewed with some alarm the increasingly imperialistic claims of science: "Physics, chemistry, biology, geology, each separately, and all in their combination, [have] reached a point where they thrust forth their arms to claim man as a mere fact within the world of nature, the realm of events in space and time." Scientists, Dewey claimed, were no longer content to restrict their special inquiries; they now frequently sought to create a "mechanical philosophy" and even a scientific ethics. The basis of a scientific ethics would be "the ascertained and demonstrated laws of the universe." The advocates of such an ethics claimed that it eliminated the arbitrariness of theological ethics and that it would set morality upon the same solid footing as science itself.[25]

Whatever the appeal of a scientific ethics, Dewey found himself "unmoved" and unconvinced. He remained certain that "the cause of theology and morals is one" and that "the physical interpretation of the universe is one which necessarily shuts out those ideas and principles which are fundamental to ethics." The standpoint of science, the physical interpretation of reality, was "fatal at once to the categories of morals and to the attitude of the practical life of morality." Moral considerations, Dewey argued, must be based on three elements which were antithetical to the physical sciences: "(1) activity for an end, that which has a purpose or aim, in technical phrase teleological action; (2) activity from choice, from the decision of personality, volitional action; and (3) activity towards an ideal, that which is not, but which ought to be." Despite the power of the physical sciences in their proper realm, they are incapable of meeting these three tests for establishing an ethics. As Dewey argued, "we cannot admit the claims of physical science to be the founder of the ethical system for the coming man," because "(1) ethics deals with an end, and there is no place for an end in nature as confined to space and time; and because (2) even if there were an end in the universe, this would not of itself constitute the ideal for human conduct; and because (3) science is utterly unable to establish the essential feature of the ethical ideal, its insistence upon the identity of humanity in their relation to it."[26] In this essay Dewey not only attempted to limit the claims of science, he also more clearly differentiated the spheres of philosophy and science. Though his approach was not wholly at odds with subsuming science under an all-inclusive philosophy, his emphasis here was to demarcate the respective responsibilities of the two modes of inquiry.

In the late eighties and early nineties Dewey began to move away from the absolute idealistic conception of science which had marked his early essays. This tendency is evident in his differentiation of ethics and science and becomes more pronounced in his studies on logic. Dewey still firmly rejected a dualism in subject matter or even method, but he was now more willing to give to science and to logic a standing independent of some greater philosophical absolute. For Dewey, the method of science and the method of logic were not identical, though they shared a number of crucial characteristics.

Dewey's view of logic may show the influence of Peirce, with whom he had studied at Johns Hopkins.[27] Less insistent than Peirce on the primacy of logic, Dewey nonetheless argued that logic was a fundamental characteristic of scientific thought and a necessary method in the pursuit of truth. He acknowledged the prevailing scientism of the era and believed that "logical theory must be the endeavor to account for, to justify, or at least to reckon with this scientific spirit." Dewey believed that the newer methods in logic were cognizant of contemporaneous developments in science and that the newer logicians concerned themselves with establishing a method based on facts and capable of producing truth. This, Dewey noted, was "the Logic of science, *i.e.*, of actual knowledge."[28]

Dewey opposed any implied bifurcation of the universe into the logical and nonlogical, or scientific and nonscientific. He postulated a continuum in which all modes of observation and inquiry deal with the same universe, but within which certain methods of inquiry, the logical and the scientific, achieve higher degrees of truthfulness because the investigators are self-conscious about their methods. The world, for Dewey, was "but one world, the world of knowledge," and that "one world is everywhere logical." In our ordinary modes of inquiry, the logical aspects are "undeveloped" and "latent" and the results, consequently, are often erroneous. In scientific investigation, the underlying logic is more conscious, more "explicit," and so the approach to truth is closer.[29] The process of inquiry in science and nonscience alike is similar, though in the case of science it is more self-conscious and self-reflective. Originally, in every subject matter and in every science, "idea and fact are at one." But problems and contradictions inevitably arise to separate fact and idea. The mind seeks to reunite idea and fact and by "observation, experiment, and all the other means at its disposal, makes its idea as definite and coherent as possible, and thus frames a hypothesis or theory." But this unification of fact and idea is only provisional and temporary until new contradictions appear. Nonetheless, it is through this process, "the actual process of knowledge, of science," that we build up "the universe, the realm of experience." Knowledge, then, "whether in the form of ordinary observation or of scientific thinking, is logical." According to Dewey, "the only difference is in the degree of development of the logical functions present in both."[30]

Dewey's clear rejection of dualism in his consideration of scientific and logical thought did not preclude greater awareness on his part of the distinctiveness of logical and scientific methodology. Those methodologies might lie on the same continuum with ordinary common-sense observation, but they are nonetheless distinguished by their greater self-consciousness, rigor of technique, and standards of verification. Dewey did not go so far as Peirce in reducing all philosophy to logic, but by the late 1880s he had separated scientific and logical thought from ordinary observation and had installed the former as a surer method for achieving truth.

Dewey's descriptions of science in the 1890s are less idealistic and are closer to what a working scientist might accept. In an address, "Reconstruction," first delivered to the Students' Christian Association at the University of Michigan, Dewey applauded the achievements of science in reaching truth. Science he defined as "a method of inquiry, as an organized, comprehensive, progressive, self-verifying system of investigation." These new methods and instruments have given the world "an almost boundless confidence in the possibility of the human mind to reach truth." Still, implicit in Dewey's view was the notion that science was a method to achieve some truth greater than that which could be gained within the boundaries of any special science. There may truly be no limits to the method of science, but it is a method pursued in hopes of approaching ever closer to "the actual incarnation of truth in human experience and the necessity of giving heed to it."[31] Truth, as a universal, still eluded the inquiries of the special sciences, however efficacious their methods.

Philosophy, for Dewey, became the necessary complement to the special sciences. Both science and philosophy properly "report the actual condition of life, or experience. Their business is to reveal experience in its truth, its reality. They state what *is*." Despite this common purpose, philosophy and science differ, since philosophy reports "the more generic (wider) features of life" and science "the more detailed and specific." Science and philosophy are thus "intimate allies" in the search for truth. Philosophy is the self-conscious "claim of the individual to be able to discover and verify truth for himself" while science is "the practical belief at work engaged in subjugating the foreign territory of ignorance and falsehood step by step." The achievement of truth depends upon both the "detailed and concrete" work of science as well as the "earnestness and courage" fostered by "the wider, even if vaguer, operation of philosophy."[32]

Dewey still sought to reconcile the dual aspects of the pursuit of truth, but he no longer found that resolution in an absolute self-consciousness. Beginning in the nineties, he postulated instrumentalism as the mode of reconciliation. "*Reality*," he wrote, "*is not to be read in terms of knowledge as such, but in terms of action*." Only action, Dewey argued, could "reconcile the old, the general, and the permanent with the changing, the individual, and the new." Dewey saw action "as progress, as development" and knowledge as a "tool." Increasingly, "the dominant interest becomes the *use* of knowledge; the conditions under which and ways in which it may be most organically and effectively employed to direct conduct."[33]

Dewey's nascent instrumentalism of the 1890s, with its view of science as the concrete methodology of action applied to human conduct, was a significant departure from his Hegelian idealism, which merged philosophy and science in a higher synthesis. Dewey had gradually sharpened his understanding and definition of science and had brought it into closer accord with the accepted scientific outlook. His developing instrumentalism meant a greater separation of philosophy and science as modes of inquiry, but Dewey stoutly resisted the temptation to divide sharply the two disciplines. To so divide science and philosophy would have introduced an unacceptable dualism into the universe and into the process of seeking knowledge and truth. Dewey gradually shifted his focus from the absolute to the world around him and sought a reconciliation of science and philosophy in instrumentalism. Philosophy remained the broadest category of inquiry, concerned especially with finding meaning in and giving meaning to life. Science became the method of inquiry, the means by which knowledge is gained and problems solved. Synthesis, then, was no longer to be found in some higher state of the absolute, but in action directed to the improvement of the human condition.

Dewey's intellectual journey in the last decades of the nineteenth century differed significantly from that of James. Whereas James had sought to walk a middle path between the alluring claims of science and of faith, Dewey's path took him away from the idealism of his early writings toward the instrumentalism of the end of the century. Like James's, Dewey's struggle was in part a contest between faith and science. Dewey's early faith in absolute self-consciousness gave way to reliance on the efficacy of scientific method in reforming the world. Dewey and James both believed that science could not be complete in itself, that there was more to the world than what science revealed. James defended faith against the scientific materialists, while Dewey sought a reconciliation in action directed toward improving human life. For both men, philosophy and science remained distinct enterprises, however intimately allied they might become. The same, however, cannot be said of Charles Sanders Peirce.

Charles Peirce wrote little on the relation of science and philosophy in the 1880s, but it again became a theme in his work of the 1890s. Much of this latter work was a recapitulation of and elaboration on ideas he had developed earlier. Science was primarily a method, he emphasized, a method for achieving a closer approach to truth, to reality. For Peirce the method was more important than any particular results, and it was in fact a defining characteristic of a science. Science progresses not only by the careful exercise of method, but through intuitive leaps of genius which set science on a new course of discovery. Though Peirce believed in scientific progress, it was not progress toward some humanitarian or utilitarian goal; only nature can determine the goal of science, and the best we can hope for in any lifetime is to take some steps toward achieving that undetermined goal in some indefinite future. Philosophy, for Peirce, was part of that pursuit of truth so long as the philosophers pursued it in a scientific spirit, and that meant basing philosophy on logic.

The method of science, the *pursuit* of knowledge and truth, defined science for Peirce in the 1890s. Knowledge by itself is nothing more than "a dead memory; while by science we all habitually mean a living and growing body of truth." What constitutes knowledge is constrained by time and culture; the astronomical facts of Ptolemy, for example, are no less examples of scientific knowledge for having been superseded. "That which constitutes science," Peirce concluded, "is not so much correct conclusions, as it is a correct method." The scientific method itself is a product of human thought and thus must be preceded by "the scientific spirit, which is determined not to rest satisfied with existing opinions but to press on to the real truth of nature."[34]

Scientific inquiry and the pursuit of truth were for Peirce the preserve of scientific men, those individuals imbued with the spirit and practicing the method of science. Science is marked by "diligent inquiry into truth for truth's sake." Not knowledge, "but the love of learning," characterizes the scientific man. Peirce wrote that "if a man burns to learn and sets himself to comparing his ideas with experimental results in order that he may correct those ideas, every scientific man will recognize him as a brother, no matter how small his knowledge may be." Here Peirce returned to his idea of a community. Scientists in general form a community, but within that larger grouping are smaller communities of more specialized inquiry. Those who pursue a particular science "herd together. They understand one another; they live in the same world, while those who pursue another branch are for them foreigners."[35] The members of a particular scientific community cooperate with each other, and each contributes his bit to that "living historic entity," truth. But the scientific community is never satisfied with present truth and seeks ultimately to conquer the last bastions of truth. "The idea of science," as Peirce graphically described it, "is to pile the ground before the foot of the outworks of truth with the carcasses of this generation, and perhaps of others to come after it, until some future generation, by treading on them can storm the citadel."[36]

Just as a military campaign is marked by long periods of inaction punctuated by strategic or tactical breakthroughs, so science progresses by ordinary work in the laboratory and, more importantly, through interpretive "leaps" by individuals of genius. As Peirce put it, science "advances by leaps; and the impulse for each leap is either some new observational resource, or some novel way of reasoning about the observations." The "active scientist" does not simply operate within the ordinary, accepted framework of science, but also "entertains hypotheses which are almost wildly incredible, and treats them with respect for the time being." The scientist engages in such behavior because the hypotheses will be quickly put to the test and discarded if erroneous. But the hypotheses, however outrageous, might be true, and their potential truth can only be tested by their postulation and by subsequent experimentation. For the true scientist, retroduction (provisionally adopting a hypothesis; often called abduction by Peirce) is not just a wild guess; it is set forth "upon the hope that there is sufficient affinity between the reasoner's mind and nature's to render guessing not altogether hopeless, provided that each guess is checked by comparison with observation."[37] Like James, Peirce found that fringe beyond the bounds of ordinary science to be the most fruitful and challenging, but also like James, he sought to bring the fringe under the understanding of science by applying to its problems the methods of science.[38]

Was philosophy a part of the army of science? Peirce definitely considered philosophy, or at least philosophy properly conducted, to be a legitimate science. He acknowledged, however, that contemporary philosophy, and especially metaphysics, was in a "deplorably backward condition." This backwardness could be attributed neither to the difficulty and abstraction of metaphysics nor to the impossibility of observing its objects of inquiry. As Peirce noted, "the abstracter a science is, the easier it is," and "the things that any science discovers are beyond the reach of direct observation." Only "the premises of science," Peirce wrote, "not its conclusions . . . are directly observed." It was thus not any intrinsic difficulty which prevented philosophy from becoming a science, but rather the absence of philosophers imbued with the scientific spirit and trained in the scientific method. Peirce was convinced that "the present infantile condition of philosophy . . . is due to the fact that during this century it has chiefly been pursued by men who have not been nurtured in dissecting rooms and other laboratories, and who consequently have not been animated by the true scientific *Eros*."[39]

The scientific philosopher is concerned only about truth for truth's sake and must ignore and reject moral, idealistic, or utilitarian considerations in a single-minded pursuit. To bring in these extraneous considerations would be to "barricade the road of science with empty books and embarrassing assumptions." The true philosopher as scientist tries "to make such conjecture as to the constitution of the universe as the methods of science may permit, with the aid of all that has been done by previous philosophers." The best Peirce hoped to accomplish was "to supply a hypothesis, not devoid of all likelihood, in the general line of growth of scientific ideas, and capable of being verified or refuted by future observers." As for his own work, it was "serious research to which there is no royal road." His philosophy, he wrote William James, "and all philosophy worth attention, reposes entirely upon the theory of logic." Peirce felt his rigorous standards were not often upheld, and he chided James and his Harvard colleagues for their neglect of logic: "People who cannot reason exactly (which alone *is* reasoning), simply cannot understand my philosophy,—neither the process, methods, nor results."[40]

The one Harvard philosopher to whom Peirce gave good marks for his understanding of logic was Josiah Royce. In his review of Royce's monumental *The World and the Individual*, Peirce credited Royce with "doing good service" toward bringing about a unification of philosophical and scientific or mathematical thought on the question of the nature of the universe. What was needed, according to Peirce, was "a really scientific logic and metaphysics" united in the thought of one man. If Royce did not fulfill all the qualifications, he nonetheless enjoyed "the esteem and sympathy of the theological metaphysicians" and was "thoroughly alive to the ideas of science and . . . thoroughly versed in all the more philosophical part of modern mathematical speculation."[41]

Royce's work gave Peirce hope that philosophy might soon begin to acquire the character of a science. From his special perspective Peirce had come to believe "that metaphysics has at length reached a point in its disorderly march at which it can now discern, through the haze upon the distant hill, the place at which it is destined to join company with the orderly army of science. Surely that reunion must take place sometime." The "vital condition" which, for Peirce, would make this goal achievable was for the "scientific man" to continue to hang "upon the lips of nature, in order to learn wherein he is ignorant and mistaken: the whole character of the scientific procedure springs from that disposition." This must also become the procedure of the metaphysician if philosophy is to join science on the hill. In preferring the method of science over the traditional methods of metaphysics, Peirce was not advocating an empty materialism. "The scientific man is eager," he wrote, "to submit himself, his ideas, and his purposes, to the Great Power which, no doubt, penetrates his own being, but is yet all but wholly external to him and beyond anything that his poor present notion could ever, of itself, develop unfructified."[42] As his review of Royce reveals, Peirce did not believe religion and science to be incompatible. Murray Murphey, in fact, has observed that one of Peirce's major aims was "to construct a philosophy which would effect a reconciliation between religion and science and permit scientific men to believe once more . . . that science is the study of God's works."[43]

The widespread conflict of religion and science in late nineteenth-century America lay at the center of these speculations by James, Dewey, and Peirce on the relationship of philosophy and science. All three men recognized the power of scientific method and sought to appropriate it for at least some part of their philosophy. But while seeking to use the methods of science and even to enhance that method's credibility as the road to truth, all three philosophers also tried to preserve a place for religion, for belief, and for morals. Science was limited, though in its own proper sphere its methods and conclusions were unassailable. There was still room for faith and belief, for humane and ethical action, and for a realm into which science could not inquire. None of the three were materialists, not even Peirce, and all rejected the dogmatic materialism of the more extreme advocates of science. So too, they rejected a sharp dualism between the material and the spiritual; they tended to view the world as all of a piece, even as science broke off fragments for particular study. Though James was the most explicit in seeking to find a middle way between the extremes of faith and science, Dewey in instrumentalism found a way to unite scientific fact and moral impulse in ameliorative action, and Peirce held that the particular truths were only part of some larger truth, some wider realm beyond our limited understanding.

Although James and Peirce had a more thorough grounding in science than Dewey, all three men were preeminently philosophers. They willingly wrestled with the broader problems of truth and meaning; they dealt with issues easily deferred or ignored by the special scientist in the laboratory. As men of the last half of the nineteenth century, James, Dewey, and Peirce could not ignore science, but neither could they ignore religion and belief. The problem they faced was how to yoke together religion and science at a time when the scientists in their success and their arrogance were less and less dependent upon the religious, the spiritual, and the philosophical. It was no longer enough simply to assert the right to believe. That right had to be won in contest with science, on grounds and with weapons largely chosen by science. If James, Dewey, and Peirce did not completely succeed in reconciling science and religion in these decades, they established a foundation on which the debate could continue in the new century.

FIVE

Treating Psychology as a Science: Toward the Separation of Psychology and Philosophy

In 1850 few philosophers in the United States would have drawn a sharp distinction between philosophy and psychology. Yet over the next half century philosophy and psychology became recognizably distinct disciplines, each with its own adherents and advocates, its own professional institutions and commitments, and each beginning to develop relatively independent of the other. Relations between the two disciplines remained close well into the twentieth century because of overlapping interests and concerns and because of close personal tries between the first generation of professional philosophers and psychologists. But the two groups gradually established separate identities as the psychologists carved out an independent realm in the academic landscape. A widening divergence between those interested primarily in philosophical questions and those interested in psychological ones was perhaps inevitable in the late nineteenth century, but the intellectual and institutional conditions in American colleges and universities fostered the split.

The appeal of science, institutional pressures, and the differing personal ambitions of turn-of-the-century psychologists and philosophers shattered the long-standing marriage of philosophy and psychology. The two fields had long been considered different approaches to the same set of problems, with the difference being a matter of emphasis. Psychology had attempted to explain the role and workings of such particular phenomena as emotion, sensation, and willing. It was an introspective science of the soul. Philosophy had long cast a wider net of understanding over the same phenomena and had framed understanding of the immediate in a more comprehensive context. The rise of nineteenth-century experimental science provided the psychologists with the model of a science for emulation and the physiological tools, however primitive, for conducting scientific experiments. For psychology, long considered only a "colonial outpost" of philosophy, the methods and values of the physical sciences now opened a road to independence.[1] Institutional pressures in both the reorganizing colleges and the newly created universities of the period fostered the separation of philosophy and psychology. In the competition for funding, staffing, students, and space, the psychologists quickly realized the advantages of independence. They could best assert their scientific credentials and defend their academic turf in their own department, unfettered by the lack of interest and occasional hostility of the philosophers. Finally, the ambitions of strong-willed men like William James, John Dewey, G. Stanley Hall, Edward B. Titchener, and J. McKeen Cattell almost required separate spheres of activity. The philosopher-psychologists, James and Dewey, wanted to preserve for philosophy a wider, more comprehensive stance of understanding, leading ultimately to action. The psychologists, especially Hall, Titchener, and Cattell, wanted to put aside fruitless metaphysical speculation to pursue scientific knowledge obtained by experimentation. Although philosophy and psychology could have remained more intimately connected, the appeal of a scientific model, institutional demands, and personal ambition drove the two disciplines apart between 1875 and 1925.

The shift to a more scientific psychology in the United States was prefigured and influenced by developments in German psychology. By midcentury German psychologists had begun to transform their study into an experimental science based in the laboratory. As in the United States, psychology in Germany had long been considered a subdiscipline of philosophy. According to R. Steven Turner, four changes within the German university system brought a split between philosophy and psychology. First, the discoveries of the natural and physical sciences were translated into institutional reality in terms of funding, staffing, and departmental identity; the process provided psychologists with a successful model for emulation. Second, new discoveries in physiology so enhanced the understanding of sensory perception that the affiliation of psychology with physiology became a paramount concern. Third, the invention by Gustave Fechner of techniques of psychophysical experimentation in the 1860s promised psychologists the tools they needed to create a true science of psychology. Finally, the intellectual climate put a premium on scientific values and methods and increasingly discredited metaphysical speculation. Gradually chairs of psychology were established, or psychologists took over chairs that had once been philosophical. Institutes and experimental laboratories were set up, and graduate students were trained. Though many American psychologists took their inspiration from their reading of the German academic scene, the formal separation of the two disciplines in Germany proceeded slowly. By the early twentieth century, German psychology possessed only some of the attributes of autonomy.[2] Ironically, American psychologists, many of whom had studied in Germany, sought and achieved institutional autonomy more quickly and more completely than their German mentors.

The scientific impulse of German psychology provided a model for American psychology, but the Americans were not slavish imitators of German practice. When aspiring young American psychologists first encountered the German science in its laboratories, their prior education shaped their understanding of the experience. In addition, their own career goals and the institutional demands being placed on them as they sought positions in American universities influenced their responses to German psychology. For example, when William James encountered German psychology firsthand in the late 1860s, he had already completed the bulk of his medical training. He had planned to study with both Herman von Helmholtz and Wilhelm Wundt, but his recurrent neurasthenic attacks prohibited more than a glance into their physiology laboratories. Nonetheless, while in Germany he read widely in the new physiological psychology and came away convinced of its importance. When James fought to secure his position at Harvard in the mid-1870s, his knowledge of German psychology was a key weapon in his arsenal.

Although James's initial appointment was in physiology, he soon began to shift his responsibilities in the direction of psychology. In 1874, in his second year as a full-time instructor, James offered a graduate course entitled "The Relations between Physiology and Psychology." In 1875, while angling for a permanent place in Harvard's plans, James outlined to President Charles W. Eliot his views on the proper place of psychology and physiology. He argued that the new physiological psychology warranted formal recognition by the college and that the subject should be taught by a person who combined thorough knowledge of both fields; someone, in short, like himself. James's arguments helped him win appointment as assistant professor of physiology in 1876. At the same time, he was transferring more of his teaching to psychology. He offered his first undergraduate course in physiological psychology in 1876–77, and in the following year his psychology instruction was moved to the department of philosophy. In 1875 James established what was apparently the world's first psychological laboratory. However primitive, it preceded Wilhelm Wundt's 1879 institute at Leipzig and G. Stanley Hall's 1881 laboratory at Johns Hopkins. Although James remained somewhat skeptical that physiological research could solve all psychological problems, he clearly recognized that the new discoveries were forcing "a change in the method and *personnel* of philosophic study." It had already reached the point, he wrote, when "to criticise these 'new developments' at all, one must have gone through a thorough physiological training." James's advocacy of physiological psychology in the 1870s was thus a response to the successes of the new science, to the changing institutional climate at Harvard, and to his own desire to secure a permanent position on the Harvard faculty.[3]

G. Stanley Hall's adoption of psychology as a profession grew out of similar mixed motives. Hall first encountered modern psychology through his studies with Adolf Trendelenberg in Germany in 1869–70 and through reading Herbert Spencer's *Principles of Psychology*. It was, however, Wundt's *Grundzüge der physiologischen Psychologie,* published in 1873, that opened to him the road to a scientific psychology. Unable to finance study in Germany, Hall took his Ph.D. in psychology under James in 1878. Hall conducted a long campaign to secure a position at Johns Hopkins in the late 1870s; his training in the new psychology was a key part of his argument. As John O'Donnell has observed, Hall was "not particularly proselytizing for the advancement of the science of psychology; he was merely campaigning for his own philosophic future." By 1879, Hall had committed himself to psychology. His advocacy of a scientific psychology not only suited his own ambitions, it met the needs of Daniel Coit Gilman, president of Johns Hopkins. Under community pressure because of alleged materialism at the new university, Gilman was seeking a science which could bridge the gap between the physical sciences on the one side, and philosophy and theology on the other. In Hall, Gilman found a man and a version of psychology cognizant of the new developments and comfortable with more traditional concerns. Hall's persistence and Gilman's needs won Hall an appointment as lecturer at Hopkins in 1881, when he established his first laboratory, and a permanent appointment as professor of psychology and pedagogics in 1884.[4]

James and Hall are illustrative of the unstable mixture of philosophy and psychology in the 1870s, on the eve of the appearance of professional disciplines. Both men, as we have seen earlier, were of a philosophical inclination, but circumstance and upbringing precluded immediate entry into the philosophical professoriate. Psychology, especially in its new scientific trappings, provided a convenient and significant way station for both men and ultimately a successful career for Hall. The new physiological psychology coming out of Germany offered several advantages to these men and to the universities in which they sought employment. In an era of increased "science-envy," the scientific credentials of the new psychology were far stronger than anything offered by contemporary philosophy. At the same time, psychology still retained its close ties with philosophy. It promised that some traditional problems, such as perception and the acquisition of knowledge, might be better explained and understood as the result of a modern and scientific inquiry. However, neither James nor Hall in their early psychological studies considered psychology as a science sufficient unto itself. It provided scientific data for philosophic contemplation, for the creation of reasoned plans of practical action, and for pedagogical purposes. The conception of psychological science as antecedent to other studies and purposes was more typical of the United States than of Germany, where the ideal of a pure science was stronger.[5]

The founding years of professional psychology in the United States were marked by the adoption of physiological methods and the creation of experimental laboratories. Physiological psychology was, according to John O'Donnell, the "most conspicuous" element of the emerging science. But it was only one part of a "volatile mixture of philosophy, physiology and social science." Psychology and psychologists in the last quarter of the century retained close links to traditional philosophical concerns, while forging ties to the nascent reform impulse of the period. The adoption of laboratory experimentation and the creation after 1875 of laboratories devoted specifically to scientific psychological research marked a shift in emphasis for the developing science. The formation and building of psychological laboratories was, however, often more symbolic than productive of significant experimental results. As O'Donnell has observed, "The esoteric laboratory provided its practitioners with a scientific passport to professional autonomy, an entering wedge into an academic world that offered status, security, and financial support for pursuits that often bore little substantive relation to experimental endeavor."[6]

William James revealed his ambivalence toward the scientific aspect of the new psychology in his Lowell lectures of 1878. He acknowledged the achievements of science and in particular the discoveries of physiology which had illuminated some of the workings of the nervous system and the brain. But these achievements, he argued, were diminished unless they were understood within a larger philosophical context. His recent experience in being "obliged to teach a little anatomy, a little physiology, [and] a little psychology" had convinced him that no one approach had a monopoly on knowledge. While the physiologist and philosopher each owned "a lot in the field of human knowledge," James urged his listeners "to aspire to the attitude of one who should own both lots . . . We are alike proprietors of a body and a mind. We are . . . interested in having [as] sound a science of the one as of the other." For James, psychology was neither a traditional, introspective science of the soul nor a physiological science founded on "the twitching of frogs' legs." James believed that a psychology worthy of the name would study both the mind and the brain, would be both introspective and physiological, and would, as Gerald Myers has noted, include "an inescapable subjective element." "It must be," James wrote, "that truth is one, and thought woven in one piece."[7] Only by remaining open to all possible sources of truth can we hope to achieve understanding; physiological psychology is only a piece, albeit an important piece, of the puzzle.

James was not alone in his efforts to keep a foot in both physiological psychology and philosophy. John Dewey's encounter with the new psychology in Hall's Johns Hopkins laboratory forced a reorientation in his thought. Initially skeptical of the value of psychology, Dewey nonetheless felt it might "furnish grist for the mill, if nothing else." Finding himself more attracted to physiological psychology than he had anticipated, Dewey in the early 1880s attempted to come to terms with the science and to uncover its implications for philosophy.[8]

Dewey's initial effort to explain the significance of the new psychology was published in 1884 in the *Andover Review*, a journal addressed more to theologians and ministers than to scientists. After reviewing the progress of psychology from the eighteenth century to his own day, Dewey focused his attention on the impact and importance of physiological psychology. He proposed to clarify the then-prevalent confusion regarding the significance of the new science. He rejected the "popular opinion" that "physiological psychology is a science which does, or at least claims to, explain all psychical life by reference to the nature of the nervous system." Physiological psychology by itself, as a science, explained nothing: "Explanations of psychical events, in order to *explain*, must themselves be psychical and not physiological." If physiology failed to provide an explanation for psychological phenomena, it was nontheless valuable for having given psychology "a new instrument, introduced a new *method*,—that of experiment, which has supplemented and corrected the old method of introspection." Physiological psychology gave the investigator of "psychical facts" wider and more effective "means of ascertaining what these facts are and how they are conditioned." In addition, physiology provided "an indirect means of investigation" into "the nature of mental activities and their causes."[9]

If physiology embraced one wing of the new psychology for Dewey, the practical social sciences comprised the other wing. The new psychology was closely tied to "the growth of those vast and as yet undefined topics of inquiry which may be vaguely designated as the social and historical sciences,—the sciences of the origin and development of the various spheres of man's activity." These "sciences of humanity" provided a "method of objective observation." Coupled with experimentation, these new methods of psychology "indefinitely supplement and correct the old method of subjective introspection." For Dewey it was no longer adequate to have a psychology based only on abstract logic, on introspection, or even on experimentation; the new psychology was valuable because, in addition, it "bears the realistic stamp of contact with life."[10]

Dewey's essay in praise of the new psychology picked up important themes in the domestication of psychology as a science. Dewey recognized that the older, introspective methods were no longer adequate; they needed to be supplemented by newer, more effective techniques. But note, Dewey did not here completely reject the older method. While acknowledging the validity of the results of scientific experimentation, Dewey was careful to point out that those results in themselves were not an explanation of psychological phenomena. The new science, in other words, could not be completely divorced from philosophical considerations. Finally, there is in this early essay of Dewey's a hint of the practical side of psychology which became so important to American practitioners. Psychology was not some abstract isolated science, but one intimately tied to other studies of human experience and activity. By "regarding life as an organism in which immanent ideas or purposes are realizing themselves through the development of experience," the new psychology could assist in the coming reconstruction of society.[11]

In his *Andover Review* article, "The New Psychology," Dewey described a psychological science that would have been welcomed in the world's leading laboratories, even as he proposed a broad reforming agenda for it. Two years later, in two essays published in the British journal *Mind*, "The Psychological Standpoint" and "Psychology as Philosophic Method," he defended an idealistic conception of psychology in which the physiological elements were barely recognizable. Psychology, he acknowledged, was the "scientific and systematic account" of experience. Because a valid philosophy must be rooted in experience, and because psychology was the science of this experience, psychology became, "in short, *philosophic method*." Dewey, as we have already noted, conceived of philosophy as the science of absolute consciousness and of psychology as the science of individual consciousness. Because we have no direct access to the absolute, we can only study the individual and the immediate through the science of psychology. Just as physiology enables us to make certain indirect inferences about the mind, so psychology allows us to make certain analogies regarding the absolute. Psychology as a "positive science" is grounded in "certain facts and events" and based on "systematic observation, experiment, conclusion and verification." But Dewey argued that psychology was much more than a special science: it was "the highest *of* sciences: it appears as *Science* itself, that is, as systematic account and comprehension of the nature of conscious experience."[12] By conceiving psychology as the grand science of the individualized absolute consciousness, Dewey here lost sight of the new science of psychology being developed in the experimental laboratories of Europe and America. Though he claimed to root his psychology in experience and fact, his psychology of consciousness hearkened back to the older psychology of the soul rather than forward toward an experimental science.

Dewey's three essays reveal the unstable mix that was psychology and philosophy in the 1880s. We see Dewey struggling to come to terms with the newer psychological methods. The Hegelianism of his study with H. A. P. Torrey and George Sylvester Morris found expression in his higher synthesis of psychology and philosophy, but his exposure to the experimental psychology of G. Stanley Hall took root in his advocacy of the new psychology. The triumph of the new science was by no means an inevitable or even desirable outcome for Dewey in the mid-1880s. The mixture of the old and the new was very much in evidence in *Psychology*, the text that Dewey published in 1887.

Dewey began writing his text in psychology in 1885 shortly after taking a position at the University of Michigan. He seems to have conceived of the book both as an introduction to the field and as a defense of his idealistic conception of the discipline.[13] In the preface of *Psychology*, Dewey acknowledged the intimate ties between philosophy and psychology and attempted to clarify them in light of recent developments. Psychology had only recently "attained any independent standing," having earlier been "largely a compound of logic, ethics, and metaphysics." This earlier compound had, however, "made psychology a good introduction to the remaining studies of the philosophic curriculum." But if psychology could now stand alone, Dewey was still unwilling to "leave behind all purely philosophic considerations, and confine [himself] to the facts of scientific psychology." Metaphysical considerations would inevitably be smuggled into the text, and Dewey thought it better to be open and clear about the philosophical element. In addition, Dewey remained convinced that psychology was a useful path into the realm of philosophy. His objective for his text was to "make our psychology scientific and up to the times, free from metaphysics—which, however good in its place, is out of place in a psychology—and at the same time make it an introduction to philosophy in general." His book would thus attempt both "to reflect the investigations of scientific specialists in this branch" and "to develop the philosophic spirit." Psychology, he was convinced, remained "the best possible introduction to all specific philosophic questions."[14]

Dewey's first chapter, "The Science and Method of Psychology," echoed his earlier statements on psychology as a science. Psychology is the "*Science of the Facts or Phenomena of Self."* The fundamental characteristic of self is "the fact of *consciousness.*" Consciousness per se can be neither defined nor described, and psychology is limited to studying "only the various *forms* of consciousness, showing the *conditions* under which they arise." Psychology differs from the other sciences in that the facts of consciousness are always individual and unique; unlike the other sciences, it deals with no universal facts. Psychology is the science of self, whereas all other sciences deal with "facts presented *to* the selves or minds which know them." Dewey argued that psychology's subject matter gives it a dual relationship to the other sciences. First, "it is co-ordinated with other sciences, as simply having a different and higher subject-matter than they. . . . Thus considered, psychology is evidently simply one science among others." Second, psychology is the central science, "for its *subject-matter,* knowledge, is involved" in all the other sciences.[15] Psychology is at one both similar to and more than a special science.

Psychology, like any discipline, requires a proper method in order to constitute a science. Though it deals with "the facts of self," those facts must be "systematically collected and ordered with reference to principles" so that they may be explained. Psychology embodies four forms of method: introspective, experimental, comparative, and objective. Dewey argued that since "the study of consciousness itself must be the main source of knowledge of the facts" of consciousness, introspection is an indispensable method for psychology. In fact, introspection "must *ultimately* be the sole source of the *material* of psychology." Notwithstanding the widely recognized difficulties of introspection, Dewey felt that this method could become a "scientific process." The key to making introspection a scientific act is to reflect critically upon experience, to analyze and classify experience. The experimental method is a useful supplement and corrective to introspection, even though the psychologist "cannot experiment directly with the facts of consciousness." It is possible, however, to "experiment, indirectly, through the connection of the soul with the body." The experimental method has two branches: "One, *psycho-physics,* deals with the quantitative relations between psychical states and their bodily stimuli, while the other, *physiological psychology,* uses physiological processes for the sake of investigating psychical states." The comparative method enables the psychologist to move beyond the confines of the individual mind and to understand the normal mind "of the average human adult" by comparing it with the consciousness of animals, children, abnormal individuals, and individuals of different cultures and races. Finally, there is the "study of the objective manifestation of mind," which Dewey described as "the broadest and most fundamental method of correcting and extending the results of introspection." The mind, he argued, was not simply "a passive spectator of the universe, but has produced and is producing certain results." These results are all the manifestations of culture and civilization, such as language, science, art, politics, and religion. It is in studying "these wide departments of human knowledge, activity, and creation that we learn most about the self."[16]

In thus dividing his psychology into four methodological modes, Dewey revealed something of the confusion in his own conception of the science and in psychology's status as a discipline. His fundamental reliance upon introspection, however scientifically conceived, was a holdover from the traditional psychology of the soul, which had relied upon introspection almost exclusively. His treatment of experimental psychology as a useful corrective and supplement to introspection acknowledged its achievements as a physiological science but denied any fundamental identity between physical and mental processes. At best, physiological psychology gave us only indirect knowledge. With the comparative and objective methods, Dewey sought to place psychological explanation within a wider frame. The comparative method offered the psychologist a vital perspective on his science. The objective method hinted at Dewey's own developing sense of psychology and philosophy as tools for rational, practical action. As he noted, the mind is not passive; it is active, a builder, a doer, and only in action can the psychologist understand the self. If we begin the psychology of self by looking inward, we must end it by being active, by looking and moving outward.

In the body of his text Dewey mixed discussion of the results of psychological experiment with philosophical reflection. His notes reveal a wide familiarity with the new physiological psychology. Wundt, Helmholtz, James, Hall, and Ladd, among others, are frequently cited. However, the thrust of his chapters is to place experimental discoveries in an idealistic, explanatory framework. They are useful only in "elevating us above what is purely contingent and accidental in self-consciousness, and revealing to us what in it is permanent and essential; what, therefore, is the subject-matter of psychology." Perhaps the most scientific of his chapters is the third, "Elements of Knowledge," which reviews research into sensations. But even while reporting on the results of various stimulus-response and other sensory experiments, Dewey quickly discounted any materialistic explanation in favor of an idealistic one, in which sensation is the active response of the soul to some external stimulus. The physiological explanation of stimulus and response is inadequate; true psychological explanation must be found in a study of the mind and soul.[17]

Dewey divided the subject of his book into three main topics: knowledge, feeling, and will. After discussing the processes by which knowledge is acquired, Dewey examined five stages of knowledge—perception, memory, imagination, thinking, and intuition. Knowledge culminates in intuition of God, "for it involves a unity of the real and the ideal, of the objective and the subjective." Feeling, which involves the "*internal* aspect" of mental life, was Dewey's second major category. The various types of feeling—sensuous, formal, qualitative, intellectual, aesthetic, and personal—culminate in "feeling as social judgment, conscience." Conscience, for Dewey, was "the experience of personality that a given act is in harmony or in discord with a truly realized personality." To act requires will, the subject of the last section of Dewey's text. Broadly speaking, the will is "all psychical activity having a mental and not merely a physiological stimulus." More narrowly conceived, the will involves an "action arising from an idea and ending in making this idea real." The will, for Dewey, "connects the content of knowledge with the form of feeling." In discussing the will he took up, in turn, sensuous impulses, volition, physical control, prudential control, and moral control. Dewey concluded that "the unity of the self is the will . . . The will, in short, constitutes the meaning of knowledge and of feeling; and moral will constitutes the meaning of will." The moral will is the highest expression of the self and is "the conscious realization by man that the real and the ideal *ought* to be one, and the resulting attempt to make them one in specific acts and in the formation of character."[18]

Although Dewey acknowledged in *Psychology* the discoveries of the emerging science, they take a distinctly subordinate role to his larger purpose. One comes away from the text with a greater sense of the synthesis of knowledge and feeling in the will than with an understanding of psychological processes. Dewey was not so much laying the groundwork for a new science as for a new ethics based on up-to-date explanations of physical and psychological phenomena. Though cognizant of the new psychology, Dewey bent its results to his moral and ethical purposes in justifying an active and moral will. Despite its title, the book was more a philosophical and ethical treatise than a scientific psychology.

It is no surprise, then, that the book was greeted warmly by idealists and criticized harshly by experimentalists. G. S. Morris, Dewey's mentor and colleague, declared, for example, that it was "a real contribution to self-knowledge." *Psychology* was soon adopted as a text in a number of colleges and universities. If one of Dewey's teachers liked the book, another, G. Stanley Hall, was extremely critical. Hall criticized Dewey's method of always interpreting psychological facts in light of his system, rather than giving them an independent scientific legitimacy. Hall found the book old-fashioned and the physiological illustrations too pat. Dewey's skill in reading psychological facts into Hegelian idealism did not make his book, in Hall's view, a scientific treatise. Hall concluded that "students inclined to immerse themselves in an ideal view of the world" would find *Psychology* "very stimulating, but dire will be the disappointment of those who hope to find in it the methods or results of modern scientific psychology." William James began the book with enthusiasm, but that soon turned to disappointment. He faulted Dewey for trying "to mediate between the bare miraculous self and the concrete particulars of individual mental lives." Dewey's treatment of the particulars smudged the hard edge of their reality without providing adequate compensation.[19]

James's comments on Dewey's *Psychology* were framed with the knowledge that his own unfinished text would attempt more directly to lay a scientific foundation for a new psychology. James had undertaken the task of writing a textbook on psychology in 1878 at the invitation of the publisher Henry Holt. Both men anticipated that the book would be published in two years. Instead, it took James twelve years to produce *The Principles of Psychology*, in two weighty volumes. The delays were not caused simply by James's laborious method of composition, nor by periods of inactivity occasioned by revival of his neurasthenic symptoms. They also resulted from James's efforts to assimilate the latest and very best scientific results then being published in ever-swelling volume both in Europe and in America. And, as he put it, his book "has in the main grown up in connection with the author's class-room instruction in Psychology." Parts of the eventual text were initially published throughout the 1880s, as James finished a section or sought critical reaction to his ideas. Some of these essays appeared nearly intact in *The Principles of Psychology*, but most were extensively revised, and all were made part of the overall scheme and viewpoint of the book.[20]

James felt that he had suffered great anxiety in giving birth to this "enormous *rat*" and even at this distance one can sense his relief at its completion. James was, however, somewhat ambivalent about his accomplishment and thought the result was far too long. He wrote to Henry Holt that *The Principles of Psychology* was "a loathsome, distended, tumefied, bloated, dropsical mass, testifying to nothing but two facts: *1st,* that there is no such thing as a *science* of psychology, and *2nd,* that W. J. is an incapable." James more accurately assessed the significance of his achievement in letters to other correspondents. He told his wife that despite his own limitations he had written "the biggest book on psychology in any language except Wundt's, Rosmini's and Daniel Greenleaf Thompson's." When he wrote his brother Henry, James was even more perceptive: "As 'Psychologies' go, it is a good one, but psychology is in such an ante-scientific condition that the whole present generation of them is predestined to become unreadable old medieval lumber, as soon as the first genuine tracks of insight are made."[21]

From the outset, James sought to rest his text on experimental results and in the process to help create a science of psychology. In an early letter to Holt, James proposed to call his book *Psychology, as a Natural Science*. In the preface to the book James clarified his stance. "I have," he wrote, "kept close to the point of view of natural science throughout the book." James thought every science had to make certain assumptions which were unquestioned, at least within the science. "Psychology, the science of finite individual minds, assumes as its data (1) *thoughts and feelings,* and (2) *a physical world* in time and space with which they coexist and which (3) *they know.*" These points can be argued, but such an argument takes place on a metaphysical level and is outside the limits of his study and book. Psychology as a natural science is limited, according to James, to "the empirical correlation of the various sorts of thought or feeling with definite conditions of the brain." His book would present no "closed system," but "mainly a mass of descriptive details, running out into queries" posed for some future metaphysics. For now, "the best mark of health that a science can show is this unfinished-seeming front."[22]

Compared to Dewey's text, James's *Principles* has the appearance and the gait of a scientific volume. James began by defining the scope of psychology broadly within the limits of his conception of a science. "Psychology," he asserted, "is the Science of Mental Life, both of its phenomena and of their conditions." The phenomena are such familiar things as feelings, desires, thoughts, and decisions. James discounted the traditional faculty and associationist accounts of psychological phenomena and acknowledged the relevance of physiology to a study of mental phenomena. But, for James as for Dewey, physiological explanation was not alone a sufficient account of mental phenomena. He noted that the "boundary-line of the mental is certainly vague," but given the state of psychological science, he saw that as beneficial: "At a certain stage in the development of every science a degree of vagueness is what best consists with fertility." How then to attempt a demarcation of the mental and the physical? As James put it, "*the pursuance of future ends and the choice of means for their attainment are thus the mark and criterion of the presence of mentality* in a phenomenon."[23] This functionalism would be the touchstone of James's psychological science.

James devoted the first chapters of *Principles* to a detailed review of the physiology of brain function and its implications. "The minute anatomy and the detailed physiology of the brain are," he wrote, "achievements of the present generation." However, he recognized that "many points are still obscure and subject to controversy." He described numerous experiments to identify and isolate certain brain functions and to correlate brain activity with the sensations of touch, smell, and sight. In addition, he discussed stimulus-response experiments and some electrical and chemical theories offered to explain brain behavior, without finding them persuasive. While surveying what was known about habit, James found evidence for the "plasticity" of organic structures in responding to external stimuli and to conscious choice. The unrestrained workings of the brain can be bent to human purposes by habit. The ability to acquire habits is an ethically neutral function of brain activity, but habits do have a moral and ethical dimension. The greatest need in education is to *"make our nervous system our ally instead of our enemy"* and to make *"automatic and habitual, as early as possible, as many useful actions as we can."*[24] We become, in the end, what our habits are.

Though James was cognizant of current physiological research and found the results of that research valuable for understanding the functioning of the brain, he rejected materialism and the suggestion that we are mere conscious automata. The theory of conscious automata, as espoused by Thomas H. Huxley and William K. Clifford, held that states of consciousness, feelings and emotions were "immediately caused by molecular changes of the brain substance." James also quoted Huxley to the effect that "there is no proof that any state of consciousness is the cause of change in the motion of the matter of the organism."[25] Though James recognized that reasons could be advanced in support of this theory, he found them unconvincing. James found fault with the theory due to metaphysical considerations regarding causation. Since David Hume, the whole causal relationship had been problematical, and the automatists simply had no good metaphysical grounds for denying psychical causation while upholding material causation. Metaphysically, both were equally suspect. James preferred to argue that there was merit in the common-sense view that "ideas *seem* to be causes" and psychology could best proceed by provisionally granting causal efficacy to ideas and to feelings. The brain was likely to remain for some time "a sort of vat in which feelings and motion somehow go on stewing together," and of which we could only glean bits of indirect knowledge. The language and attitudes of common sense were, James felt, compatible with the current state of both psychology and physiology. Lacking persuasive proof, the Huxleys and the Cliffords were reduced to asserting the conscious-automata theory on "purely *a priori* and *quasi*-metaphysical grounds" and thus committing *"an unwarrantable impertinence in the present state of psychology."*[26]

Though James clearly rejected materialistic automatism, he was under some obligation to offer an explanation of the relationship of mental and physical processes. He argued that the theory of the soul possessed certain logical advantages and corresponded well with common-sense belief. The soul, as a "spiritual agent," could be the "medium upon which . . . the manifold brain-

processes *combine their efforts.*" James asserted that "to posit a soul influenced
in some mysterious way by the brain-states and responding to them by conscious affections of its own, seems to me the line of least logical resistance." But
this theory, though "less positively objectionable," still "does not strictly *explain* anything." The best that a scientific psychology could do was to postulate
a psycho-physical parallelism between *"the succession of states of consciousness with the succession of total brain-processes."* This was *"the last
word of a psychology which contents itself with verifiable laws, and seeks only
to be clear, and to avoid unsafe hypotheses."* Such a position, even if only provisional, would keep his psychology "posivitistic and non-metaphysical." Here
James's pluralism came to the fore, in his willingness to let others draw what
metaphysical conclusions they would on the basis of his psychological science:

> The spiritualistic reader may nevertheless believe in the soul
> if he will; whilst the postivistic one who wishes to give a
> tinge of mystery to the expression of his positivism can
> continue to say that nature in her unfathomable designs has
> mixed us of clay and flame, of brain and mind, that the two
> things hang indubitably together and determine each
> other's being, but how or why, no mortal may ever know.[27]

James's pluralism regarding the metaphysical implications of a science of
psychology reflected not only the diversity within contemporary psychology,
but also James's own divided mind on the subject. His struggle to achieve psychological stability, his efforts to come to terms with his father's religious
beliefs, his scientific training, and his resistance to positivism meant that
James himself embodied some of the tensions in nineteenth-century psychology. The text of *The Principles of Psychology,* as Mark Schwehn has pointed
out, mirrors the tension between James's view of psychology as "a positivistic
science, an uncritical discipline, a search for ultimate laws of relation between
thought and physiological states of the brain" and his desire "to develop a
view of consciousness that would legitimate moral and religious experiences
as authentic and irreducible aspects of the life of the mind." Just as Dewey's
Psychology reflected his Hegelian heritage, so James's *Principles* bore traces of
his intellectual and psychological struggles. Because James had personally experienced "the stresses of his culture, especially the tension between science
and religion" in the complex dynamics of his family and "within the precincts
of his tortured psyche," his text spoke powerfully to both contending sides in
the debate over the scientific character of psychology. Schwehn concludes that
in the *Principles* James was unable to take a definitive stance, to "separate
psychological study from philosophical speculation." Instead, in writing the
book, James "sought to provide a reasonable therapy for divided souls, for

those who, like himself, felt the full force of the imperial claims of science even as they longed to follow the promptings of their hearts."[28]

James's divided mind regarding the science of psychology is reflected in the language of his exposition of the methods of psychology. James, unlike Dewey before him, outlined only three methods in psychology: introspection, experimentation, and comparison. His rhetoric in discussing these methods reveals his faith in the traditional technique of introspection, even as he acknowledged the achievements of the newer approaches of experiment and comparison. Introspection remained the fundamental method of psychology: *"Intro-spective Observation is what we have to rely on first and foremost and always."* The point was so obvious that James thought it required no argument. "Everyone *agrees,*" he wrote, that when we look into our own minds *"we there discover states of consciousness."* This belief was so basic that he summarily dismissed "all curious inquiries about its certainty as too metaphysical for the scope of this book." He admitted that introspection is *"difficult and fallible"* and that his text would amply illustrate those difficulties, but he also thought that *"the difficulty is simply that of all observation of whatever kind.* Something is before us; we do our best to tell what it is, but in spite of our good will we may go astray." The ordinary citizen and the scientist alike are prone to error. Echoing Charles Peirce, James wrote that the "only safeguard is in the final consensus of our farther knowledge about the thing in question, later views correcting earlier ones, until at last the harmony of a consistent system is reached." As the sole method of psychology, introspection belongs to the "youth of our science" when the texts of Locke, Hume, Mill, and Bain were "still untechnical and generally intelligible, like the Chemistry of Lavoisier, or Anatomy before the microscope was used."[29]

Even though *The Principles of Psychology* is a masterful summary of contemporaneous experimental work in psychology, James's general comments regarding experimentation betray his deep ambivalence toward the method. His rhetoric reveals his own distaste for scientific experimentation and his suspicion that it is hostile to a broader, more humane view of nature. James admitted that by engaging in minute experiments, by compiling a massive record of repeated experiments, by recording a myriad of physiological and psychological responses, and by generating statistical analyses of these results, experimental psychology had amassed a considerable body of fact and had entered a new, "less simple phase." Although he willingly accepted the results of such research, he was clearly disenchanted with the method itself. Perhaps reflecting on his own brief experience with German science, he wrote that "this method taxes patience to the utmost, and could hardly have arisen in a country whose natives could be *bored,*" as the Germans "obviously cannot." James's language pictures psychological experimentation as a brutal assault on the human mind: "The simple and open method of attack having done what it can, the method of patience, starving out, and harassing to death is tried: the Mind must submit to a regular *siege*, in which minute advantages gained night and day by the forces that hem her in must sum themselves up at the last into her overthrow." He implicitly and unfavorably contrasted the laboratory style with his own more literary prose when he complained that "there is little of the grand style about these new prism, pendulum, and chronograph-philosophers. They mean business not chivalry." James grudgingly allowed that the results obtained by this warfare against the mind could produce some useful discoveries. He noted that the older method, which chiefly consisted of inspired introspection, had not answered all questions, and he supposed that the experimentalists' "spying and scraping, their deadly tenacity and almost diabolic cunning, will doubtless some day bring about" greater insight into nature.[30] One finishes the paragraph wondering if such an assault is worth the cost, whatever value the results might have. That thought, however, must be balanced by the thousand-plus pages in which James himself, despite his personal feelings, relied on the results of such experimentation to summarize what was then known about the mind and its relations with the body.

When James moved to discuss the third method of psychology, comparison, his language was less harsh, but it still reflected his skepticism. He acknowledged that in trying to understand the major aspects of psychological phenomena, it was "of the utmost importance to trace the phenomenon considered through all its possible variations of type and combination." Still, he wondered whether the method and the subjects studied were all relevant: "So it has come to pass that instincts of animals are ransacked to throw light on our own; and that the reasoning faculties of bees and ants, the minds of savages, infants, madmen, idiots, the deaf and blind, criminals and eccentrics, are all invoked in support of this or that special theory about some part of our own mental life." If that were not enough, James believed that the custom of using questionnaires in psychological research was likely to spread and had the potential to become one of "the common pests of life." Again, James recognized that these methods produced results, but he cautioned investigators to beware of "the great sources of error in the comparative method." Interpreting the "psychoses" of others is "wild work" in which the scientist's own "personal equation" is likely to affect the outcome. For example, "a savage will be reported to have no moral or religious feeling if his actions shock the observer unduly." The only protection against such bias is "to use as much sagacity as you possess, and to be as candid as you can."[31]

James, despite his avowed intention to make psychology into a science, did not reject the more traditional methods of introspection and comparison in favor of exclusive, or even heavy, reliance upon the experimental method. His language, in fact, betrays his attachment to introspection, carefully and rigorously performed. His comments on the experimental method reveal not only his distaste of and unsuitability for laboratory work but also his conviction that physiological or psycho-physical fact was not in itself an adequate explanation of mental phenomena and of consciousness. Being scientific for James did not mean exclusive reliance upon laboratory experimentation, so long as the other methods were carried out in a scientific spirit, with scientific rigor, and with full knowledge of their faults and weaknesses. James's willingness to rely upon introspection and comparison opened him to criticism from more experimentally-minded psychologists who felt that he was thereby compromising the science.[32] But for James, pluralism of method was essential if final consensus about the mind, the brain, and the body was ever to be achieved.

The publication of *The Principles of Psychology* in 1890 marked a significant stage in James's intellectual development, in the development of psychology as a natural science, and in the growing rift between psychology and philosophy. For James, the *Principles* signified the culmination of his physiological and psychological studies. He had never been fond of laboratory work and now wished to put it behind him. To Hugo Münsterberg James confided that "I naturally hate experimental work," and to his friend Theodore Flournoy he wrote that he had "always felt that the occupation of philosophizing was with me a valid excuse for neglecting laboratory work, since there is not time for both." James did not, of course, immediately and completely abandon psychology for philosophy. He responded to several of the reviews and critiques of his book and in 1892 published the revised and shortened *Psychology: A Briefer Course,* designed specifically as a text for classroom use. But increasingly, James turned to developing those metaphysical implications which had been lurking on the fringes of his psychology and which he had hitherto downplayed in attempting to make psychology more scientific. His advice to Flournoy—"Your work as a philosopher will be more *irreplaceable* than what results you might get in the laboratory out of the same number of hours"— applied to himself as well.[33] The scientific foundation was established; now James could move on to the more intriguing and significant metaphysical problems.

From the time it was published, sympathetic readers and critics alike have recognized *The Principles of Psychology* as a significant accomplishment and as a watershed for the field. James's volumes were applauded even as they were criticized. G. Stanley Hall, for example, expressed his distress at the looseness of James's science, at his tendency to be certain where other scientists doubted, and at his failure to state adequately what was more definitively known. Hall conceded that the book's "very inconsistencies and incoherencies" reflected the unsettled character of the field, but he also feared that James's unsystematic treatment would "greatly magnify all the unrest, distraction and conflicts of the present hour." Despite his reservations, Hall, not surprisingly, concluded that the book by his graduate advisor was "on the whole and after all the best work in any language." The very qualities that distressed the experimentalist Hall delighted William Dean Howells, the novelist and editor of *Harper's* magazine. Howells celebrated James's "poetic sense of his facts" and his "artistic pleasure in their presentation." For Howells, the philosophical aspects of *Principles* stood out: "If Psychology in this work is treated philosophically rather than scientifically, there can be no question but it is treated profoundly and subtly, and with a never-failing, absolute devotion to the truth."[34]

Two philosophical colleagues, Charles Sanders Peirce and George Trumbull Ladd, both found fault with the book, though Peirce, at least, acknowledged its importance. Peirce, writing in the *Nation*, charged, among other things, that James's description of scientists accepting their data uncritically was a seriously flawed view of scientific procedure. Scientists must always subject the phenomena of their study to "rigid criticism," and James's method, if adopted, would "make a complete rupture with accepted methods of psychology and of science in general." Peirce, in spite of the critical tenor of his review, recognized that James had produced a significant work. A definitive judgment would require time, but Peirce was confident that *The Principles of Psychology* was "the most important contribution that has been made to the subject for many years." George Trumbull Ladd, a Yale philosopher who had published his own *Elements of Physiological Psychology* in 1888, attacked James's conception of a psychological science for being too narrow. In a long review published in *Philosophical Review*, Ladd found the book interesting, frank, and provocative, but also lacking the unity of a scientific treatise. He was most disturbed by James's conception of psychology, which he regarded as "so narrow, that a consistent adherence to it compels us to admit the utter impossibility of establishing psychology as a natural science." Ladd cited, in particular, James's failure to connect adequately the mental and physical, while seeming to make such a connection the key to the new science. In addition, Ladd criticized James's tendency to admit metaphysics into his science. Ladd concluded that "as descriptive science, the work is admirable . . . As explanatory science also,—wherever it departs most widely from its own conception—it is generally admirable. As explanatory science, without metaphysics, . . . it is, at best, *not science at all.*"[35]

Near the end of his review Ladd raised the question which James had discussed in the preface to his book: Was psychology a science, or could it
become a science? Ladd believed that "modern psychology is amply entitled
to be called a science; and even—if you please—'a natural science'." It has a
field of phenomena—"states of consciousness"—and data for description
and explanation. The science of psychology also has "the task of tracing the
evolution of mental life": "When we point out uniform relations, the dependence of mental state on mental state, of one stage of mental life on other
stages of mental life, we render psychology scientific." He charged that James
was ready to surrender this explanatory mode without offering any more
powerful explanations. "Cerebral physiology," he argued, was little more
than a "'mess of pottage'." In the end, Ladd cast doubt on the possibility of a
psychological science without metaphysics and without the soul: "But may
we pursue psychology as a 'natural science' without postulate of a soul, and
without any metaphysical implicate or postulate whatsoever? Possibly: I am
not prepared to say that we cannot; but the way is straight and narrow and
there are few, if any, who succeed in finding it."[36] And Ladd, in the end,
doubted that the James of *The Principles of Psychology* had found that narrow
path.

In his reply James protested that he had "never claimed, . . . as Professor
Ladd seems to think I claim, that psychology as it stands to-day, *is* a natural
science, or in an exact way a science at all." Psychology was only in the early
stages of becoming a science, much like physics before Galileo and chemistry
before Lavoisier. The discipline of the late nineteenth century consisted of "a
mass of phenomenal description, gossip, and myth," but there was enough
"real material" to justify the hope that it might become "worthy of the name
of natural science at no very distant day." James "wished, by treating Psychology *like* a natural science to help her become one." He defended his contention that psychology must approach some of her data uncritically. All natural
science, he argued, "is a mere fragment of truth broken out from the whole
mass of it for the sake of practical effectiveness exclusively." Psychology, if it
was ever to become a science, must necessarily "renounce certain ultimate solutions" and simply accept such "facts" as the existence of a physical world
and of states of mind. James conceded Ladd's point that there was as yet no
"'science' of the correlation of mental states with brain states," but, he coun-
tered, such a goal was the "*program* of a science well limited and defined." If
the science of psychology did not yet exist, James wanted to "cheer those on
who are working for its future" and to urge them to "aspire" to create the
science.[37]

The publication of *The Principles of Psychology,* even more than the establishment of primitive psychological laboratories, marks a watershed in the

development of psychology as a science in the United States and in the relationship of philosophy and psychology. In his two volumes James managed to survey the field, to summarize the latest scientific information, and to give encouragement to the future development of psychology as a science. Although his science was current, the book was not a dry treatise; nor was it a polemical tract. James wrote his book cognizant of a larger intellectual context, aware of a historically intimate relationship between philosophical and psychological inquiry, and supportive of the growing efforts to make psychology into an independent science. The book thus spoke to several audiences. The experimentalist could find in its pages his results cited and could come away encouraged in his laboratory pursuits. The philosopher could easily read the volumes as a psychological prolegomenon to some future metaphysics. James had constructed a scientific foundation, and it was now the philosophers' task to build upon on it. Even the theologian and the religiously inclined could take comfort in James's repeated assertions that nothing in psychology precluded belief in the soul, even if that belief could not be established scientifically. James's greatest accomplishment in *Principles* was not so much in establishing the state of the science, as in writing a volume that expressed aptly the pluralism, even confusion, of an era slowly and painfully shedding its reliance on theology and philosophy as the touchstones of culture and yet not ready to declare full allegiance to science.

If *The Principles of Psychology* marks an intellectual divide, it also marks a disciplinary one. Psychology had been, as Joseph Jastrow observed, a "colonial outpost" of philosophy.[38] Its researches had traditionally been seen as providing data for the philosopher's informed speculation. That attitude is clearly present in Dewey's *Psychology*, but it is evident as well in James's *Principles*. Both men, significantly, turned away from psychology after publishing their texts to devote their energies to philosophical inquiry. But if these philosophers could still see psychology as a springboard to metaphysics, the psychologists took from James's work a very different message. While acknowledging that psychology was not yet a science, James had been determined to help it become one. The younger psychologists, and especially the experimentalists, took up James's challenge, in part because he had demonstrated how scientific psychology had already become, and in part because he confirmed in their minds the conviction that the future of psychology lay in experimentation and in alliance with the natural sciences, especially physiology, rather than with philosophy.

The early 1890s, then, mark a parting of the ways for philosophy and psychology. Even those philosophers most attracted to a scientific psychology found it inadequate for answering the larger questions and put it aside to pursue their metaphysical studies, studies often imbued with the knowledge gained from psychology. The psychologists, finding the intellectual and institutional ties to philosophy increasingly confining, sought ways to establish the independence of psychology as a science and as an academic discipline. Through the 1880s in the United States the history of the two fields had been congruent. Scholars took their degrees in one field and wrote and taught in the other. Psychologists could most often be found in departments of philosophy, and sometimes even in chairs of philosophy. The two fields were seen as mutually dependent intellectually, even when it was conceded that philosophy was the higher pursuit. But following the publication of *The Principles of Psychology* in 1890, and in part because of its publication, philosophy and psychology diverged to become rival academic disciplines and competitors in understanding the workings of the mind and brain.

SIX

From Colonial

Outpost to

Academic Rival:

Psychology

and Philosophy

at the Turn

of the Century

The publication of William James's *The Principles of Psychology* in 1892 was a turning point in the relationship of philosophy and psychology in the American university. The book was both an end and a beginning. James's syncretic style, mixing metaphysics, science, ethics, and even religion, culminated in his *Principles*. James had successfully melded the older synoptic approach with the newer experimental method, but his was a success that brought an end to the tradition of which it was a part. At the same time, James's reliance upon, even celebration of, the methods and discoveries of scientific physiology and psychology encouraged those younger scholars who had already given their allegiance to scientific approaches to the study of the mind. James's science of psychology did not provide all the answers, but it did demonstrate conclusively the potential inherent in an experimentally based psychology. By summarizing as he did the state of the discipline, James had demonstrated how much had been accomplished, how much remained to be done, and how best to go about the task.

The Principles of Psychology did not in itself give birth to a new science of psychology. James, after all, had written his book based on what the science had already achieved. But in the United States, at least, the book gave intellectual warrant to the scientific approach to psychology. In the decades following, psychologists moved quickly to ensure the intellectual standing of their field, to separate themselves definitively from the more metaphysical philosophers, and to establish their discipline as a recognized and respected academic specialty within the American university. Psychologists no longer saw themselves occupying a "colonial outpost" of philosophy; they were building and occupying academic fortifications of their own.[1] More laboratories were being established, separate departments of psychology were being created, and in 1892 the American Psychological Association was founded to give a disciplinary focus to these efforts.

The philosophers were, of course, well aware of the efforts of the psychologists to differentiate themselves and to establish an independent academic identity. Their response, however, was slow, sometimes uncomprehending, and ineffectual. Throughout the 1890s and even well into this century, many philosophers continued to assert the intimate connection between the two disciplines. They still saw philosophy as the premier field, although they welcomed and utilized the achievements of the new psychology. By the first decade of this century some philosophers, at least, had come to recognize that mere assertions of primacy were inadequate to protect what they perceived as philosophy's diminishing role in American universities. The philosophers' response varied. Some asserted with renewed vigor their conviction that philosophy was as much a science as psychology and entitled to equal standing on those grounds. Others reasserted philosophy's traditional, synoptic role centered in metaphysics. Both groups, however, found some merit in emulating the disciplinary accouterments of psychology. Steps were taken to establish new journals, to defend departmental prerogatives, and, in 1901, to create the American Philosophical Association. In order to compete successfully for scarce university resources and for recognition and prestige, the philosophers at the turn of the century found themselves in the uncomfortable role of copying the psychologists.

Psychology in the 1890s began to mature into a separate discipline within the American academic context. It had long been part of the course of study at American colleges, but until the end of the nineteenth century psychology had typically been subsumed under philosophy. Psychology had been the science of the soul, or of mental phenomena, whose results were vital to the construction of a philosophical system. As psychology began to move out from under the shadow of philosophy, the goal of its practitioners was not so much to reject this past as to establish an independence commensurate with the field's new methods and recent successes. As John O'Donnell has observed, "This search for autonomy was essential to psychology's institutional survival and constitutes the keystone of its intellectual development after 1892."[2] In the American context, intellectual independence was closely tied to institutional autonomy; for psychology, as well as for philosophy, professionalization provided a means whereby both could be achieved and protected.

The German model in psychology provided an essential impetus to the creation of a separate field. The work of German pioneers, such as Herman von

Helmholtz and Wilhelm Wundt, formed the methodological underpinnings of the new science. Their studies and experiments in physiological psychology enabled psychology to become more than an introspective inquiry and to acquire the features and the appearance of a science. German psychology provided not only a model, but also a training ground for American psychologists. Many Americans studied in German laboratories and some returned with German degrees. In a few cases American universities imported German psychologists, such as Hugo Münsterberg at Harvard, to undertake research and teaching. What Americans seem to have taken most from German psychology were a commitment to experimentalism and a conviction that psychology ought to forge closer links with the sciences.[3]

The role of the laboratory in the transformation of American psychology has been the subject of much debate, almost from the time of the establishment of the first one. James and Hall in the 1890s disagreed publicly over who had established the first psychological laboratory in the United States—James at Harvard in 1875, or Hall at Johns Hopkins in 1881. The dispute was not simply a matter of faulty memory; it also involved the question of what properly constituted a laboratory. James apparently had set aside a small room with a few pieces of apparatus as early as 1875 and had conducted some primitive experiments and experimental demonstrations on the equipment. Hall's first laboratory was, however, more prominently and publicly established. By the early 1890s eighteen psychological laboratories had been established in the United States. The laboratories seemed to signify the arrival of psychology as a discipline and the modernity of the colleges which housed them.[4]

The dispute between James and Hall over primacy in establishing the first psychological laboratory is emblematic of the symbolic importance of the laboratory to late nineteenth-century psychology. That the laboratories were used more frequently to conduct demonstrations and to train graduate students than to pursue significant research does not diminish their importance. The laboratory was the discipline's "vital center." It provided experimentalists with "a scientific passport to professional autonomy, an entering wedge into an academic world that offered status, security, and financial support for pursuits that often bore little substantive relation to experimental behavior." In addition, the laboratory proved to be an important training ground for new psychologists. The laboratory was, O'Donnell argues, "not a stable community of the competent but a springboard for a vocationally mobile profession."[5] Work in a laboratory validated the scientific credentials of the experimentalist. The establishment of a psychological laboratory signified the recognition of the new scientific discipline by a university.

Between 1885 and 1895 psychology acquired many of the characteristics of a self-conscious profession. G. Stanley Hall had taken the lead in proselytizing for the new science and in providing vehicles for professional advancement. He established its first journal, the *American Journal of Psychology,* in 1887. Five years later, after he had become president of Clark University, Hall issued the invitation which led to the formation of the American Psychological Association. The initial membership was heavily weighted toward people who had close ties to Hall, but also included the leading directors of laboratories and philosopher-psychologists including James, George Trumbull Ladd, and Josiah Royce. Membership was restricted to those committed to advancing psychology as a science. Although it would have been impossible for Hall to have secured a consensus on the definition of psychology as a science, the new organization nonetheless "symbolized the advance toward professionalization." Hall and the other founders of the association had "created a forum for ensuing debate while providing to other professional organizations and potential patrons the appearance of a unified scientific community dedicated to common goals." The *Psychological Review,* a second journal dedicated to publishing the results of the new science, was established in 1894.[6]

The last decade of the century saw a significant expansion in the personnel and resources devoted to the science of psychology. Whereas seventeen Americans had obtained doctorates in psychology in both American and German universities between 1884 and 1892, ninety had by 1899. Although the number of laboratories also increased, the rate was less rapid. Nineteen laboratories had been established by 1892, and thirty-three by 1899. O'Donnell has pointed out that the number of doctorates in psychology far exceeded the number of laboratories and that partly as a result, many psychologists turned away from experimental research to the practical application of psychology, to problems of education, society, politics, and economics. Leading psychologists in the period were quick to develop connections with state bureaus of education and other public and private institutions which relied upon, or could be persuaded to rely upon, the expert advice of the experimentally trained psychologist. Such a strategy not only provided employment for psychologists who could not find places in the laboratory, it also forged a pattern of "social support of the discipline."[7]

This portrait of a discipline acquiring the characteristics of a profession should not obscure the important differences among the leading psychologists at the turn of the century. Historians of the discipline have stressed the variety of approaches which characterized the work of the leading practitioners and the lack of unanimity regarding the scientific characteristics of the field and the practical applicability of experimental results. The studies of both Daniel Bjork and John O'Donnell, for example, reveal a discipline divided by significantly different conceptions of science, by the strong-willed ambitions of the first generation of professional psychologists, and by rival notions of how psychology could best serve the larger society. Bjork has examined the very different conceptions of science held by James, Münsterberg, Edward B. Titchener, and J. McKeen Cattell. O'Donnell has found three broad conceptions of psychology developing in the 1890s—research, utility, and humanistic study. Disagreements as to the primacy of one approach over another ultimately focused, according to O'Donnell, on two fundamental issues: "Whether psychology could or should become an exact natural science, and whether it was to be devoted primarily to theoretical or to practical problem solving." These often heated debates did not mean that psychology could not become a profession, or even a science, only that the issues had not yet been resolved and those goals achieved. The growing number of doctorates, the increase in laboratory research, the new journals, and even the American Psychological Association did not of themselves mean that the psychologists at the turn of the century had become self-conscious and confident professionals.[8] But like James, who hoped his text would help make psychology a science, the founders of these departments, institutions, and journals hoped their actions would make psychology both a science and a profession.

Philosophers were, of course, well aware of the psychologists' efforts to create a new science and to establish a profession. Philosopher-psychologists like James, Dewey, and Ladd had written some of the first psychology texts to take notice of the new developments and to foster the science. The philosophers could not miss the separatist tendencies of many psychologists who were establishing their laboratories and departments and beginning to compete for university resources. The new journals and the American Psychological Association, even when they welcomed philosophical contributions, did so with a sufferance that was sometimes irksome.[9] Many philosophers, as we have already seen, shared with psychologists an urge to make their own discipline more scientific and to secure it a permanent place in the new universities, but they also felt compelled at the turn of the century to confront the psychologists' claims to independence. Some, like James, were content to let the experimentalists go their own way, confident that philosophy's task was ultimately more significant. Others reaffirmed philosophy's traditionally intimate ties with psychology in hopes of stemming the defections. Finally, some philosophers set out consciously to imitate the professional characteristics of the psychologists in the belief that they would thereby strengthen philosophy against further losses of intellectual authority, personnel, and prestige in the university.

In the aftermath of publishing his *Principles of Psychology*, James turned his attention to philosophical and metaphysical problems and gave up directing the work of the Harvard psychological laboratory. He also recognized, however, that Harvard could not afford to be without a first-rate laboratory and an experimentalist. As James put it to Hugo Münsterberg when asking him to consider a possible position at Harvard, "We are the best university in America, and we must lead in psychology." James had already raised forty-three hundred dollars for improvements and had supervised the transfer of the laboratory to new, larger, and better equipped quarters.[10]

James not only had a personal antipathy to sustained laboratory work, but he was also skeptical of the results obtained there. He cautioned his contemporaries not to put too much faith in experimental work. His attitudes are clearly revealed in correspondence with George Holmes Howison, a philosopher at the University of California who sought James's advice on the establishment of a psychological laboratory. In 1893 James wrote Howison to console him on the lack of a laboratory: "I don't think that the *results* ground out of all the labor have so far been important." Still, a laboratory was useful to bring students "in touch with the concrete facts of the human organism" and he urged Howison to develop a demonstration laboratory. The following year he again wrote Howison, this time to discuss the responsibilities of George M. Stratton, who had just been hired at California. Again he urged Howison to "give up the notion of having a laboratory of *original research*. My private impression is that the business is being overstocked in America, and that the results are not proportionate to the money expended." Stratton, he suggested, could acquire in two years' study what psychology he needed in order to teach and to run demonstrations in the laboratory.[11]

James wanted a skilled experimentalist for the Harvard laboratory, but he saw no compelling reason why people lacking skill or interest should chain themselves to the laboratory. Writing his Swiss friend Theodore Flournoy, James urged him not to get too deeply involved in research "if you find that ideas and projects do not abound." He wrote Flournoy that "your work as a philosopher will be more *irreplaceable* than what results you might get in the laboratory out of the same number of hours"; he felt that the same applied to his own situation.[12] Because he was certain that philosophical reflection was his proper calling and because he remained confident that philosophy would retain its central place in American thought, James could view the impending divorce of experimental psychology and philosophy with equanimity. Others, however, were less confident about the impact of the divorce on philosophy.

The anxieties felt by philosophers less confident than James are evident in Jacob Gould Schurman's prefatory remarks in the first issue of the *Philosophical Review*. Schurman and his colleagues at Cornell University set out to provide philosophy with the same opportunities for publication as characterized the other sciences and professions. Philosophy, he lamented, lacked both a journal and a professional organization. Despite these failings, Schurman discerned a "philosophical renascence" in the making. In support of his conviction he cited "the establishment of new philosophical professorships and schools with a corresponding increase of material equipment," an increase in the number of graduate students, and a growth in the number of philosophers conducting research and writing. But in describing the revival of philosophy, Schurman counted psychology as a branch of philosophy. To be sure, psychologists pursued their own investigations, but they were simply partaking of "the spirit of specialization [which] has taken possession of Philosophy." The scope of the new journal would embrace psychology as well as the other branches of philosophy such as ethics, logic, epistemology, and metaphysics. Psychology, by becoming more scientific had, Schurman acknowledged, "within the last decade probably outstripped every other province of human knowledge in the rate of its growth." Nonetheless, there was still need for "a general philosophical magazine to bring to a focus the light generated in the several provincial centres and to reflect it upon the wider undertakings of the federal executive."[13]

Psychologists in the 1890s would not have granted philosophy the role of federal executive, but some were still willing to acknowledge intimate ties to philosophy. Men like James Mark Baldwin, then at Princeton, and George Trumbull Ladd at Yale hearkened back to an older pattern of science closely linked to philosophical inquiry. Though both men had established laboratories and had conducted experiments, they also sought to preserve the fruitful integration of philosophical and psychological inquiry. Baldwin in an essay exploring the past and present status of psychology described this period as "the age of scientific method." The scientific temper had become so pervasive that "any class or school of philosophic thinkers who do not face toward the scientific east are steering up-current and will be absent when science and philosophy enter a common barge and together compass the universe of knowledge." The application of scientific methods had proceeded further in psychology than in philosophy. In fact, the modern psychologist no longer needed to be grounded in philosophical theory, though his psychological facts would continue to have major impact on "general philosophy." Baldwin used the image of a chemical precipitate to describe how psychological questions ought to be separated from the mass of speculation and handed over to the psychologist for special treatment. Even though he urged psychologists to take up their separate scientific tasks, Baldwin retained his faith in the tie to philosophy. The new philosophies, he asserted, could be made "richer and more profound by reason of the lessons of the new psychology." Baldwin concluded that "the traditional connection with philosophy is not severed by the new directions of our effort, but on the contrary they are made more close and reasonable."[14]

George Trumbull Ladd took the occasion of his 1894 presidential address to the American Psychological Association to call for renewing and strengthening the ties that bound psychology and philosophy. He conceded that it was an age of science, but he argued that "science and philosophy will always exist; neither can expel the other from the region of human interests and human endeavor; indeed, no rigid demarcation can ever permanently divide them; each will flourish only in dependence upon the other." Philosophy, Ladd asserted, was "but wild and mischievous speculation, unless it build itself upon the concrete and particular sciences," and science without philosophy was "but the unsatisfying husk of knowledge." These considerations bore on the relationship of psychology and philosophy because psychology was generally conceded to be the science closest to philosophy and there was then considerable sentiment to separate metaphysics from it. For his part, Ladd believed that the line between philosophy and psychology was all but "invisible," and that the intimacy of the ties made it impossible to separate the disciplines. Philosophical assumptions lay behind most psychological experiments, and "so intimate and binding" were the ties between the fields "that not one of the larger psychological problems can be thoroughly discussed without leading up to some great debate in the field of philosophy." Psychology, he thought, was "naturally propaedeutic to philosophy." Granting these links between philosophy and psychology, Ladd nevertheless acknowledged that the American Psychological Association had been "formed in the interests of a science of psychology" and should not be expected to "occupy its time and energies largely in the discussion of philosophical problems." Still, he urged the membership to "add the philosophical spirit to our scientific interest" and to be "tolerant and generous toward the various possible expressions of philosophical views."[15]

Despite the assurances of Baldwin and Ladd, philosophers rightly feared that the balance of intellectual and institutional authority might be shifting in the direction of psychology. Ladd's successor as president of the American Psychological Association, J. McKeen Cattell, was more committed to and outspoken on the superiority of science to philosophy. Psychology as a science was, properly conceived, "the gateway to architectonic philosophy." Although the final questions of philosophy remained beyond the reach of science, "the world-view of each of us depends increasingly on what the natural and exact sciences contribute to it." Those philosophies developed without the aid of scientific experiment no longer had a claim to truth and were to be admired only as poetry. The traditional philosophic inquiries, such as epistemology, ethics, logic, and even aesthetics, now relied heavily on psychology. This, Cattell thought, was as it should be. There was, in fact, only one way to prevent the demise of philosophy: "The twilight of philosophy can be changed to its dawn only by the light of science, and psychology can contribute more light than any other science."[16]

These conflicting claims by psychologists created some confusion, if not anxiety, among contemporary philosophers. A. C. Armstrong's two surveys of the state of philosophy in American colleges and universities, in 1895 and 1897, reveal the uncertainty within the field. In his first essay he noted the growth and progress of psychology as a science and conceded its considerable impact on philosophy: "There is no more prominent feature of our recent development and our present condition than our devotion to the newer methods of attacking psychological questions." Psychology had pushed the philosophers to develop their own "empirical tendencies" and to neglect the deeper, more fundamental problems. What prevented a more complete rupture of psychology and philosophy were, he thought, the emerging "metaempirical interpretations" based on scientific inquiry and fact. Two years later, Armstrong pointed to a revival in philosophy spurred by academic competition with the other disciplines, especially psychology. A revived philosophy, he was convinced, could compete in the new scientific world and could continue to lay the metaphysical foundations for the special sciences.[17] Although Armstrong's hopes were not out of line with the thoughts of Baldwin and Ladd, they betrayed little recognition of the more independent stance taken by experimental psychologists such as Cattell. The time was quickly approaching when mere assertions of intimacy would no longer serve to keep the two disciplines yoked together.

At the end of the century John Dewey, in an address before the Philosophical Union of the University of California, reexamined his conception of the relationship of psychology and philosophy in light of the decade's developments. Dewey took up the assertion that psychology could and should be separated from philosophy and that it should conduct its scientific inquiries in relative isolation from the larger philosophical issues. Dewey conceded that such a conception of psychology had some appeal, for "such a view seems to enroll one in the ranks of the scientific men rather than of the metaphysicians." There was no denying that many psychologists set certain scientific limitations on their field, and while Dewey did not wish to reject totally his colleagues' beliefs, he remained convinced that those limitations concerning the philosophical import of psychological science were not finally and firmly established. Scientific inquiry into consciousness or states of consciousness was, he argued, "the open gateway into the fair fields of philosophy."[18]

Dewey recognized the value of specialized scientific inquiry and had no desire to press philosophical considerations upon every active psychologist. But at the same time Dewey rejected the building of walls between the two disciplines. Postevolutionary science demanded a seamless web between the inquiry into particulars and the analysis and generalization that stood at the pinnacle of scientific method. Dewey rejected any dualism between psychology and philosophy. The conclusions of a psychological science fed naturally into the development of philosophy, just as philosophic assumptions helped shape psychological inquiry. For Dewey in 1899 psychology had become a tool in the social reconstruction of society, in the reshaping of democracy. Psychology supplied "knowledge of the behavior of experience" which was essential to "the ordering of life in response to the needs of the moment in accordance with the ascertained truth of the moment."[19]

A role in the building of a stronger democracy would, thought Dewey, require a transformation of philosophy as well as of psychology. Philosophy would have to surrender its claim "to be the sole source of some truths and the exclusive guardian of some values." Philosophy must become "a method; not an assurance company, nor a knight errant." Although philosophy should not be sacrificed to the popular appeal of science, "there is a sense in which philosophy must go to school to the sciences; must have no data save such as it receives at their hands; and be hospitable to no method of inquiry or reflection not akin to those in daily use among the sciences." Psychology is important to philosophy because psychological science reveals how possible experience becomes real in the life of specific individuals. And it is that knowledge which philosophers require if they are to become a force for social change and the reconstruction of society.[20] Without a continuing intimate connection with psychology, philosophy was in real danger of losing contact with the real and the actual, of becoming irrelevant.

Departing from his 1880s conception of psychology as philosophic method, Dewey had here reinstated the primacy of philosophy. Psychology was an important tool for philosophers; it was the science of individual experience. But the findings of psychological science must be merged into the philosophic effort to provide a grounding for the reconstruction of society. Psychology was a way to measure and to examine the validity of philosophic conceptions, but Dewey no longer saw psychology as the method of philosophy, as he had earlier. Unlike some of the more experimental psychologists, Dewey maintained the intimate ties between the two fields; but for him at the turn of the century, the continuum from psychology to philosophy left philosophy triumphant and psychology subservient.

Notwithstanding the professions of linkage asserted by philosophers and philosophically-minded psychologists, many psychologists in the 1890s more sharply differentiated their science from philosophy. One of their major vehicles for accomplishing the separation was the American Psychological Association, which had been organized in 1892. The annual meetings of the association provided an opportunity for members to assess and to celebrate the state of their science, to exhort themselves and their colleagues to greater progress, and to develop a community of like-minded scientists. The association fostered the image of psychology as a science when it forged official ties with the American Society of Naturalists in 1895 and with the American Association for the Advancement of Science in 1902. As Thomas Camfield has observed, the purpose of the American Psychological Association was "to symbolize the distinctiveness of their special field, give structure and corporate weight to their common goals, and promote, in a multiplicity of ways, both the scientific and social progress of their discipline."[21]

The psychologists' efforts to create a professionalized science had a direct bearing on the philosophers' slightly later drive to create a profession and an association of their own. On the twenty-fifth anniversary of the founding of the American Philosophical Association, H. N. Gardiner, the long-time secretary-treasurer of the association, recalled the steps which had led to the establishment of a separate philosophical organization. He noted that from the inception of the American Psychological Association some of the more philosophical psychologists had offered papers that were "of a distinctly philosophical character." The practice continued at subsequent meetings of the psychological association, and Gardiner estimated that in some years the philosophical presentations amounted to between one-third and one-half of the total. Gardiner remembered that this situation was "satisfactory neither to the philosophers nor to the psychologists." The philosophers felt "their claims were allowed only on sufferance" while "the psychologists were disposed to regard these claims as an impertinence and to resent the intrusion of the philosophical camel into the psychological tent." As early as 1896 proposals were advanced within the American Psychological Association to establish a separate philosophical association or at least a separate philosophical section at the annual meetings. Though some psychologists were clearly dissatisfied with the makeshift arrangements, no formal moves were taken within the psychological association to drive the philosophers out.[22] Instead, it was the philosophers who ended what was becoming an intolerable situation by creating their own association.

The American Philosophical Association came into being in 1901 in response to the pervasive climate of professionalization and specialization and to the feelings of inferiority engendered by the meetings with the psychologists. There was an initial meeting at Cornell University in the fall of 1901, followed by a larger meeting in New York in November attended by representatives of nine colleges and universities. The first annual meeting was held in April 1902 at Columbia University, and forty of the ninety-eight charter members attended. Gardiner recalled that in organizing themselves the philosophers had no intention of cutting themselves off from contact with other scholars and associations. He noted that in the early years of the philosophical association the philosophers held joint sessions with the psychologists in 1902, 1904, 1905, and 1913. On three occasions the philosophers met at the same time and place as the American Association for the Advancement of Science. Despite these efforts to maintain scientific ties, Gardiner felt that some of the best meetings were those held alone, "free from the confusions and dispersions of interest which commonly accompany the larger gatherings." These meetings, whether alone or in concert with other professional associations, provided the philosophers with a disciplinary focus which, if it did not significantly advance philosophical thought, gave them a sense of participating in one of the major academic tendencies of the period.[23]

J. E. Creighton, the Cornell idealist, was elected first president of the American Philosophical Association. In his presidential address Creighton outlined some of the purposes of the new association. He cautioned his listeners not to expect the association to become "a kind of universal panacea for all the ills from which philosophy suffers." Creighton argued that modern scientific work required cooperation among scientists and had given rise to the proliferation of associations. Philosophy, however, had traditionally been more of an individual enterprise, and thus the philosophers had been slow to see the advantages of organization. Recently philosophers had come to realize the potential benefits of cooperation, especially as they had "abandoned the attempt to deduce a philosophy of the world from fundamental first principles, by means of deductive arguments, and have frankly adopted the inductive method of procedure." Creighton believed that "for the majority of men at least, intellectual contact and personal intercourse with their fellow workers in the same field are essential conditions of complete sanity of view."[24] If nothing else, the new association would promote that fruitful exchange of ideas and criticism among philosophers.

Although encouraging cooperation in the spirit of scientific inquiry was an overarching goal of the association, Creighton suggested that the "main purpose" of the association should be "to promote and encourage original investigation and publication." He also hoped that the American Philosophical Association could become the vehicle for improving the standing of philosophy in the university. Creighton deplored the fact that "philosophy does not enjoy the general recognition, even among educated men, that is accorded to many other sciences" and that in "many colleges and universities the place of philosophy is only grudgingly conceded." He attributed philosophy's decline in public and academic esteem to the philosophers' "lack of zeal in original investigation" and to the commonly held belief that philosophy had been "barren of real results." Though Creighton proposed no practical steps the association might take to remedy philosophy's precarious standing, he expressed the hope that its actions would help raise "the standing of philosophy in the learned world and in the esteem of the general public."[25]

Creighton concluded his address by taking up the question of philosophy's proper affiliation with the other sciences. He thought philosophy could benefit by widening its scientific affiliations, particularly with groups like the American Association for the Advancement of Science. He stressed that "our relations should be close and intimate with the American Psychological Association, to whose courtesy philosophical interests in the past have owed so much, and by means of whose fostering care the present organization has grown up." In spite of the obvious advantages of affiliation, Creighton cautioned his colleagues not to forsake philosophy's unique standpoint nor to adopt that of "other sciences in the attempt to imitate their procedure, no matter how fruitful or successful these methods may appear to be when applied in other fields." No good could come from "a blind faith that if we are fervent in protesting our love for natural science, and our determination to follow the road that it has marked out, all will go well." For Creighton, "philosophy, to be philosophy at all, has to *humanize* its facts, that is, to look at them from the standpoint of complete and self-conscious human experience."[26]

Creighton typified the ambivalence that surrounded the establishment of the American Philosophical Association. There was, on the one hand, the anxiety that philosophers were losing out in the academic competition with the ascendant sciences, for prestige, resources, and power. The philosophical association was a defensive measure designed to deter future defections from the camp of philosophy and to reassert, more aggressively, philosophy's standing within the university and its ability to contribute something of value to the larger community. On the other hand, there was Creighton's clearly expressed fear that in emulating the other sciences philosophy would lose its traditional standpoint and role. Creighton, for one, did not want philosophy to become just another special science, though, as we have seen, his contemporaries held a variety of views on this point. Creighton was right in at least one respect. The American Philosophical Association could not be a panacea for all the ills of philosophy; but at least it gave philosophers a measure of disciplinary unity, a focal point for debate, and an organizational structure comparable to other disciplines. Whether it could restore philosophy's standing as queen of the sciences was more problematical.

Although the establishment of the American Philosophical Association in 1901 brought to the surface the academic rivalry between philosophy and psychology, it also permitted each discipline to focus on its strengths without being tied to an encumbering and not always welcome ally. The establishment of the philosophical association left the more scientifically inclined psychologists in firm control of their organization. Freed of the metaphysical tinge of philosophy, the psychologists in the early twentieth century exhibited "an extremely self-conscious and relentless concern for full-scale development, and for stature, as a science and profession." They also began to shift their social appeal from "the promise of ultimate scientific achievements" to the promise of the "practical value" of their science. The efforts to achieve scientific stature were not entirely successful in the years before the first world war, due to the psychologists' inability "to reach agreement among themselves as to the definition of their field and its phenomena, or with regard to proper methods of investigation."[27] Psychology's internal coherence as a science was thus far less established than it appeared to those in philosophy, which had even less standing as a science.

However much the psychologists might wish to separate themselves from the philosophers, the philosophers were determined, by and large, to maintain the traditionally intimate links between the two disciplines. In 1904 a new journal appeared, the *Journal of Philosophy, Psychology, and Scientific Methods,* edited in the philosophy department at Columbia. The very title of the journal suggests its ambitious range. The editors proposed to cover "the whole field of scientific philosophy, psychology, ethics and logic." Critically important to the establishment of the journal was the editors' conviction "that the relations between philosophy and psychology should remain intimate, and that the fundamental methods and concepts of the special sciences . . . should be kept in touch with philosophy in its historic development." The journal retained its inclusive title until 1921, when it became simply the *Journal of Philosophy,* thereby reflecting more accurately its subject matter.[28]

Just as F. J. E. Woodbridge and his colleagues at Columbia were launching the *Journal of Philosophy, Psychology, and Scientific Methods,* there began to appear in the psychological journals retrospective analyses of the recent rapid development of psychology as a science. Edward F. Buchner reviewed psychology's progress for the *American Journal of Psychology* and in the process revealed the extent to which the psychologists held a significantly different view of their discipline's ties to philosophy from that of most philosophers. He celebrated psychology's recent achievements and in particular its new affiliations with the physical and physiological sciences. By becoming more scientific, psychology had managed to escape "the buffetings from philosophical systems." In the past, Buchner wrote, psychology had been "given a small corner in a philosophical system," but now psychology was no longer dependent upon philosophy: "*Now* one's philosophy depends upon his psychology, upon his recognition of the psychological facts of experience and his methods of interpreting them." Buchner was convinced that "no one who has not blown the psychological trumpet can gain the attention and respect of his philosophical contemporaries."[29]

The programmatic statements of philosophers in the *Journal of Philosophy* and of Buchner in the *American Journal of Psychology* overstate the arguments from their respective viewpoints. They are, nonetheless, instructive of the state of the relationship between philosophy and psychology in the early twentieth century. The philosophers, in large measure, sought to retain their traditional interpretive superiority while recognizing the particular successes of the science of psychology. In their minds, the philosophical point of view was necessary to place the concrete results of scientific experiment in a larger, comprehensive framework. The traditionally intimate ties between philosophy and psychology ought to be maintained, in part because philosophers needed the data developed by psychologists, but even more importantly, because the experimental psychologists required the metaphysical foundations that, in the philosopher's view, could only be provided by philosophy. But as Buchner's essay revealed, the psychologists were inclined to reverse the significance of the ties to philosophy, if they were to be maintained at all. Buchner suggested that psychology could develop quite nicely without any links to philosophy. Rather, it was philosophy which required the maintenance of those ties so as not to lose all contact with the concrete and actual in experience. Although both sides agreed that some ties were useful, their divergent interpretations of the significance of those ties made mutual understanding and cooperation difficult. Over the next several years, philosophers and psychologists periodically discussed the existing state of interdisciplinary relationships and offered ideas on how the two fields might profitably interact. The philosophers, responding to their perceived loss of influence, typically argued for the value of intimate ties to psychology and for a relationship beneficial to both fields. The psychologists were increasingly inclined to view their discipline as a science and to urge their colleagues to increase the scientific character and practical utility of their work.

Frank Thilly, a Princeton philosopher, expressed a representative philosophical viewpoint in his 1906 essay, "Psychology, Natural Science, and Philosophy." Thilly recalled philosophy's glorious past as "monarch of all she surveyed." Philosophy had been "the mother science," giving birth, one by one, to the more specialized sciences. In his own day, Thilly lamented, philosophy had been significantly diminished by specialization: "Philosophy, the sometime queen, has become a dowager; her children have deserted her, all but a few barren daughters, we are often told, for whom nobody cares." Even psychology, so long an intimate part of philosophy, was being urged to "cut loose from her old-fashioned sisters, and set up an establishment of her own or go to live with the natural sciences."[30]

Thilly recognized that there were appealing reasons why psychologists might want to break their traditional ties to philosophy. Experimental methods had given psychology a more scientific character and had created a greater affinity between psychologists and scientists. Since scientists were "apt to smile at the pretensions of the philosophers," Thilly could understand, if not fully accept, the appeal of being identified as a scientist. He acknowledged, too, that some psychologists were arguing that psychology was, in fact, a natural science, though he remained skeptical. Finally, he recognized that the separation of psychology from philosophy had certain practical benefits for both fields in the competition for university resources, students, and recognition. Despite the reasons that could be offered to support a divorce between philosophy and psychology, Thilly remained convinced that "the proposed separation" would be "beneficial neither to philosophy nor to psychology itself." The continuing relationship ought not to be "one of absolute dependence on either side," but rather one of fruitful and cooperative independence.[31]

Thilly argued against the affiliation of psychology with the natural sciences on two grounds: first, the subject matter of psychology and natural science differed, and second, despite the introduction of experimental methods into psychology, the methods of psychology and those of science were not identical. In terms of subject matter, Thilly believed that psychology was primarily a science of "thoughts, feelings, and volitions," whereas natural science took as its subject "material objects." Though he recognized that mental phenomena were "somehow related to a physical and biological environment," mental facts could be studied independently of the physical phenomena of interest to the natural scientist. Thus, psychology could not legitimately be reduced to "a branch of physics or biology." If the subject matter of psychology could not be reduced to that of a natural science, neither could the methodology. Although "the general method of psychology is the same as that of every other department of research," there is "a specific difference between the method of psychology and that of natural science. The method of psychology is primarily subjective or introspective, the method of science is objective." Even the introduction of experimental method into psychology failed to eliminate this distinction; the object of experimentation, in Thilly's view, was "to facilitate introspection, to render it more exact, to correct it, to bring it under control, to verify it." For these reasons, Thilly concluded that "psychology is not a natural science either in subject matter or in method, and that there is no reason for affiliating it with natural science." Though it was conceivable that psychology "should cut loose from its historical association with philosophy and proclaim its independence," there was "no good reason why this should be done." Thilly thought that it was in "the interest of both parties that the old friendly relations be continued. Philosophy needs the companionship and example of psychology to do fruitful work, and psychology cannot fail to benefit by such association herself."[32]

Four years after Thilly's defense of the traditional relationship between philosophy and psychology, Robert M. Yerkes, the Harvard comparative and animal psychologist, attempted to clarify psychology's relationship to science and, by implication at least, her ties to philosophy. Yerkes spoke from the perspective of one who thought psychology was at least capable of becoming a science, if it had not yet attained that status. To test his own conception of psychology's relationship to the sciences, Yerkes surveyed the views of twenty noted biologists as to whether they considered psychology a part of physiology and as to how they would define psychology. Of his nineteen respondents, four admitted they had no opinion; eight, with qualifications, believed psychology to be a branch of physiology; and seven thought that psychology was "an independent science, differing essentially in materials or methods, or both, from the biological sciences." Among the last group Yerkes found a difference between those who argued that the methods of psychology were those of the natural and physical sciences and those who felt that they were different. Yerkes concluded that many scientists were still unconvinced that psychology merited status as a science and that the burden of persuading them otherwise lay with the psychologists. Successful scientific work would be more persuasive than rhetoric.[33]

Having gathered the biologists' views, Yerkes set forth his own conception—one shared, he believed, by many of his psychological contemporaries. Yerkes developed his conception in response to four questions he posed: (1) Is the "material" of psychology "essentially different" from that of the other sciences? (2) Are the methods of science applicable to psychology? (3) Are the "aims or purposes" of psychology the same as those of the other sciences? and (4) "Is the scientific investigation of consciousness, as such, worth while?" In response to the first question Yerkes argued that the material of psychological study—psychic phenomena or states of consciousness—was not essentially different from the material of the physical sciences; every science deals with a restricted group of phenomena, whether those phenomena have a physical or only psychical existence. Second, Yerkes argued that like the natural sciences, psychology sought to observe "its objects under natural and experimentally controlled conditions" and to gain "a description of its materials which is quantitatively accurate, which is verifiable, which forms a basis for the prediction of events, and which explains phenomena by revealing their causal relations." There was no denying that in the present state of psychology the results of the science were "crudely inexact in comparison with those of the physical sciences." But Yerkes insisted "that it need not be true" and that with "ingenuity, insight, and persistent effort" the psychologists could achieve the levels of exactitude and verifiability characteristic of the hard sciences. He concluded that there was "no essential difference in the methods" of the psychical and physical sciences. Both kinds of science are "observational, experimental, quantitative, causal in their explanations; both are in process of development, but in degree of development the psychical sciences are inferior to the physical sciences." The last two of his questions Yerkes answered more summarily. He asserted that psychology did share the aims and purposes of all science, which he defined as "to give accurate descriptions of its objects, to correlate its phenomena, to discover their laws, and to explain everything causally." Finally, he declared that the "scientific investigation of consciousness" was, in fact, worthwhile. Although he doubted that he could justify his belief before all skeptics, he remained convinced that "the study of consciousness is worth while, if we can achieve the goal of science."[34]

Personally convinced that psychology was a science, although somewhat undeveloped in certain respects, Yerkes nonetheless conceded that "the current American psychology of to-day is a dismal mixture of physiology and psychology." The biologists and other scientists had every right to be confused about psychology's status as a science. The key to remedying this situation, Yerkes believed, was for psychologists to "deal with psychological objects thoroughly and in a rigorously scientific manner instead of devoting most of our time to premature attempts to correlate physiological and psychological phenomena." The psychologists would have to narrow their field of inquiry and explanation if they were to win credibility as a science. Yerkes attributed the "extremely unsatisfactory" state of his discipline to four "preeminently important reasons." First, he cited the lack of "a generally and unquestioningly accepted body of presuppositions or postulates" to undergird the work of psychology. Second, he pointed to the absence of "strong and research-impelling faith in the value of the aims of psychology and in the possibility of attaining those ends by available scientific methods." Third, he suggested that psychologists were still too steeped in philosophical methods rather than rigorously trained in scientific methods. And finally, he criticized poor teaching, especially that which presented psychology as "a collection of bizzare phenomena or as a philosophical discipline instead of as a science similar to the physical sciences in aims and methods."[35]

What becomes clear in Yerkes's critique of the discipline is the lack of unanimity among the practitioners of psychology as to the state of the science, its characteristics if it was a science, or even the extent it could or should be a science. Though philosophers tended to see psychology in monolithic terms, as a coherent science presenting a serious challenge to their legitimacy, the testimony of Yerkes and others reveals a discipline that, like philosophy itself, had some pretensions to science, but that had not yet reached that lofty goal. If Yerkes did not despair for the scientific future of his field, that was in part because he hoped by his own work and his essays to push his colleagues and his discipline further along the road to becoming a recognized and accepted science.[36]

By the second decade of the century the debate and rivalry between philosophy and psychology had settled into a predictable pattern. The psychologists fought to increase their scientific and utilitarian credentials and to distance themselves from the philosophers. The philosophers, for their part, sought to retain their traditionally intimate ties to psychology, to be seen as a higher, more complete version of that science. The tensions between the two disciplines remained very much alive over the decade as philosophers and psychologists in particular universities and colleges attempted to work out more appropriate arrangements for the sharing or dividing of resources and power. Christian Ruckmich's 1912 survey of the status of psychology revealed that affiliation with philosophy was still common, and in many cases still satisfactory to both parties. Relations were most satisfactory at schools where the affiliation was "partial and for the most part theoretical." It was least satisfactory, from the psychologists' point of view, where philosophers imposed curricular requirements in philosophy or where the psychology taught was the nonempirical variety. In these situations, the psychologists advocated affiliation with the sciences.[37]

The urge to make psychology into a science and to break all links to philosophy and introspective psychology lay behind John B. Watson's behaviorist revolt, launched in 1913. John O'Donnell's study has documented the origins of behaviorism in the complex intellectual and institutional context of late nineteenth-century psychology. Behaviorism, in O'Donnell's view, was less a sharp break with the recent past than an effort on Watson's part to enhance psychology's scientific credibility and to "make his own field of investigation more secure as a branch of academic psychology." O'Donnell acknowledges that Watson created something new in his version of behaviorism, but the particulars of his version were ultimately less persuasive to many psychologists than his "general conceptualization of psychology's purpose and scope." The broader concept of behaviorism was a psychology of practical utility grounded in an experimental science. The practical value of applied psychology won the field widespread support outside the university, while its scientific, laboratory-based methods gave it greater scientific warrant both within the university and without. As these developments unfolded in the teens and twenties, the likelihood of a rapprochement of philosophy and psychology dimmed. The psychologists, in particular, had little to gain from a reunification with the philosophers.[38]

Some philosophers refused to bid psychology farewell. The familiar arguments concerning the traditional ties, the shared assumptions, and even shared subject matter and method were repeatedly rehearsed between 1910 and 1930. For example, in 1914, J. E. Creighton in a long essay, "The Standpoint of Psychology," argued it was "essential that the connection between philosophy and psychology that has in recent years been somewhat weakened should be restored and strengthened. A close intimacy and a constant give-and-take association is essential to the fruitful development of both these subjects." Writing three years later, George M. Sabine argued that the recent advances in philosophy had been largely "the result of new methods and new subjects of scientific investigation." The result, he thought, was that philosophy was showing "a tendency toward re-establishing its connections with science," including psychology. Only in that way could "a higher degree of system" be eventually achieved. Though Sabine granted the various sciences their necessary independence, it was only in the higher synthesis of the philosopher that truth ultimately would be found. In Sabine's view the new philosophy was dependent upon the new sciences, including psychology, yet philosophy would eventually emerge triumphant, as it had throughout most of its history.[39]

John Dewey's view of the relationship of philosophy and psychology in the second decade of the century was more cognizant of their institutional and intellectual rivalry. He recognized the legitimacy of the emerging disciplinary boundaries and yet remained certain of some continuing interdependence between the two fields. Speaking to a joint session of the philosophy and psychology associations in New Haven, Dewey disavowed "any attempt to pass upon what psychology must be or ought to be; I am content that psychology should be whatever competent investigators in that field *make* it to be in the successful pursuit of their inquiries." Philosophers, however, might legitimately inquire into philosophy's past influence upon psychology and pose questions about the continuing implications of that influence. Dewey believed that given the subject matter of the two fields and recognizing the interests and beliefs of thinking human beings, some relationship of philosophy to psychology is inevitable. Students come to philosophy with well-established beliefs in the existence of both physical and psychical realms. The science of psychology can tell us something about sensations and images, and this knowledge has direct bearing upon the resolution of epistemological problems in philosophy. In light of the relevance of psychological science for current philosophical inquiry, Dewey concluded that a philosopher had to "admit that his philosophizing is infected with psychology beyond all cure, or else challenge the prevailing conceptions about the province, scope, and procedure of psychology itself."[40]

Dewey argued that philosophers might legitimately examine "a science for survivals of past philosophies" and reflect upon "their worth in the light of subsequent advance in science and art." In taking a brief look at the newly emerging behaviorist movement, Dewey discerned some philosophical baggage embedded in the movement, which had the potential for undermining its achievements. He argued that the narrow interpretation of behavior in limiting it to "the activities of the nervous system" was a "by-product of the older problem of the relations of mind and body." Dewey saw no reason, except for the history of philosophic influence, why behavior might not be seen "to be as wide as the doings and sufferings of a human being." Dewey argued that the behaviorist was a prisoner of his philosophical past. Although behaviorism was potentially revolutionary, the nature of the revolution was shaped by what it was revolting against. Dewey preferred to throw out this philosophical past and to start with a new definition of behavior, which encompassed "the sum total of life-attitudes and responses of a living being." In holding to their more restrictive conception of behavior, the behaviorists failed to break completely free from the presuppositions of the past; "They are perpetuating exactly the tradition against which they are nominally protesting."[41]

Dewey's recognition of the separate inquiries of philosophy and psychology did not lessen his conviction that philosophers in the early twentieth century had "a deep concern with the way in which psychology is developing." What happened in psychology was bound to have an impact on philosophy, and the philosopher was within his rights to keep close watch on the new developments in psychology and to criticize faulty philosophical assumptions. He encouraged philosophers and psychologists to make "psychology a theory of human nature as it concretely exists and of human life as it is actually lived." Any such psychology would contribute to the "emancipation of philosophy."[42] Here, then, was a more mature and sophisticated view of the relationship. Dewey, while recognizing the independence of the fields, argued that philosophers and psychologists shared the same world, that both sought truth according to their best methods, and that the research and conclusions in one field might well have implications for the other. Dewey's vision of the relationship was no longer one of superiority and inferiority, or even mutual dependence but of a fruitful interdependence, which grew out of their common past and which, if employed properly, pointed to an even greater future for both disciplines.

By the second decade of this century the relationship of philosophy and psychology had begun to mature into the pattern suggested by Dewey's essay. Practitioners of each discipline increasingly recognized the legitimacy of their separate claims to a place in the modern university and perhaps even to status as a science. There were still psychologists and philosophers who were avid supporters of other patterns. The experimental and behavioral psychologists still fought vigorously to affiliate their science with the natural and physical sciences and to disavow any substantial ties to philosophy. On the other side, traditional philosophers like J. E. Creighton continued to assert the desirability and even existence of an intimacy that had all but disappeared. The reconceptualization of the relationship of philosophy and psychology had grown out of the intellectual and institutional context of the preceding forty years. The increasing prestige of scientific authority had forced both psychologists and philosophers to rethink their theoretical underpinnings and methodologies. Because certain types of psychological inquiry lent themselves particularly well to experimental and laboratory investigation, the scientific turn in psychology occurred faster and more completely than in philosophy. The intellectual issues at stake in making these two fields into sciences were quickly translated into institutional pressures leading to separation. Although colleges and universities were expanding in the period, resources were not limitless, and those fields which were more scientific appeared to have a better claim to support and status. Institutional realities fostered an academic differentiation that in turn fed into the emerging intellectual separation.

By 1915 the separation was by no means total, nor did it become complete even over the next several decades. The problems studied by psychologists and philosophers were too similar; fruitful interdependence, such as that envisioned by Dewey, would enliven both fields. Still, the signs of separation were unmistakable. The academic landscape had been significantly altered. Psychology had established its institutional independence and had marked its achievement with new laboratories, departments, journals, and a professional association. Although philosophers lagged behind, they, too, quickly saw the advantages of academic organization in defending what was left of their shrunken preserve. Although the philosophers emulated the professional characteristics of the other sciences and organizations, their own efforts to strengthen philosophy as an academic discipline could not resolve the still-nagging question as to whether philosophy was a science or whether it could or should become a science. That question dominated the philosophers' efforts to respond to the intellectual and institutional challenges of the early twentieth century.

The separation of psychology from philosophy and the attendant anxiety among philosophers regarding their place in the universities and the broader intellectual community at the turn of the century were part of a larger phenomenon. Thirty years of debate on the question of philosophy's proper relationship with science and the sciences had raised the central issues and had established the importance of resolving philosophy's status in a scientific age. Propelled by the defections from philosophy, by fears of growing irrelevance, by a desire to emulate the successful sciences and academic professions, and by a genuine desire to incorporate, in some sense, the values and methods of science, many philosophers after 1900 struggled with the challenge of science to philosophy. The stakes seemed high—the survival of philosophy as they knew it or reconceived it—and the prospects for success were uncertain. The result was a crisis of confidence among American philosophers.

Characteristics of the crisis was an inability to define precisely and consistently what science or its methods were and how they properly related to philosophy. Most philosophers were willing to accept the appellation "scientific" if it meant simply careful, rigorous inquiry; but that, philosophers often claimed, had long been characteristic of philosophy. Some philosophers, such as Charles S. Peirce, Arthur O. Lovejoy, and Christine Ladd-Franklin, argued that philosophers ought to create a community engaged in scientific pursuit of truth. This would have entailed the adoption by philosophers of scientific values and methods and a communal mode of inquiry dedicated to arriving ultimately at the truth.

SEVEN

Science and the Crisis of Confidence in American Philosophy

121

John Dewey and his followers shared the admiration for science, but did not want to transform philosophy into a science. Philosophers must, according to their view, rely upon the facts of science and even upon the method of science, but philosophy was much more than a pursuit of pure truth. Philosophy must assume a practical aspect; it must make a difference in society. Philosophers must use science to improve society along the line suggested by philosophy. Not all philosophers in this period thought that the way out of the crisis of confidence was to place even more faith in science. William James and several other men remained skeptical of the more extreme claims of the advocates of science. They reaffirmed the indispensable role of the individual philosopher and his unique vision. For them philosophy was more important for its vision and insight than for its method or result. Within each of these broad categories there were, of course, many individual variations. It is not too much to say that each philosopher had his or her own conception of science and its proper relationship to philosophy.

The combination of often inconsistent views on the nature and role of science was not unique to philosophy in this period. Contemporary psychologists, as we have seen, often had very different views about science and its proper place in their discipline. Professionalizing historians at the turn of the century were equally captivated by the promise of science. The historians, as Richard Hofstadter has discovered, were no more precise than the philosophers or psychologists in defining what they meant by science: "The language of science was ubiquitous, the deference given to it almost universal, but historians did not always mean the same thing when they spoke of it." David Hollinger has noted that among late nineteenth-century academics the urge to be regarded as scientific was widespread, even though "procedures and operating assumptions differed from discipline to discipline." Despite these differences, academics saw science as a "single, if amorphous entity."[1] The triumph of scientific and professional values in the wake of Darwin had undermined the standing of philosophy and the other liberal arts and had shaken the confidence of their practitioners and advocates. Those who did not join the community of science attempted to build bulwarks against the invasion.

The anxieties of the philosophers and their humanistic colleagues were not entirely self-induced. College presidents celebrated the spreading influence of science in their universities, and scientists frequently asserted superiority over the liberal arts in general and over philosophy specifically. As far back as 1878 Charles W. Eliot, president of Harvard, claimed that the "typical scientific mind" had "come to be the only kind of mind, except the poetic, which commands the respect of scholars, whatever their department of learning." Eliot noted that "in every field of study, in history, philology, philosophy, and theology, as well as in natural history and physics, it is now the scientific spirit, the scientific method, which prevails." Although he overstated the situation in philosophy, few could miss the implication that the scientific spirit ought to prevail where it did not yet dominate. Some thirty years later, E. J. James, at his inauguration as president of the University of Illinois, argued that his university "must become, in all departments of professional life, a great center of scientific research and investigation."[2]

Scientists, if anything, were more outspoken than college presidents on the superiority of science. R. S. Woodward, a physicist and president of the Carnegie Institution in Washington, applauded the spread of scientific methods as they "gained a footing of respectability in almost every department of thought, where, a half-century ago, or even twenty years ago, their entry was either barred out or stoutly opposed." Where science had not yet strengthened scholarship, Woodward urged the adoption of its methods and values. "The so-called humanities," he wrote, "must be broadened, purified and elevated if possible to the intellectual level of the more highly developed sciences." The Harvard embryologist Charles S. Minot conceded that "in an ideal world philosophers and scientists would be identical." However, in the actual world of the early twentieth century, "philosophy is dependent upon the progress of science" and "scientific progress must come first." Ira Remsen, a chemist and president of Johns Hopkins, believed that "the intellectual progress of a nation depends upon the adoption of scientific methods in dealing with intellectual problems . . . We need it [scientific method] in every department of activity." Laurence Veysey has rightly noted that American academics did not give universal assent to these claims of the research scientists.[3] Nonetheless, the attitudes expressed by respected college presidents and scientists at national meetings and in the pages of *Science,* as well as at faculty meetings and in casual conversation, fostered among philosophers an uneasiness that their discipline as traditionally practiced was no longer central to the intellectual life of the academy or of the nation.

In addition to the pervasive scientism, professionalization characterized American higher education in the post-Darwinian era. Philosophers joined with their academic colleagues in using professionalization to assert and protect their authority and social role. The religious and theological authority on which professors had earlier relied was no longer available to them. Scientific discoveries had limited the realm of theological authority, and in the wake of Darwin science had become, in many intellectual circles, a counter and ascendant authority. The rise of scientific values precipitated "profoundly disruptive changes in the habits of causal attribution, in the criteria of plausibility, in the relation of the man of knowledge to his clientele—[and] finally, changes in the very notion of truth itself." Professionalization accompanied this change in values as "part of a broad movement to establish or reestablish authority."[4] In philosophy, as in the other disciplines, scientific values and methods became the basis on which the new authority was established: "The word 'scientific' then seemed to epitomize the very essence of the professional idea—expert authority, institutionally cultivated and certified."[5] In such a context there were compelling reasons for philosophers to find scientific methods and values alluring.

Professionalization has two components, one institutional and the other substantive. The institutional aspects are fairly well defined: academic journals, advanced degrees, organized associations, and regular meetings. More elusive, the substantive dimension embraces the broad intellectual consensus and methodological framework within which recognized professionals work. The degree of substantive coherence will strongly influence the institutional coherence and vigor of a profession, at least in its early years.

Professionalization and specialization developed slowly within academic philosophy. The first professional organization, the Western Philosophical Association, was established in 1900, followed a year later by the American Philosophical Association. As previously described, the American Philosophical Association was formed in part in response to the discomfort philosophers felt when they met as part of the American Psychological Association. Although their experience with the psychological association was the immediate impetus to the philosophers' establishing their own organization, both the Western and the American Philosophical associations rose out of a twin desire to prevent further splintering of new disciplines from philosophy and to provide a professional framework and common forum in which the increasingly specialized philosophers could cooperate to mutual benefit. Unlike the newer disciplines of economics, sociology, political science, and psychology, which were formed by breaking away from nineteenth-century moral philosophy, academic philosophy professionalized in response to these challenges to its traditional domain. Whereas for the other disciplines professionalization represented progress and the achievement of an independent intellectual and institutional identity, philosophic professionalization was defensive—an attempt to prevent further defections from the traditional preserve of moral philosophy by making philosophy itself more specialized, more scientific, and more professional.[6]

There was little disagreement among philosophers over the institutional aspects of a profession; by the first years of this century most of the trappings were in place. The philosophers, however, failed to achieve a substantive coherence—any minimal consensus on methodology, subject matter, important questions, or the place of science—within the institutional framework of the American Philosophical Association. The philosophers also failed to create a strong institutional apparatus. Philosophy was the only academic profession whose association did not publish a journal and the only one to begin with two associations, add a third (the Pacific Division in 1924), and to achieve a coherent national organization only in the 1960s.[7]

The inability to attain greater professional coherence, especially in the substantive sense, was rooted in sharply differing conceptions of what philosophy was, or ought to become. The philosophers achieved and maintained institutional professionalization largely because of the imprecision and ambiguity that marked much of the debate on the nature and role of science. The ambiguity was both fruitful and debilitating: fruitful in that it allowed the creation and maintenance of the institutional dimension of professionalization; debilitating in that it hindered the development of even a minimal substantive consensus. Only so long as the debate was ambiguous and lacked resolution could most philosophers, of whatever orientation, consider themselves professional philosophers.

In the first years of this century two rival conceptions of the role of science in philosophy framed the debate. Although both Charles Sanders Peirce and John Dewey are considered leading advocates of pragmatism, their conceptions of the proper place of science within philosophy differed significantly. For Peirce, science was a mode of life especially adapted to the pursuit of truth by well-tested methods. Peirce recognized that philosophy was not yet a science, but he saw no reason why scientific values and methods could not be adapted to philosophic inquiry, why philosophy might not itself become a science. As he wrote his friend William James, "I think philosophy is, or should be, an exact *science,* and not a kaleidoscopic dream. . . . Philosophy is either a science or is balderdash."[8] While Dewey shared Peirce's admiration for the methodology and achievements of science, he parted company with Peirce on the issue of making philosophy into a science. Dewey believed that the methods of science promised intellectual control, but that science alone was not sufficient to resolve the broad range of problems confronting the philosopher in society. Dewey argued that while the methods of science and of philosophy were identical in kind, the problems each addressed were different. While Peirce was interested in using scientific method in pursuit of pure truth, Dewey wanted to resolve practical problems and to reconstruct society along the lines suggested by both the moral and the scientific aspects of philosophy.

Peirce considered himself to be primarily a scientist, and it distressed him that philosophy had not yet achieved the rigor of method nor certainty of result which characterized the sciences. Philosophy, according to Peirce, was still "in that stage in which fundamental principles are disputed," and consequently it was "still far from having reached the status of a mature science progressing in an orderly manner." Nonetheless, Peirce discerned some basis for optimism. Metaphysics, he believed, had finally "reached a point in its disorderly march at which it can now discern, through the haze upon the distant hill, the place at which it is destined to join company with the orderly army of science. Surely, that reunion must take place sometime." The reunion of science and metaphysics would be achieved when "all human research" was "conducted upon some unitary plan."⁹ That plan, Peirce felt, was the program of science.

The program of science embraced a commitment to the pursuit of "cosmical truth," adherence to the methodology of science above any particular results, and dedication to the communal nature of scientific inquiry. Peirce rejected utilitarian justification for the pursuit of scientific truth. Neither a desire for social stability nor an increase in pleasure is sufficient warrant for the scientist. Rather, a "deep impression of the majesty of truth, as that to which, sooner or later, every knee must bow" impels scientific inquiry. The scientist, as he follows out his research, "becomes better and better acquainted with the character of cosmical truth" and gradually "conceives a passion for its fuller relevation." Though every scientist must recognize that he can contribute only "small steps" toward the achievement of truth, he is content. The true scientist "hopes that by conscientiously pursuing the methods of science he may erect a foundation upon which his successors may climb higher. This, for him, is what makes life worth living and what makes the human race worth perpetuation."¹⁰

Despite Peirce's commitment to the ultimate achievement of "cosmical truth," he put more emphasis on the methodology of science than upon its particular results. "The wonderful success of modern science" was due, he thought, to considering "science as living, and therefore not as knowledge already acquired but as the concrete life of the men who are working to find out the truth." Science, Peirce wrote, was "a mode of life whose single animating purpose is to find out the real truth." The scientist pursues truth by "a well-considered method" based upon results already achieved and through "cooperation" with other scientists. The ultimate achievement of truth may lie in the distant future, but that makes little difference to the immediate activity of the scientist. Peirce believed that the scientist's spirit of inquiry is more important than the mistakes which mar his conclusions: "It makes no difference how imperfect a man's knowledge may be, how mixed with error and prejudice; from the moment he engages in an inquiry in the spirit described, that which occupies him is *science*."¹¹

Although the individual may be animated by the spirit of science, the progress of science toward truth is dependent upon the work of the community of scientists. "The veritable essence of science," for Peirce, was the cooperative nature of the enterprise. Peirce envisioned "the scientific world" as "like a colony of insects, in that the individual strives to produce that which he himself cannot hope to enjoy." Each scientist adds his mite to the ever-accumulating body of evidence: "One contributes this, another that. Another company, standing upon the shoulders of the first, strike a little higher, until at last the parapet is attained." This steady progress toward truth is "built up out of surmises at truth."[12] Peirce urged those who "deplore the present state" of philosophy to help bring it to

> a condition like that of the natural sciences, where
> investigators, instead of contemning each of the work of
> most of the others as misdirected from beginning to end,
> cooperate, stand upon one another's shoulders, and
> multiply incontestible results; where every observation is
> repeated, and isolated observations go for little; where
> every hypothesis that merits attention is subjected to severe
> but fair examination, and only after the predictions to
> which it leads have been remarkably borne out by
> experience is trusted at all, and even then only provi-
> sionally; where a radically false step is rarely taken, even
> the most faulty of those theories which gain wide credence
> being true in their main experiential predictions.[13]

Science is like a vast, self-regulating organism, each element of which contributes its part to the overall goal of achieving truth. Philosophers, Peirce hoped, would soon join ranks with their scientific brethren in this collective enterprise.

The notion of science as a living process in a community of scholars echoed elements of Peirce's earlier writings on science and philosophy. There was, however, a new dimension to his thought in the early years of the century. Peirce had become even more convinced of the need for philosophy to develop a specialized, technical vocabulary if it was to become a science. As he put it in 1906, "If philosophy is ever to stand in the ranks of the sciences, literary elegance must be sacrificed—like the soldier's old brilliant uniforms—to the stern requirements of efficiency, and the philosophist must be encouraged—yea, and required—to coin new terms to express such new scientific concepts as he may discover."[14] Philosophy, Peirce argued, could not become scientific "until it provides itself with a suitable technical nomenclature, whose every term has a single definite meaning universally accepted among students of the subject, and whose vocables have no such sweetness or charms as might tempt loose writers to abuse them."[15] One thinks, of course, of "'pragmaticism', which is ugly enough to be safe from kidnappers," distinguishing Peirce's philosophy from the looser pragmatisms of James and F. C. S. Schiller.[16]

In spite of Peirce's image of philosophy as an austere science framed with a forbidding terminology, he derived a sense of joy and pleasure from the pursuit of scientific philosophy and expected that others would share in the pleasure. Philosophy, he wrote, ought to be studied in the same spirit as all the sciences; that is, in "the spirit of joy of learning ourselves and in making others acquainted with the glories of God." Peirce acknowledged that "it is not a sin to have no taste for philosophy" as he defined it. However, he was convinced that "each person will feel this joy most in the particular branch of science to which his faculties are best adapted," and that most people did have "an interest in philosophical problems."[17] Science and a scientific philosophy were thus much more than accurate description and analysis of physical processes. They were a way of life, a means of getting in touch with the deepest spiritual mysteries, of becoming "acquainted with the glories of God." The roadway might be austere, but for Peirce the promised reward was illumination and understanding on a spiritual as well as on a scientific level. Although his prescription for a scientific philosophy looked forward to the professional, scientific, and analytic philosophy characteristic of the twentieth century, Peirce's own goals for his scientific pursuit of truth remained firmly grounded in an older tradition of seeing the handiwork of God in the discoveries of science.

John Dewey, like Peirce, emphasized scientific method and process. Unlike Peirce, who exercised the method in pursuit of "cosmical truth," Dewey sought to apply the method and conclusions of science to the improvement of society. Science, for Dewey, was not a body of knowledge cut off from the practical problems of the world. Science was a means of intellectual control, of bringing to bear on the problems of the world the best minds and a proven method. Even though they shared a methodology, science and philosophy were not in Dewey's view identical. The method of science gave us facts about and knowledge of the world; the scientific method of philosophy was a means of effectively addressing the recurrent problems of mankind. Although science and philosophy intersected for Dewey, he maintained their distinctiveness and philosophy's vitally important social and practical role.

Dewey's writings on science and philosophy in the first years of this century reflect clearly his conviction that the acknowledged accomplishments of science did not set science apart from the broad sweep of human concerns. The sciences, Dewey wrote, are "the outcome of all that makes our modern life what it is. . . . They did not grow out of professional, but of human, needs." There is no doubt that the development of the sciences represents "a profound modification and reconstruction of all attained knowledge—a change in quality and standpoint." Still, "in spite of confusion and conflict, the movement of the human mind is a unity. . . . The body of knowledge is indeed one; it is a spiritual organism." The early twentieth century was for Dewey "a period of applied science" in which "the practical occupations of men" were "more and more infused with reason; more and more illuminated by the spirit of inquiry and reason. They are dependent upon science, in a word."[18] In the universities of his day Dewey saw hopeful signs that the insights and methods of science were being applied to the practical, human needs of society.

Dewey accepted the commonplace notion that "science is a body of systematized knowledge." This conception of science might be regarded in two different ways: science might be conceived as "a property which resides inherently in arranged facts," or it might "mean the intellectual activities of observing, describing, comparing, inferring, experimenting, and testing, which are necessary in obtaining facts and in putting them into coherent form." Both aspects of science were included in Dewey's conception of a body of systematized knowledge, but the method had primacy over the results since the method determined the results. As he defined it, "'scientific' means regular methods of controlling the formation of judgments regarding some subject-matter." Dewey had great faith in the profitability of the scientific method and in its applicability beyond the relatively narrow bounds of the physical and natural sciences. Science was not for Dewey "a peculiar development of thinking for highly specialized ends; it *is* thinking so far as thought has become conscious of its proper ends and of the equipment indispensable for success in their pursuit."[19]

Dewey knew that many critics would reject his contention that scientific methods were applicable in all areas of inquiry and that science was shaped by values. Dewey did not seek to reduce morals, ethics, or other considerations of value to the physical sciences. Rather, he argued that the scientific method of inquiry was appropriate to "matters of conduct" as well as to "physical matters." In "Logical Conditions of a Scientific Treatment of Morality," Dewey took up the question of the proper intersection of value and scientific method. Science, he argued, is "absolutely dependent for logical worth upon a moral interest: the sincere aim to judge truly." Because the appropriate use of resources and reliance upon scientific methods depend "upon the interest and disposition of the judger, we have only to make such dependence explicit, and the so-called scientific judgment appears definitely as a moral judgment." In addition, he argued that even when scientific method is employed with regard to "objects as objects" and without "conscious reference whatever to conduct," there is an implication that the use of the method is "for the sake of the development of further experience." This meant, for Dewey, that the practice of science is *"regulated activity, i.e.;* conduct, behavior, practice." All science, even the physical sciences, have "reference to change of experience, or experience as activity," and when this reference is applied to controlling consciously the nature of change it becomes ethical. Thus for Dewey there was a *"continuity of experience"* in which science and ethics were essential aspects of the effort to control change rationally.[20]

Dewey held that the primary object of science is "to give intellectual control—that is, ability to interpret phenomena—and secondarily, practical control—that is, ability to secure desirable and avoid undesirable future experiences." But for philosophy the question of practical control assumes primacy. Philosophy conceived primarily as method means the establishment of a "philosophy which shall be instrumental rather than final, and instrumental not to establishing and warranting any particular set of truths, but instrumental in furnishing points of view and working ideas which may clarify and illuminate the actual and concrete course of life." Philosophers should not constitute "a separate and monopolistic priesthood" guarding and revealing truth, but rather they much "organize . . . the highest and wisest ideas of humanity, past and present" to interpret effectively "certain recurrent and fundamental problems, which humanity, collectively and individually, has to face."[21] Only then could there be any hope of resolving perennial problems and of restructuring society upon rational grounds. And that, Dewey insisted, was the real task of philosophy and the philosopher.

Peirce and Dewey each made a case for the philosopher's reliance upon the methods and conclusions of science. Peirce's advocacy of the scientific method as a way of life pointed toward the subordination of philosophy to science. While Dewey relied on the method and results of science, he continued to argue that the philosopher's task complemented the scientist's but was not subordinate to it. Both were necessary for effective social reconstruction. Not all philosophers, however, shared the enthusiasm of Peirce and Dewey for the methods and values of science. Dissenting voices urged philosophers to uphold hard-won metaphysical positions and to resist the urge to narrow the scope of philosophy to fit scientific requirements.

F. J. E. Woodbridge, the Columbia realist and naturalist, soon to be editor of the *Journal of Philosophy*, urged his colleagues not to abandon the legitimate claims of metaphysics. Philosophers, he thought, had too often succumbed to the temptations of science: "We have, in my opinion, looked with a too jealous glance on science and its achievements. We have coveted a name which has won distinguished glory apart from our participation and aid. We have blushed at the imputation of not being scientific in our work." Where Peirce and Dewey sought to incorporate the method of science within philosophy, Woodbridge argued for the historically significant independence of metaphysics. Metaphysicians "have a claim of our own to recognition quite independent of the revelations of science, a birthright by no means to be despised." Woodbridge saw his own work as a philosopher taking place in "a totally different sphere" from that of the scientist. "Scientific knowledge" and "metaphysical knowledge," he claimed were "widely different": "Science asks for the laws of existence and discovers them by experiment. Metaphysics asks for the nature of reality and discovers it by definition."[22] Woodbridge's vigorous defense of metaphysics was a direct response to the more sweeping claims of science and of the scientifically oriented philosophers. However, one detects in his language a fear that science had already triumphed, that metaphysics as traditionally practiced was doomed despite the best efforts of its advocates.

William James, despite his closer ties to the world of science, remained opposed to the narrowing of philosophy to the methods and conclusions of a science. He believed that "the claims of the sectarian scientist are, to say the least, premature." Religious and other experiences showed "the universe to be a more many-sided affair than any sect, even the scientific sect, allows for." James argued that there was no one key "for unlocking the world's treasure-house." Why, he asked, "may not the world be so complex as to consist of many interpenetrating spheres of reality, which we can thus approach in alternation by using different conceptions and assuming different attitudes." We needed, James thought, different types of thinking appropriate to the situation: "Common sense is *better* for one sphere of life, science for another, philosophic criticism for a third; but whether either be truer absolutely, Heaven only knows."[23] For James, then, a pluralism of outlook and method was more likely to produce fruitful results than a single-minded reliance upon science.

Notwithstanding these dissents, many philosophers in the early twentieth century were attracted to the claims of science, to the notion of philosophic progress achieved by scientific means, and to the idea of establishing a profession on a par with the other scientific disciplines. For them the adoption of scientific methods and values and the achievement of professional coherence on the model of the natural and social sciences promised progress in philosophic inquiry and status within the university. In spite of the establishment of the American Philosophical Association in 1901 and subsequent efforts to use the association to forge disciplinary coherence, the achievement of progress and status remained elusive.

Formed to combat feelings of inferiority engendered by meeting with the psychologists and to foster a professionalized philosophical discipline, the American Philosophical Association soon became a focus for debate on the direction philosophy ought to take in response to the scientism, specialization, and professionalization increasingly characteristic of American university life. Some philosophers saw in the association an opportunity for philosophy to demonstrate its contemporary vitality and usefulness and thus to regain some of its lost stature within the academic community. Others argued that philosophy should not demonstrate contemporary relevance by becoming an academic profession and science. Merely to emulate the other disciplines and sciences would destroy the traditional strengths of philosophy without offering compensating advantages.

From the very outset of the association, the advocates of professionalization stressed the importance of communal inquiry in the achievement of philosophic progress. J. E. Creighton set the tone of the debate in his inaugural address as president, when he called for the rejuvenation of philosophy through cooperative enterprise. If philosophers were to become scientific professionals it was necessary for them "to combine forces and to work, not as a number of isolated individuals, but as a group of coöperating minds." But despite his call for cooperation on the model of the sciences, Creighton, as we have seen, continued to believe that philosophy had its own distinctive role and methodology: "Philosophical science is not 'natural science'."[24] His ambivalence concerning the methods and standpoints appropriate to philosophy in the twentieth century marked the debate on philosophy's proper role as an academic profession and its proper relationship to science.

The advocates of philosophic progress developed Creighton's notion of co-operation along the lines outlined in the 1870s and after by Charles Peirce. Peirce had argued that the sciences relied upon the collective achievement of truth and urged philosophers to adopt similar cooperative methods and goals. For Peirce, truth was achieved when "all intelligent and informed doubt has ceased and all competent persons have come to a catholic agreement." In philosophy, the individual was incapable of attaining the "ultimate philosophy"; that could be sought only "for the *community* of philosophers."[25] The language of the advocates of scientific progress clearly echoed the ideas of Peirce. Dickinson S. Miller, for example, called for the adoption of cooperative scientific methods for philosophic inquiry. Arguing that "the social development of philosophy has only begun," Miller asserted that "philosophy will not be a science until it has achieved a consensus of experts, *i.e.*, a tested method and tested principles." The philosophers' most immediate task was "to reach common ground." Christine Ladd-Franklin, who had studied logic with Peirce at Johns Hopkins, lamented the philosophers' unwillingness "to secure *common assent* among those (they may be few in number) who are in a condition to form well-grounded judgments in a given domain." Science, she argued, "consists of *knowledge* . . . which represents at a given time, the best result of the combined effort of all scientists,—hypothetical always, . . . but nevertheless of a high degree of probability, and only to be displaced by wider and more profound experience." She hoped that a closer study of these methods would "put the philosophers on a safer track."[26]

The advocacy of communal inquiry took institutional form within the association as an effort to organize philosophical discussion with a view to obtaining consensus upon a particular issue. In the first ten years of the association, six of the annual meetings had discussions organized by the executive committee. Among the topics taken up were the meaning and criterion of truth in 1907 and realism and idealism a year later. These discussions were not fully satisfactory even to their partisans, for they lacked the rigor, focus, and consensus supposedly characteristic of the sciences.[27]

Not all philosophers welcomed the formation of the philosophical association or the efforts to mold philosophy into a professional academic discipline. Some, like William James, had a temperamental aversion to collective, professional activity. Others recognized that philosophy faced a crisis in withstanding the challenge of science in American universities, but rejected the idea that philosophy could best meet that challenge by emulating the sciences and the more highly professionalized disciplines. For these philosophers the crisis was sharpest, for they risked the demise of philosophy as they knew it. If they did not change, their discipline might well become irrelevant in the university, but if they joined the movement to reconstruct philosophy as a professional, scientifically-oriented discipline, then they abandoned philosophy as they practiced it. In the end, most sought to adopt the forms of professionalization without necessarily compromising the practice of philosophy.

William James's objection to the professionalization of philosophy rested on his conviction that academic organization and bureaucratic structures could only hinder the free play of thought and the pursuit of truth. James initially turned down an invitation to join the association on the grounds that "philosophical discussion proper only succeeds between intimates who have learned to converse by months of weary trials and failure. The philosopher is a lone beast dwelling in his individual burrow.—Count me out!" Three years later, James confided to his notebook his disgust with "the professional-philosophy-shop, with its faculty, its departments and sections, its mutual etiquette, its appointments, its great mill of authorities and exclusions and suppressions which the waters of truth are expected to feed to the great class-glory of all who are concerned." Though he later relented, joined the association, and became its president in 1906, James remained doubtful of the value of the communal enterprise of philosophy. As he wrote his friend Theodore Flournoy in 1908, "the collective life of philosophers is little more than an organization of misunderstandings."[28]

James was secure enough in his position not to worry about the place of philosophy in the university, but other critics of professionalized philosophy expressed their anxiety about philosophy's contemporary role even as they criticized the direction it seemed to be taking. George R. Dodson, a St. Louis writer, deplored philosophy's diminished status within the university: "It does not command the confidence of the other departments, but is regarded with dislike and distrust. Nor do the students, as a rule, think more highly of it; while in the mind of the general public philosophic thinking is a synonym for futility." Dodson rejected the notion that philosophy could regain its proper influence by becoming either a special science or a synthesis of the sciences. He asserted that in the universities, at least, "philosophy should magnify its unifying and synthetic function." J. E. Creighton, despite his early support for cooperative inquiry, soon found the emphasis on consensus and agreement too confining. He acknowledged that "the lack of any established body of results" was a "source of the wide-spread conviction that philosophy neither bakes bread nor can any longer give us 'God, freedom, and immortality'." Philosophy, for him, was not a special science, but "an attempt to understand and evaluate the standpoint and results of all the sciences and the meaning of experience as a whole." If agreement upon "an officially established creed in philosophy" was not possible, Creighton still hoped some consensus could be reached "regarding the nature of the problems that can profitably and significantly be raised and the kind of answers which they demand."[29]

Morris R. Cohen, a philosopher of science critical of the enthusiastic scientism of the period, attacked the reduction of philosophy to a science at the 1909 meeting of the American Philosophical Association in New Haven. In his first address to the association, Cohen criticized both the abandonment of the philosopher's critical stance toward the special sciences and the attempt "to make philosophic discussion itself scientific, *i.e.*, to narrow it down to certain definite and decidable issues." He strongly opposed making philosophy "into a special science, dealing with definite problems and giving definite answers."[30] Cohen pinpointed the growing professionalism within the discipline as the prime impetus to the greater emphasis on science. He traced this increasing adherence to the values and methodology of science in the successive appearance of new philosophical journals. The *Journal of Speculative Philosophy* (1867), edited by men who were not primarily academics, represented a theologically based, systematic philosophy. *Philosophical Review*

(1892), dominated by academics, represented an architectonic conception of science—a view that criticized the special sciences but built upon scientific results to create a world view. The *Journal of Philosophy, Psychology, and Scientific Methods* (1904) appeared along with the drive to narrow philosophy to the category of a special science. These changes in the journals accompanied the rise in university instruction in philosophy, which in turn increased the professionalization of the field and the acceptance of science. The new universities required a far greater degree of specialization, and the older conception of philosophy as a "kind of universal knowledge" was declining. Cohen noted that "the idea that philosophy may not be a science is so repugnant to professional philosophic teachers that it seems almost futile to maintain such a thesis." Even philosophers had succumbed to the "allurements" of the recent achievements of science.[31]

Cohen conceded that the application of science to philosophy strengthened the latter. But, he asked, was it necessary to accept science as the ideal of philosophy? Was not the philosopher's task different from the scientist's? Cohen thought some fields of philosophy—logic, for example—might be developed into a science, but that did not require the reduction of all philosophy to a science. Furthermore, not even science ensured the resolution of all philosophical disputes through empirical investigation. Without that assurance, there was even less reason to accept the construction of a scientific philosophical platform. Cohen argued that both philosophy and science possessed "*the desire to know the truth.*" The philosopher's task, however, was to take the results of the special sciences and to pull them together in the creation of a coherent world view. Such a philosophy "would aim to be scientific, but it would not be afraid to go beyond science just as life and conduct must go beyond knowledge." A broadly conceived philosophy, Cohen felt, would counter "the present anarchic tendency to over-specialization."[32]

Josiah Royce, like Cohen, faulted the advocates of professionalization for their effort to narrow the scope of philosophy. Royce valued "the right sort of philosophical communion and community" among the members of the philosophical association, and he hoped the association would "initiate methods of coöperation which, as they come to be improved by experience, will continue to grow more and more effective as the years go on." Royce, however, criticized the organizers of recent discussions for framing the terms of the debate in a way that excluded a significant body of philosophers from participation. He wanted to avoid "defining the issue or the rules or the coöperation so as to exclude anybody whose views are seriously represented in classic or current philosophical discussion."[33]

Royce's proposals for more open discussion are significant in light of his own experience in working with scientists in his Harvard seminar, where he sought to develop a "community of interpretation." In the first years of the century, Royce's seminar brought together both philosophers and scientists to examine such topics as "The Logical Analysis of Fundamental Concepts and their General Relations to Philosophical Problems" (1904–6), "A Comparative Study of those Concepts of Human Thought which have to do with the Relations of Whole and Part" (1908–9), and "A Comparative Study of Various Types of Scientific Method" (1910–12, 1913–16). In taking up a topic such as scientific method, Royce typically invited a number of scientists or experts to the seminar to describe their methodology and to participate in the ensuing discussion.[34] Thus, the philosophical issues were addressed in the company of the working scientists.

Harry T. Costello's notebooks for Royce's 1913–14 seminar provide a full record of the discussions for that year and an indication of the range of the subjects addressed. The seminar was regularly attended by nine graduate students in philosophy or psychology, including Ralph M. Blake, A. P. Brogan, T. S. Eliot and Leonard T. Troland, as well as Royce and Costello, then an instructor in philosophy at Harvard. The focus of the seminar was "comparative methodology in the field of science," and the specific topics included internal relations, causality, implication and deduction, classification of the sciences, fertility, and induction. In addition to student papers on description and explanation and on causality, the seminar discussed the presentations of the scientific visitors who "read accounts of their recent investigations." The visitors for 1913–14 were Lawrence J. Henderson, a biological chemist, who several times presented material concerning the fitness of the environment, Elmer E. Southard, a neuropathologist, who spoke both on delusions and on the scientific use of statistics, and Frederick A. Woods, an embryologist and histologist with an interest in using statistics to examine heredity, who addressed the seminar on statistical methods in studying the relationship of heredity and the environment. One of the students, Leonard Troland, who later co-invented the Technicolor process, also presented to the seminar a summary of Einstein's recently developed theory of special relativity and a paper on the use of statistical sampling in the sciences.[35] In this fashion, Royce provided a meeting place where the community of science and the community of philosophy could intersect and examine recent issues of mutual interest. It is no wonder, then, that Royce objected to the narrowly specialized discussion required of the participants at the annual meetings of the American Philosophical Association.

Royce's Harvard seminar embodied the notion of a community of interpretation which he had developed in *The Problem of Christianity*, lectures delivered at Oxford in the spring of 1913 and published later that same year. The first volume of the published work contains eight lectures that develop the ethical and psychological dimensions of the concept of the universal community, which is at the center of the two-volume work. Here he explored the relationship of the universal community to the Christian community, the importance of Christianity as a religion of loyalty, and the ways in which an understanding of the "Beloved Community" could help us deal with the moral burdens of individuals and live a Christian life. In the eight lectures of the second volume, Royce examined the relationship between Christian ideals and the real world in terms of the concept of community. Communities, for Royce, were not mystical bodies, but were very much of this world and were in fact the basis for our understanding of the world around us. Building on a recent rereading and new understanding of the work of his friend Charles Peirce, Royce developed the "community of interpretation" as a metaphysical principle and methodological procedure.[36]

Royce defined a community as those selves who shared an *"ideal common past and future."* The existence of a community depends on three conditions: the ability of the individual to consider himself intimately connected to remote past and future events, the existence in "the social world [of] a number of distinct selves capable of social communication, and, in general, engaged in communication," and the existence of at least some shared events in the "ideally extended past and future selves" of every member of the community. The essential action of such a community is cooperation. But cooperation alone does not, Royce argued, make a community. A community exists only where the members view the cooperation as an integral part of their lives and where the members can "direct their own deeds of coöperation," watch the cooperative deeds of their fellows, and "know that, without just this combination, this order, this interaction of the coworking selves, just this deed could not be accomplished by the community."[37] A community, thus, consists of self-conscious selves embarked on the cooperative attainment of goals over time.

The process of interpretation was basic to Royce's conception of community, and in developing his own ideas he drew heavily upon the work of Peirce. Although Royce relied primarily on Peirce's early essays in the *Journal of Speculative Philosophy,* he acknowledge that he had only recently appreciated their significance, and he absolved Peirce of any responsibility for the use he made of them. Royce stressed the idea that "interpretation *is* a triadic relation." Moreover, the interpretative relation always brings the three terms into a "determinate order. One of the three terms is the interpreter; a second term is the object—the person or the meaning or the text—which is interpreted; the third is the person to whom the interpretation is addressed." For Royce, the interpretative process represents more than a logical formalism; it also carries psychological implications for the participants. "First, interpretation is a conversation, and not a lonely enterprise. There is some one, in the realm of psychological happenings, who addresses some one." Second, "the interpreted object is itself something which has the nature of a mental expression"; it is what Peirce called a "sign." Third, "since the interpretation is a mental act, and is an act which is expressed, the interpretation itself is, in its turn, a Sign." New signs require further interpretation and, thus, "the social process involved is endless." This social process is "an infinite sequence of interpretations" which, "once initiated, can be terminated only by an external and arbitrary interruption, such as death or social separation."38

When the triadic relationship of interpretation consists of individuals—the interpreter, the one interpreted, and the one to whom the interpretation is offered—a community of interpretation is created. The goal of a community of interpretation is "unattainable under human social conditions, but definable, as an ideal, in terms of the perfectly familiar experience which every successful comparison of ideals involves. It is a goal towards which we all may work together." Royce's view of "that goal as a common future event" recalls Peirce's notion of the ultimate truth in some indefinite future. Sharing that common goal, the members of the community of interpretation can change position, becoming, in turn, interpreter, interpreted, and recipient of the interpretation. The key, of course, is the role of interpreter, regardless of who holds the office, for it is that individual who brings the community closer to its goal of "the ideal unity of insight." This goal can be reached only if the interpreter's neighbors can be transformed in "ideas between which his own interpretation successfully mediated." But that, of course, is never fully possible, and so the goal, although real, remains elusive.39

Having developed the concept of the community of interpretation in the abstract, Royce proceeded to examine two possible communities of interpretation, scientists and philosophers. The teamwork characteristic of modern science and the need to interpret and to substantiate discoveries through additional research mean that "the spirit of science is one of loyalty to a Community of Interpretation." An individual may make a discovery, but it is "a scientific discovery only in case it can become, through further confirmation, the property and the experience of the community of scientific observers." Disregarding the technical details of particular sciences, Royce argued that "this confirmation always involves a typical instance, or a series of instances, of Peirce's cognitive process called interpretation." This interpretive process is guided by both general and "highly metaphysical" principles which, as his seminar amply demonstrated, implicates "all the central problems of philosophy." Chief among these principles is the belief in the existence of a scientific community. Royce believed that the reality of the scientific community could never by proved by "scientific observations." Rather, "the existence of the community of scientific observers is known through interpretation" involving both ethical and social motives.[40]

At a minimum, a scientific community is made up of "the original discoverer, of his interpreter, and of the critical worker who tests or controls the discoverer's observations by means of new experiences devised for that purpose." Although seldom analyzed, Royce believed that, regardless of the complexity of the scientific enterprise, "the essential structure of the community of scientific interpretation remains definitely the same," and its existence was "presupposed as a basis of every scientific inquiry into natural facts." The scientific community is a more highly developed and self-conscious embodiment of the community of interpretation in its goal of "a certain type of spiritual unity." As Royce described this spiritual unity, it took on something of the character of Peirce's notion of truth: "The goal of the community is always precisely that luminous knowledge which we do, in a limited but in a perfectly definite form, possess, within the range of our own individual life whenever our comparisons of distinct ideas are made with clearness." Just as Peirce's ideal truth was unreachable and his provisional truth resided in the consensus of the competent, so Royce's community of interpretation could reach limited knowledge, even if the ultimate goal remained unattainable.[41]

This conclusion still left Royce with the metaphysical problem of explaining how any community of interpretation could exist. Ordinarily, Royce would have turned to his fellow philosophers for assistance, but his recent experience in philosophical debate had disillusioned him:

> The philosophers differ sadly amongst themselves. They do not at present form a literal human community of mutual enlightenment and of growth in knowledge, to any such extent as do the workers in the field of any one of the natural sciences. The philosophers are thus far individuals rather than consciously members one of another. The charity of mutual interpretation is ill developed amongst them. They frequently speak with tongues and do not edify. And they are especially disposed to contend regarding their spiritual gifts. We cannot expect them, then, at present to agree regarding any one philosophical opinion.

Still, in "the history of culture," philosophers have principally taken on the task of interpretation, rather than perception or conception. Philosophers, Royce argued, have traditionally "devoted themselves . . . to interpreting the meaning of the civilizations which they have represented, and to attempting the interpretation of whatever minds in the universe, human or divine, they believed to be real." There are, of course, other interpreters, but that does not diminish philosophy. For Royce, the "philosopher's ideals are those of an interpreter," and the "unity which he seeks is that which is characteristic of a community of interpretation." The failure of any known philosophy to escape the process of interpretation furnished all the proof Royce required.[42]

Combining the leading ideas of a philosopher into a "single ideal leading" had long been the ideal of philosophy, but, according to Royce, it had yet to be accomplished. Humans continually find themselves in situations marked by conflict, antitheses, and fragmentation requiring interpretation. *"By the 'real world' we mean simply the 'true interpretation' of this our problematic situation.* No other reason can be given than this for believing that there is any real world at all." Whenever one confronts the problem of reality, one has to compare, at a minimum, "the idea of present experience and the idea of the goal of experience" in one of its many forms. Whether stated in religious, philosophic, or scientific language, *"the question about what the real world is, is simply the question as to what this contrast is and means."* Ultimately, *"an interpretation is real only if the appropriate community is real, and is true only if that community reaches its goal."* For Royce, the community of interpretation, at the broadest level as well as for particular communities, consisted of the two antithetic ideas, present experience and the goal of experience, plus the interpreter. *"Unless both the interpreter and the community are real, there is no real world."* The multifarious communities bound together by the infinitely extended process of interpretation will eventually find expression in the "Universal Community."[43]

Royce, as already suggested, went on to develop Peirce's concept of signs as the vehicle by which the process of interpretation occurs. Although he absolved Peirce of complicity in the metaphysical scheme just sketched, Royce believed that the scheme could be summarized in Peircean terminology: "The universe consists of real Signs and of their interpretation." Events in real time are signs which are interpreted and given meaning. These interpretations and meanings become, in turn, new signs, and "the sequence of these signs and the interpretations constitutes the history of the universe." Royce's "metaphysical doctrine of signs" holds that the universe consists "in and through an infinite series of acts of interpretation. This infinite series constitutes the temporal order of the world with all its complexities." Finally, "the temporal world in its wholeness" is itself "an infinitely complex Sign."[44]

Royce's community of interpretation was more sophisticated than the other notions of cooperation which dominated the discussions of the American

Philosophical Association in these years. Building on the all-but-ignored work of Peirce and on his own close familiarity with working scientists, Royce developed a metaphysical explanation of how we can build knowledge of the world within that world and a methodological process for accomplishing the task. If the goal was still a spiritual unity, Royce acknowledged that for now we must be satisfied with the more limited levels of knowledge thus far achieved by the process of interpretation. In the end, however, the world would be built by our efforts at interpreting and reinterpreting the signs through which the process proceeded. The scientist interprets the signs of the natural world, but the role of the philosopher is even broader. Some sixty years before Richard Rorty, Royce argued that the task of the philosopher had always been and still remained interpretation, drawing not only from the sciences, but also from all the other manifestations of culture. In that sense, the philosopher as interpreter of our problematic situation creates the real world.

Royce's metaphysical investigations had little discernible impact on the efforts of the partisans of professionalization and of scientific consensus to reshape philosophy along the lines of a science. Responding instead to Royce's specific criticism of the procedures of the American Philosophical Association, the association's Committee on Discussions decided that the topic of the 1912 discussion would be agreement in philosophy. The committee proposed as the basis for discussion: Was "continuous progress toward unanimity among philosophers on the more fundamental issues" either desirable or attainable? Supporters of the possibility of consensus were asked to consider where it had been reached, why so little agreement had been achieved, and what methods of philosophical inquiry or organized cooperation would increase agreement. Those who opposed the idea of agreement were asked to discuss what prevented the possibility of agreement, whether philosophy ought to express the reactions of different temperaments upon reality, and the purpose of philosophical discussion.[45] This program reflected the influence of Royce's criticism, for the phrasing of the questions opened the debate to all views. Nonetheless, the bias of the committee was clear. The heaviest burden lay on those who argued that agreement was neither desirable nor attainable; those in the affirmative merely had to propose how greater agreement could be obtained.

The debate on agreement generated considerable interest and occupied nearly a full day of the meeting. James B. Pratt, who later joined the critical realists, noted that "there was pretty general agreement that agreement itself was at least desirable." Nevertheless, several philosophers, including Frank Thilly of Cornell, argued that the recent improvement in philosophy was more the result of disagreement and criticism than anything else. No one, of course, wanted to suppress individual opinion, but, as Pratt put it, many wanted agreement on the "old questions," if for no other reason than "to go on and disagree about new ones."[46]

Norman Kemp Smith, then at Princeton, and Theodore De Laguna of Bryn Mawr offered prepared papers opposing the possibility of agreement, while Karl Schmidt of Tufts and Walter Pitkin of Columbia supported it. Kemp Smith argued that the sciences were built on the successful isolation of problems; science was "successful specialization." Philosophy, however, stood for the "general human values . . . for the past and future as against the present, for comprehensiveness and leisure as against narrowness and haste." Philosophers considered "all those problems for which no method of successful isolation has yet been formulated." In reply, Walter Pitkin and Karl Schmidt disputed Kemp Smith's holistic approach to problems. Schmidt, for example, suggested that the history of philosophy demonstrated that at least the relative isolation of problems was possible and, given that possibility, that a "certain *modicum of agreement*" was necessary for any philosophic discussion. Schmidt hoped for agreement on both the structure of truth and on the method of attaining it.[47]

The subsequent open discussion revealed just how far the philosophers were from achieving a consensus on the possibility of agreement. The debate focused on whether the history of philosophy revealed progress toward agreement or only continual disagreement. Theodore De Laguna thought that solutions only produced new problems; no final solutions were discovered, only deeper mysteries. William Ernest Hocking, however, contended that there had been both more agreement and more real progress than was readily apparent. John Dewey pointed out that even in the special sciences there were disagreements, but they took place within agreement on more fundamental issues. The debate concluded with a discussion of the practical means of furthering agreement. Ralph Barton Perry and Arthur O. Lovejoy, among others, forecast the attainment of greater agreement if the members of the association would "give up the philosopher's traditional lonely individualism, and make an effort to coöperate with each other, and especially try to understand each other and to be understood." The philosophers in attendance generally shared those sentiments, but continued to disagree on how to achieve such cooperation. Despite the final failure to agree, James Pratt's report struck the hopeful note that the discussion had advanced "the achievement of greater coöperation, if not of greater agreement."[48]

After attempting a discussion on the relation of existence and value at the 1913 annual meeting, the philosophical association allowed the practice of organized discussion to lapse for several years. Despite extensive preparation, the results of the 1913 discussion had been disappointing and had failed to produce "that clear demarcation of problems and issues which constitutes the only end practicably attainable by such discussion." The effort to secure agreement through organized discussion was revived in 1916 during Arthur O. Lovejoy's term as president. Lovejoy was a strong supporter of making philosophy more scientific and a forceful advocate of agreement achieved through organized discussion. The topic for the 1916 meeting was the distinction between mental and physical entities, and the questions posed by the executive committee welcomed contributions from the whole body of philosophers. Again, in spite of the best efforts of the organizers, the results were meager. Albert G. A. Balz, in reporting on the discussion, found signs of hope in the near-achievement of consensus on several points, but ultimately he concluded that philosophers could not ignore the "generally depressing effect of disagreement."[49]

Although this organized discussion, like all its predecessors, failed to achieve any substantive agreement, the question of agreement as an essential element of a more scientific philosophy received careful and extended analysis in Lovejoy's 1916 presidential address, "On Some Conditions of Progress in Philosophical Inquiry." Lovejoy argued that philosophy could maintain its vital role in the university and in society only by becoming more professional and more scientific. He addressed the question, What was the matter with philosophy? The chief problem, he thought, was that "trained specialists of high abilities find themselves unable to reach any common conclusion" on plain and inescapable questions. The failure to achieve a consensus on theoretical issues was indicative of the failure of the discipline to achieve any progress. And that, Lovejoy believed, was "a standing scandal to philosophy, bringing just discredit upon the entire business in which we are professionally engaged."[50]

Lovejoy conceived of philosophy as having many of the attributes of science, but he conceded that the discipline as it then stood lacked sufficient scientific method and rigor. If philosophers were committed to maintaining their pretensions to science, then it was "sheer dishonesty of us not to play *that* game according to the rules, to be content with any lower degree of rigor in scientific method, any smaller measure of established and agreed-upon results, any greater infusion of the idiosyncrasies of our private personalities." Philosophy, Lovejoy argued, "will never acquire anything like the gait of a science until it becomes, to a much higher degree than is yet customary, methodologically self-conscious; until it becomes more systematic in its procedure, devotes relatively more attention to its technique, and, for a time, relatively less to the formulation of substantive conclusions."[51]

Lovejoy followed his call for greater methodological rigor with an outline by which it might be achieved. He suggested six steps to making philosophy more scientific: 1) the acquisition of an "inductive investigator's habit of mind"; 2) "a deliberate and systematic attempt at exhaustiveness in the enumeration of the elements of a problem"; 3) the transformation of philosophy into a "coöperative enterprise"; 4) the adoption of "a common and unambiguous terminology, and . . . of a common set of initial postulates"; 5) the phrasing of all inquiry and discussion in hypothetical form; and 6) the compilation of "a modern *Summa Metaphysica*" of all relevant considerations relating to the various philosophical problems and theses. Lovejoy recognized that some of his colleagues would consider such a philosophy nothing more than "dried, abstract, depersonalized arguments and counter-arguments, destitute of all charm of style," but he believed that such a scheme was necessary if philosophers were not to abandon their "customary pretension to be dealing with objective, verifiable and clearly communicable truths." Only by reorganizing philosophy along these lines could philosophers ensure themselves "some hope of attaining the assured and steady march which should characterize a science."[52]

Lovejoy's assumptions and proposals were soundly criticized in a symposium arranged by the editors of *Philosophical Review*. Ernest Albee observed that Lovejoy in his address was characteristic of those philosophers who felt compelled "to apologize for philosophy because it is not something else." He did not go so far as to suggest that "particular philosophers or working groups of philosophers may not be 'scientific' to their hearts' content," but rejected those standards for all philosophy. Charles Bakewell shared many of Albee's views on what philosophy ought to become. He noted that many philosophers were "chafing under the neglect, not to say ill-concealed contempt, which scientists of our day show in their attitude toward us and our work. . . . We are the pariahs of the scholarly world." Bakewell nonetheless remained skeptical of Lovejoy's proposal. Its greatest fault, he thought, was not that it would give philosophy "the appearance of a Desert of Sahara, with scarcely a redeeming oasis," but that the procedure outlined was "not a procedure which has proved its serviceableness in the field of science. That is not the way the scientists work." Only William Ernest Hocking saw merit in Lovejoy's ideas. He wanted to continue the annual discussions, thought "the more organization the better," and approved of compiling a *Summa Metaphysica*. His only reservation was that he thought the cooperative enterprise would be infinite; some questions would be answered, but more would remain to be answered.[53]

In replying to his critics, Lovejoy clarified his proposals. His colleagues had not shaken his conviction that "if philosophy is to be regarded as in any sense a science, it must share the *generic* attributes of all the sciences; it must have *some* definite method of inquiry, some systematic procedure in the observation of data and the verification of hypotheses." He now suggested that the methods of science must be adapted to the needs of philosophy; they "cannot be borrowed ready-made from any special science." Lovejoy conceded that there was a part of philosophy that was "not capable of a wholly scientific and impersonal treatment" and asked every philosopher to keep in mind whether he was "functioning as an artist or as a man of science." He remained firm in his belief that the methods of science were applicable to at least part of philosophy: "But, for my thesis, it makes little difference *what* part of philosophy is conceded to be akin to science in its purpose and ideal to aim at depersonalized and universally verifiable truth. If only there be *some* such part, then to that part, and to all of it, and to it alone, the contentions advanced in my discourse apply."[54]

Despite his contributions to the 1912 debate on agreement, John Dewey was not a major participant in the effort to achieve consensus through organized discussion. Like many advocates of agreement, Dewey had great respect for the achievements of science, but, unlike them, he did not wish to remake philosophy over into a science. Scientific values and methodology could serve as models for philosophic practice, but Dewey continued to argue that philosophers must adopt those models to their own broader, more social, role in the university and in society. In several essays published in the second decade of the century Dewey refined his evolving conception of the proper relationship of philosophy and science.

One fundamental way in which science had challenged philosophy was in the method of attaining truth. In "The Problem of Truth," Dewey argued for the applicability of scientific standards of truth to philosophical problems. In scientific inquiry truth is not simply "accepted beliefs, but beliefs accepted in virtue of a certain method." For science, "truth *denotes* verified beliefs, propositions that have emerged from a certain procedure of inquiry and testing." One important consequence of this notion of truth is that it gives warrant for believing the truths put forward by experts in a particular field. If the truth is achieved by a demonstrably scientific method, then the lay person, the non-scientist, has good grounds for accepting it. The philosopher, in other words, is justified in accepting "the results of the physicist on faith." Dewey argued that science in itself is "a purely technical matter, without any fundamental, that is to say moral or practical, meaning." However, when science affects deeply ingrained human customs and habits, then "the scientific way of designating truth becomes a matter of general, or philosophic, importance." The pragmatic idea of truth is valuable because it stands for "carrying the experimental notion of truth that reigns among the sciences, technically viewed, over into political and moral practices, humanly viewed."[55]

The implications of scientific truth reached beyond the formal boundaries of the sciences, but Dewey retained a conviction that philosophy had "a distinctive problem and purpose of its own." Because of its distinctive purpose, philosophy need not "accept in a servile fashion the materials handed over by common sense and by natural science." Dewey believed that "the standpoint and method of science do not mean the abandonment of social purpose and welfare as rightfully governing criteria in the formation of beliefs." Scientific truth can help bring about "the emancipation of goods, purposes and activities, producing the transition from a stationary society to a progressive society."[56] But however necessary to the emancipation from a dead past, scientific truth, by itself, cannot point the way to a progressive future. The takes the vision of the philosopher, and on that basis, philosophy maintains its own vitally important role in an evolving society.

Dewey did not intend to outline a "scheduled program" for philosophers to follow. Rather, he suggested, the important issues for philosophers will become evident in the ever-present "human difficulties of an urgent, deep-seated kind which may be clarified by trained reflection, and whose solution may be forwarded by the careful development of hypotheses." Philosophic thinking, properly conceived, is "caught up in the actual course of events, having the office of guiding them towards a prosperous issue." Dewey did not argue that philosophy could solve problems. Philosophy, for him, was "vision, imagination, reflection—and these functions, apart from action, modify nothing and hence resolve nothing." But action uninformed by these qualities, and lacking rigorous thought, is "more likely to increase confusion and conflict than to straighten things out."[57] The function of philosophy as he sketched it was to employ trained reflection, vision, and imagination in pointing toward the courses of action productive of solutions to pressing social problems.

Dewey clarified the practical implications of his positions on science and philosophy in his 1916 book *Democracy and Education*. He defined science as "that knowledge which is the outcome of methods of observations, reflection, and testing which are deliberately adopted to secure a settled, assured subject matter." Science, he wrote, "is the perfecting of knowing, its last stage." Dewey found science liberating; it made "possible the systematic pursuit of new ends. It is the agency of progress in action." For the scientist, past experience becomes the "servant, not the master of mind." Reason, Dewey argued, now operated "within experience, not beyond it, to give it an intelligent or reasonable quality. Science is experience becoming rational." Dewey fervently believed that science freed the human mind to take control of life and to set it on the path of progress. As he wrote, "Science represents the office of intelligence, in projection and control of new experiences, pursued systematically, intentionally, and on a scale due to freedom from limitations of habit. It is the sole instrumentality of conscious, as distinct from accidental, progress."[58] Philosophers might well employ the methods of such a science and share the high value on rigorous rational thought pursued with the goal of liberation, but Dewey refused to identify completely philosophy with science as a mode of inquiry. Philosophy had its own role to play in bringing about progress.

In *Democracy and Education* Dewey sought to make his idea of philosophy explicit. Philosophy properly dealt with "the conflicts and difficulties of social life." Regarding these issues, philosophy was "an attempt to *comprehend*—that is, to gather together the varied details of the world and of life into a single inclusive whole." Dewey defined this "endeavor to attain as unified, consistent, and complete an outlook upon experience as is possible" as the philosopher's traditional "love of wisdom." He assumed, as had philosophers for generations before him, that this was "a wisdom which would influence the conduct of life."[59]

For Dewey, it was the "direct and intimate connection of philosophy with an outlook upon life" that most clearly differentiated philosophy from science. The facts of science could and certainly did influence conduct, but they were not in themselves "a *general attitude* toward" the world. Dewey acknowledged that philosophers, like all men, must go to science "to find out the facts of the world. It is for the sciences to say what generalizations are tenable about the world and what they specifically are." But only philosophy can provide a total, consistent, and unified attitude toward the world and the facts as revealed by science. Dewey was careful to define consistency as a "mode of response in reference to the plurality of events which occur." It means adaptability to new situations and experiences, it means being "open-minded and sensitive to new perceptions," and it means "keeping the balance in a multitude of diverse actions, so that each borrows and gives significance to every other."[60] Being philosophical means reasoning from a standpoint of value, of concern for the future, and of openness to change. That philosophical attitude is what sets the philosopher apart from the scientist.

Philosophy, as Dewey here conceived it, was not knowledge but thinking. Knowledge, and especially grounded knowledge, he argued, "is science; it represents objects which have been settled, ordered, disposed of rationally." Thinking is "prospective in reference. It is occasioned by an *un*settlement and it aims at creating a disturbance." The philosopher at his task thinks "what the known demands of us—what responsive attitude it exacts. It is an idea of what is possible, not a record of accomplished fact." Thinking "presents an assignment of something to be done—something to be tried." Thinking does not furnish solutions, which, Dewey argued, can be achieved only through action; its value lies in "defining difficulties and suggesting methods for dealing with them." Dewey described philosophy as "thinking which has become conscious of itself—which has generalized its place, function, and value in experience."[61]

Pure science, Dewey believed, is indifferent to the social and human value of its discoveries and facts. Its "disclosures" might as easily destroy life as to foster it. Science thus needs something beyond itself, something to connect it to the values and goals of the community in which it is found. Philosophy finds its functions in this broader world, mediating between the values of society and the achievements of science. The task of philosophy is twofold: to criticize "existing aims with respect to the existing state of science, pointing out values which have become obsolete with the command of new resources, showing what values are merely sentimental because there are no means for their realization"; and to interpret "the results of specialized science in their bearing on future social endeavor."[62]

By the late teens, the crisis of confidence in American philosophy had been largely overcome. Some philosophers, such as Peirce and Lovejoy, had taken the first significant steps to remake philosophy into a science. Much remained to be done, but the advocates of a scientific philosophy were more confident than before that the essential groundwork had been laid and that some philosophers, at least, now conducted their inquiry in the spirit of and with the methods of science. Others, such as Dewey and his followers, admired the achievements of science, acknowledged the usefulness of scientific knowledge, and sought to apply that knowledge, guided by the values of a philosophical position, to the practical problems of society. They were confident that the recent achievements in merging the knowledge of science with the insight and values derived from philosophy presaged an imminent rational reconstruction of society. There remained, of course, a substantial group of men and women for whom the appeal of science had never been very strong. These opponents of the scientization of philosophy found a home, paradoxically, in the specialized academic discipline which superseded moral philosophy. In the pluralistic context of American higher education both the more traditional philosophers and the advocates of new methods and values found a safe, academic haven under the roof of a professionalized philosophy.

The crisis of confidence, then, had affected all philosophers. It had inspired the advocates of a more scientific philosophy to refine their views and to attempt to institutionalize them in the practice of philosophy. The crisis forced more traditional metaphysicians and ethicists to defend their conception of philosophy, their independence, and their rightful place as members of an academic discipline. Most philosophers, with a few notable exceptions, found in the professionalization of their discipline an effective means to academic security, status, and even authority. Their role and status had changed dramatically from that of the mid-nineteenth-century moral philosopher, but by acquiring the accouterments and characteristics of an academic profession, philosophers carved out a secure if diminished niche in American higher education.

Although the institutions and behavior characteristics of an academic profession were largely in place by 1920, the philosophers' failure to develop a substantive professional consensus to complement the institutional structures kept philosophy weak and relatively powerless. There were, as we have seen, significant differences among philosophers regarding the appropriate role, subject matter, and method of the discipline. Even the advocates of a more strongly science-based, professional philosophy found themselves divided between the partisans of a pursuit of pure truth and the supporters of a scientific, rational reconstruction of society. In the absence of any fundamental agreement on the purposes and role of philosophy in the university and society, the profession could do little more than protect philosophy's new position as another academic discipline.

In some measure, the diminution of philosophy's role increased the philosophers' authority within their specialty. By taking on the characteristics and methods of the specialized disciplines, philosophers lost their traditional and broader functions of grounding all inquiry or of providing grand syntheses. Instead, they acquired the authority that now accrued to all recognized specialists in their particular fields. The audience for their work shrank and suspicions about philosophy's usefulness grew among the uninitiated, but within the discipline, and to some extent within the larger academic community, the philosophers' work was recognized for contributing to the development of scientifically-based knowledge. In this, philosophy as an academic profession began to conform more closely to Charles Sanders Peirce's conception of philosophy and science as a linked community of inquiry. Not all philosophers, however, were willing in the 1920s to accept this more constricted conception of philosophy. John Dewey, in particular, continued to advocate philosophy's broader social responsibilities. His views, and the ideas of other philosophers such as Morris Cohen, provided a valuable corrective in that decade to narrow specialization and professionalization. But Dewey's voice was raised against a growing acceptance of philosophy as an academic discipline of philosophic specialists which had surmounted the crisis of confidence which gave it birth.

EIGHT

The Triumph of Professional Philosophy

Philosophy's crisis of confidence was pushed into the background in 1917 by the national crisis of war with Germany. Although the debates over whether to pursue organized discussion and over whether philosophy should emulate science had perhaps run their natural course by the time the United States entered the war in April 1917, the war diverted the attention of philosophers and other academics from their own professional concerns to the national war effort. When the war ended some nineteen months later, the old issues lacked their former urgency. To some, the question of a scientific philosophy seemed settled; the task now was to get on with the business of doing philosophy in the new mold. For others, new issues and topics came to the fore and their work went in directions only marginally connected to the old debates. There were, to be sure, some vestiges of the former controversies. The older versions of philosophy as the study of values, as the search for highest generalizations, and as a vision of reality were defended in the 1920s as a backlash against the ascendancy of the more technical and specialized philosophical inquiries. C. I. Lewis at the end of the decade developed a theory of knowledge in which the concept of community played a key role. And from John Dewey the view that philosophy as a system of values ought to guide the reconstruction of society using the tools furnished by the sciences received a powerful exposition. Some of the issues which had shaped the crisis of confidence thus lingered into the postwar period, but the intensity of feeling and of the debate lessened as the philosophers settled into their roles as specialized professional academics.

From its beginning in 1914, World War I forced scholars to rethink their intellectual, academic, and national commitments. The warring nations of England, France, and Germany represented the intellectual heritage of many scholars; more direct ties, in terms of study at European institutions or degrees received from foreign universities, were common. On some campuses, foreign-born colleagues brought the war home even more personally. Philosophers, as much as any group, felt pulled by the course of war in Europe.

Like most of their colleagues, the philosophers generally supported the Allies, England and France, during the years of American neutrality. American scholars tended to identify the political, economic, and cultural interests of the United States with those of England and, to a lesser extent, of France. In addition, they generally agreed that Germany had been the aggressor. Intellectual ties to German scholarship and culture made it more difficult for many academics to side with the Allies than for their nonacademic compatriots. Still, philosophers, with the rare exception such as the German-born and educated Hugo Münsterberg at Harvard, early and eagerly joined in the condemnation of German aggression and in the chorus of support for the Allies. Scholarly detachment and the spirit of rational inquiry were often abandoned, even before American entry into the war.[1]

The war in Europe increasingly diverted philosophers from their scholarly pursuits to a consideration of the consequences and implications of the fighting. For several individuals, scholarly activity almost ceased in favor of supporting the Allies, urging United States involvement, and, after April 1917, putting talents at the service of the state. For example, as early as 1914 Arthur O. Lovejoy condemned German scholars for their unswerving and unquestioning loyalty to their nation. Thereafter, he threw himself into trying to secure American involvement in the effort to preserve western civilization. Over the next five years Lovejoy wrote some twenty essays in such journals as the *Nation,* the *New Republic,* and the *New York Times* in defense of the allied war effort.[2]

Lovejoy was not alone. Ralph Barton Perry and Josiah Royce at Harvard and John Dewey at Columbia were among the other philosophers who devoted significant attention to war-related issues. Perry and Royce, like Lovejoy, were appalled by German actions and called for stronger American support for the Allies. Perry elaborated the argument that German idealism had led inexorably to the aggressive state of the early twentieth century. In addition, he was active in supporting and publicizing American preparedness. Royce was shocked by the reports of German atrocities and tried to come to terms with this "betrayal of the community of nations." Royce found his ability to work "very greatly hindered, and at times almost wholly inhibited, by the war, and by its chaos of sorrows and of crimes." He was so intellectually indebted to German thought that his own sense of betrayal was evident when he charged Germany with being the "willful and deliberate enemy of the human race." For him, it was "impossible for any reasonable man to be in his heart and mind neutral." Before his death in 1916, burdened by the vision of a world calamity, Royce urged his fellow citizens to do all they could to secure an Allied victory.[3]

Of these philosophers, only Dewey remained somewhat detached during the years of neutrality. Dewey's efforts to understand the reasons for German actions, to support the United States' efforts to mediate the conflict, and to prepare the nation for the possibility of war were more measured than those of his colleagues. In an essay written shortly before American entry, Dewey counseled his readers to take pride in the nation's hesitation in joining the war: "We have continued to be uncertain just because we were certain that our destiny had not declared itself. . . . Never has the American people so little required apologizing for, because never before has it been in such possession of its senses." Dewey, unlike Lovejoy, Perry, and Royce would not force American participation, but when the "clearly proffered challenge" came, he, like his fellows, willingly supported his country.[4]

Once the United States declared war, the philosophers, in company with their colleagues and institutions, threw themselves into war-related work. As Carol Gruber has noted, "The institutions of higher learning donated their intellectual and physical resources to the war effort almost without reservation."[5] The philosophers' major contribution came in the effort to shape public opinion and to sustain enthusiasm for the war. Lovejoy, for example, along with the historian Albert Bushnell Hart, edited a *Handbook of the War for Public Speakers* for the National Security League, a private patriotic organization. The editors described the task of scholars as one "of informing the understanding, of awakening the moral vision and moral passion, of the entire people, concerning the cause for which they fight." Later Lovejoy worked with the Military Morale Section of the War Department and served briefly as field director of the Maryland Council of Defense and as director of lectures and war-aims instruction for the YMCA. Perry took a leave from Harvard to serve as secretary of the Committee on Education and Special Training in the War Department. Here he first directed the training of enlisted men and then the recruitment of officers from college campuses. Perry was also instrumental in the establishment of the Reserve Officers Training Corps. His colleague William Ernest Hocking served as District Director of the War Issues Course Program and wrote a psychological handbook, *Morale and Its Enemies,* for army use. Dewey was less directly involved in the war effort than many philosophers, but even he contributed to a series of "war papers" published by Columbia University's Division of Intelligence and Publicity. His contribution was "Enlistment for the Farm," calling attention to potential food shortages and the need for adequate manpower on American farms.[6] The philosophers, like most of their academic colleagues, were only too willing to put aside scholarly restraint and scientific inquiry to demonstrate their enthusiasm for and commitment to the war.

With the armistice in November 1918 philosophers turned their attention back to their scholarly pursuits and professional careers. The profession they returned to had changed, in part due to the passing of the first generation of academic philosophers. James had died in 1910, Peirce in 1914, Royce and Münsterberg in 1916. But part of the change was due to a maturation of philosophical inquiry. The persistent questions about philosophy's standing in the university and vis-à-vis science now seemed settled. The journals in the postwar period saw nothing resembling the earlier discussion of the proper role of science. Rather, they concentrated increasingly on technical and specialized studies. Bruce Kuklick has found a similar shift among graduate students in philosophy at Harvard. Whereas only 16 percent of the Ph.D.s granted from 1893 to 1906, and 32 percent of those awarded from 1907 to 1918, were in technical fields, as opposed to religious and moral philosophy or metaphysics, 51 percent of the Ph.D.s received from 1920 to 1930 were in technical fields of interest such as logic and epistemology.[7]

C. I. Lewis was one of the scholars who did not turn away from his studies during the war. Unlike those of Lovejoy or Dewey, Lewis's publications during the war were almost exclusively philosophical. He spent these years working on logic and in 1918 published *A Survey of Symbolic Logic*. Only the single essay "German Idealism and Its War Critics," originally read before the Philosophical Union of the University of California, betrayed an awareness of the conflict. But, even here, Lewis addressed his fellow philosophers more than the public in cautioning them not to draw too tightly the connections between German philosophy, especially idealism, and the causes of the war. He criticized Dewey and Santayana for misconstruing German idealism, for ignoring the "complexity of modern life," and for exaggerating "the possible connection between nationality and philosophic doctrine." He concluded that it "seems absurd to trace any noteworthy connection between German Idealism and the present crisis." Such attempts, he suggested, could only contribute to the recent "sorry enough chapter in the history of critical discussion."[8]

The publication of *A Survey of Symbolic Logic* in 1918 and Lewis's return to Harvard as an assistant professor in 1920 marked a shift in his thought. His interests turned to epistemology, perhaps influenced by the two years he spent living with and reading through the Peirce papers, which had recently come to Harvard. He later recalled that this experience turned his thought in a more pragmatic direction. Lewis's writings on logic and epistemology in the 1920s, as his earlier studies in logic, were addressed to his professional colleagues and culminated in his important statement of "conceptual pragmatism" in *Mind and the World-Order* in 1929.[9]

Not all philosophers turned to more technical studies in the discipline. Arthur O. Lovejoy, for example, devoted most of his energies in the 1920s to essays in the history of ideas, including such influential pieces as "On the Discrimination of Romanticisms" in 1924. His more specifically philosophical writings were rigorous critiques of the technical arguments of certain pragmatists and behaviorists. In his Carus lectures of 1928, published as *The Revolt Against Dualism,* Lovejoy launched a major critique of epistemological monism and a defense of epistemological and psychophysical dualism, in four-hundred closely reasoned pages.[10] Even this leader of the drive to make philosophy more scientific now saw no need for further manifestoes.

Contemporary observers sensed the change that was overtaking philosophy in the twenties. Herbert Schneider, a young philosopher reporting on the 1924 American Philosophial Association Eastern Division annual meeting, noted the increased specialization of many of the papers and the technical nature of the terminology. The general feeling, he recorded, was that "the reading and discussion of papers were on the whole less successful than the informal meetings and greetings. . . . Discussion was for the most part perfunctory, trivial, or irrelevant; there was no continuity of subject-matter among the papers; important issues were seldom raised and never debated." Too much attention, he thought, had been given to "the elaboration of terminology" and to "philosophic methods." Some philosophers thought that the state of affairs evident at the meeting meant that "the Association has run down," while others regarded the absence of significant developments as an "intellectual calm after the *Sturm und Drang* of the last few decades."[11]

Schneider, in offering his own explanation for the discomfort felt by many, pointed to a change in philosophical generations. The sessions, he wrote, were now "generally dominated by the younger generation, and even those contributors who were not young in years had relatively new interests or at least approached their problems quite independently of the terminologies and disputes of yesterday." Contributing as well to the lack of focus at the meeting was a "bewildering variety" in the subject matter of the papers. Schneider attributed this diversity to "the general tendency toward more individual pursuits and particularized fields of inquiry. Philosophic interests are diverging and philosophers consequently have fewer common problems to discuss." He astutely observed that "academic philosophy seems to be moving more in the direction of particular sciences and not in the direction . . . of a clarification of the fundamental problems of contemporary social life."[12] Though Schneider accurately discerned the major thrust of professional academic philosophy after the war, the unease he encountered at the 1924 annual meeting reflected the heritage of older patterns in philosophy, a tradition by no means wholly abandoned in the twenties.

Not all philosophers after the war focused on narrow technical studies or turned their attention to new areas of inquiry. For some, the question of whether and to what extent philosophy should be a science had not been completely and finally resolved. They still sought to preserve for their discipline something of the older tradition of broad generalization informed by values. They fought a rearguard action against the triumph of technical, specialized philosophy. Although John Dewey continued to address issues he had taken up earlier, he did not seek to turn back the clock, to recapture some golden age of philosophy. It was a time for looking forward, for clarifying and refining his earlier views, for reconstructing philosophy so it could, in turn, provide vital assistance in the reconstruction of society.

In *Reconstruction in Philosophy,* Dewey's first book published after the war, he addressed the role philosophy ought properly to play in rebuilding a world shattered by moral and physical struggle. Although direct references to World War I were few, the experience of the war lay behind Dewey's sense of urgency about setting philosophy on a new and more appropriate course. The philosophy of the future, he wrote, must "clarify men's ideas as to the social and moral strifes of their own day. Its aim is to become so far as is humanly possible an organ for dealing with these conflicts." Philosophers now had even more reason to abandon their barren dealings with "Ultimate and Absolute Reality" and to refocus their energies upon "enlightening the moral forces which move mankind and in contributing to the aspirations of men to attain to a more ordered and intelligent happiness."[13]

The world in which philosophers operated and which they tried to understand had changed. Any effort to reconstruct philosophy would be futile unless based upon the new view of the universe. The new world, according to Dewey, had been ushered in by science. It was no longer a "closed world," no longer a "fixed world" of hierarchy. Science presents modern man with a universe "infinite in space and time, having no limits, here or there, at this end, so to speak, or at that, and as infinitely complex in internal structure as it is infinite in extent." This new vision of the world has banished solidity and stability: "Change rather than fixity is now a measure of 'reality' or energy of being; change is omnipresent." The modern scientist, according to Dewey, does not try to define "something remaining constant *in* change. He tries to describe a constant order *of* change." Science now emphasizes "something constant in *function* and operation." Although scientists have reconceived the universe, the implications of that accomplishment have been seen largely in the understanding of nature and in the achievements of practical science and technology. That, for Dewey, left much undone in order to make "the new ideas and method . . . at home in social and moral life."[14]

Dewey felt that modern science and industry had entered into a fruitful alliance, which had "brought home to the contemporary mind the fact that the gist of scientific knowledge is control of natural energies. These four facts, natural science, experimentation, control and progress have been inextricably bound up together." These "newer methods and results" had, thus far, had more impact upon "the means of life rather than its ends." Human and social needs, Dewey wrote, "have so far been affected in an accidental rather than in an intelligently directed way." Dewey believed that "while we have been reasonably successful in obtaining command of nature by means of science, our science is not yet such that this command is systematically and preeminently applied to the relief of human estate." Philosophical reconstruction must, he argued, focus on the application of scientific methods and results to "the larger social deficiencies that require intelligent diagnoses, and projection of aims and methods."[15]

Science conceived as process, as experience rationalized for the purposes of control, promised to be as influential in "enabling man to effect a deliberate control" of his moral and social environment as it had been in the natural and technological. "Science, 'reason,' is not," Dewey argued, "something laid from above upon experience." Rather, it is "suggested and tested in experience" and ultimately employed "in a thousand ways to expand and enrich experience." Although science has not yet been applied to artistic and human needs, there are no fundamental reasons why it could not be: "The limits are moral and intellectual, due to defects in our good will and knowledge. They are not inherent metaphysically in the very nature of experience." When reason, viewed as "experimental intelligence, conceived after the pattern of science," is employed "in the creation of social arts," it frees humanity from the dead weight of the past. Science "liberates man from the bondage of the past, due to ignorance and accident hardened into custom. It projects a better future and assists man in its realization." The philosopher who employs "experimental intelligence" creates plans as "guides of reconstructive action." These plans are merely "hypotheses to be worked out in practice, and to be rejected, corrected and expanded as they fail or succeed in giving our present experience the guidance it requires." The key, for Dewey, was flexibility—the ability and willingness to respond to changed situations, but always employing the method of "experimental intelligence." Philosophers could not become complacent, could no longer believe they had achieved Truth, for "intelligence is not something possessed once and for all. It is in constant process of forming, and its retention requires constant alertness in observing consequences, an open-minded will to learn and courage in re-adjustment." The failure to adopt the method of experience has unfortunate consequences; "it has cultivated disregard for fact and this disregard has been paid for in failure, sorrow and war."[16]

The real influence of modern science upon modern philosophy came not so much in the particulars but in opening the possibility of a major reconceptualization of philosophy. The scientific revolutions had forced a change in the practice of science. Experimental science "became preoccupied with changes and the test of knowledge became the ability to bring about certain changes." For the experimental sciences, knowing ceased to be "contemplative" and became "in a true sense practical"; knowing now meant "a certain kind of intelligently conducted doing." This change in the sciences had, Dewey concluded, significant implications for the practice of philosophy. Unless philosophy was "to undergo a complete break with the authorized spirit of science," it too must "alter its nature. It must assume a practical nature; it must become operative and experimental." Altering philosophy in this fashion implied no "lowering in dignity of philosophy from a lofty plane to one of gross utilitarianism." The prime function of the reconstructed philosophy would be "rationalizing the *possibilities* of experience, especially collective human experience." The new philosophical practice, Dewey hoped, would "encourage philosophy to face the great social and moral defects and troubles from which humanity suffers, to concentrate its attention upon clearing up the causes and exact nature of these evils and upon developing a clear idea of better social possibilities." If that could be achieved, then philosophy could truly become "a method of understanding and rectifying specific social ills."[17]

The need for a scientifically based reconstruction of philosophy was made more urgent by the very achievements of science itself. Economic progress rested upon "the revolution that has been wrought in physical science," but as yet there was no "corresponding human science and art." Although economic and technological progress were the positive results of science, this new method of knowing also brought in its wake "serious new moral disturbances." Dewey cited "the late war, the problem of capital and labor, [and] the relation of economic classes" as three instances where an instrumental philosophy could "attempt to find an intelligent substitute for blind custom and blind impulse as guides to life and conduct." Releasing philosophy from "its burden of sterile metaphysics and sterile epistemology," from narrow technical and specialized inquiry, would, Dewey hoped, free philosophers to consider "questions of the most perplexing and most significant sort."[18]

Dewey's *Reconstruction in Philosophy* looked to a future in which the method of science—"experimental intelligence"—would be applied to pressing social and moral issues. Dewey recognized that the method of science promised more rational control, even though recent history seemed to argue otherwise. What was lacking, Dewey realized, was the standpoint of values, morality, and social needs. Scientific expertise and progress without a moral foundation and respect for humanity could easily produce social dislocation and strife, as the recent past had so vividly demonstrated. The answer was not to retreat to some ideal absolute, but to use "experimental intelligence" upon human problems, to counter the absence of values and of moral considerations with a newly rejuvenated scientific morality. This morality would change and adapt, would be flexible and responsive to change, but it would also keep human needs uppermost and so check the unbridled exercise of scientific inquiry and application of technological progress. It would succeed, Dewey hoped, because it incorporated the same method that had brought so much progress in understanding and controlling the physical world.

These views do not represent a sharp break from Dewey's earlier statements on science and philosophy. They were another step in the process of creating an instrumental philosophy cognizant of both the achievements of science and of human needs. There is, however, in these postwar statements a greater sense of urgency about the need to bring a moral perspective to bear on social problems and to infuse philosophy with scientific method. Though Dewey had few illusions about the difficulties of implementing the reconstruction in philosophy, he wanted to get on with the task. Philosophers had already wasted too much time on sterile disputes and narrow technical inquiries.

Not all philosophers in the twenties shared Dewey's vision of a reconstructed philosophy infused with the methods of science. Some sought to recapture for philosophy a measure of its former glory. The advocates of a more traditional philosophy shared Dewey's emphasis on values, but not his enthusiasm for the methods of science. Philosophy, for them, was something separate from science, however much it might depend on science for information about the physical world. Philosophy was about values, about the highest possible generalizations, and about the nature of reality. These had been the traditional areas of philosophic inquiry, and the rise of science had not, in their eyes, overthrown the philosophers' contributions to these questions. These philosophers typically acknowledged the achievements of science, but argued that science alone could not produce complete understanding of the world. Philosophy, and philosophers, had continuing and separate roles to play even in an age of science.

J. E. Creighton had been one of the early advocates of a more specialized professional philosophy and of cooperative inquiry on the model of the sciences. However, within a few years of his inaugural statement as first president of the American Philosophical Association, Creighton began to pull back from his advocacy of a more scientific philosophy. By the 1920s, when it was apparent that the values of science had largely triumphed, and narrow specialized and technical studies were commonplace, Creighton was in full retreat from his earlier positions. In three essays early in the decade, Creighton argued that philosophy and science were separate inquiries and that philosophy, not science, offered the truest vision of the real. However valuable the work of the scientist, Creighton believed that the philosopher stood the best chance of offering us a view of ultimate reality.

By 1920 Creighton was ready to disavow his earlier call for greater specialization and cooperative scientific inquiry within philosophy. Increasingly he had come "to think more of philosophy as representing an attitude of mind and a level of experience, and less of it as a 'subject' or 'science' composed of a body of propositions to be taught and learned." He had become convinced that philosophers were "following a false analogy when we seek to assimilate philosophical inquiry to that of the special sciences, and to require from philosophy the same form of practical application and of definitely marked progress that the latter are supposed to exhibit." That philosophers might learn much from the sciences in no way lessened the importance of their own study: "Each form of inquiry must do its own work, and this can not be achieved by attempts to set up philosophy as a 'science' and to demand of it the form of result that the other sciences yield." Creighton did not completely reject his earlier enthusiasm for the achievement and methods of science. He noted that one could sympathize with the motives of philosophers who wanted to make their discipline more scientific, without accepting "their somewhat pessimistic diagnosis of the condition of philosophy or approving the remedies they propose to employ." All philosophers, Creighton wrote, must pursue their studies "with systematic thoroughness and with the utmost attention to real facts and willingness to follow where the argument leads." But that statement did not mean that philosophers must abandon their "own problems and procedure and seek for a place among the sciences."[19]

If philosophy was not to be a science, then what was it? Creighton claimed that the aim of philosophy was "to construct an orderly world in terms of the relations of concrete individuals." Unlike the sciences, which abstracted the particulars into generalizations and which valued the generalization above any particular, philosophy needed to maintain the integrity and importance of the concrete and individual. Philosophers did not need to remain mired in particularity, for their ultimate goal was "synoptic vision, seeing things whole," without losing a sense of the individuality of the particular. Philosophical intelligibility, for Creighton, meant the attainment of "a concrete universal which expresses the inwardness and essence of individuals through the grasp of their constitutive relations." Philosophy conceived in this fashion was simply "the most fully integrated effort of man to establish relations with his world and thus to attain to the familiarity and confidence that come from understanding."[20] This philosophy relied less on cooperative inquiry and more on the sustained effort of the philosopher to think rigorously and to reflect seriously upon his proper place in the larger world. In some significant measure, then, each individual's philosophy would reflect a particular wisdom rather than the collective wisdom of a science.

Like Creighton, Harold C. Brown at Stanford sought to separate the task of philosophy from that of science. Brown's conception of philosophy was more dependent upon the sciences than that of Creighton. Brown held that "philosophy starts from the truths with which science ends, but its purpose is not merely to cite or to systematize." Scientific truths are instruments for action, for controlling the world around us. Philosophers are to go beyond this, to "integrate" these truths, these prescriptions for control, into a "coherent life, a condition perhaps best described as healthy-mindedness." Brown argued that where "the scientist makes discoveries, the philosopher makes interpretations." Science makes control possible, while the philosopher injects values into decisions about how that control should be exercised. Ultimately both science and philosophy are necessary: "Philosophy can not exist without science, and science loses its significance without philosophy."[21]

Brown argued that science fundamentally was description involving selection. The scientist chooses certain facts from amongst the great multitude because those facts, properly discriminated, "can serve as the basis for predictions." The real task of the scientist is to formulate "significant facts" as the descriptive basis of science. The task of the philosopher, on the other hand, is one of integration and interpretation. Philosophers take instruments of control, scientific truths, and mold them into an ideal capable of inspiring action. For Brown, "philosophic results are inspirational and win approvals." The philosopher cannot properly "criticize, correct or transform" scientific knowledge, but he can seek to build on its truths to achieve a situation in "which greater congeniality or mutual fitness can be attained in human relations and the relations of man to his environment." It is the special task of the philosopher to demonstrate that an end is "possible and desirable" rather than "to perfect the means for attaining it." Philosophers, of necessity, must "reflect upon scientific knowledge in so far as it bears upon the problems imposed by the act of living," but only as a beginning to their labors.[22] Their real task lay ahead, in fashioning a viable interpretation that establishes ideals and that gives meaning to life and to action.

William A. Brown of Union Theological Seminary and George A. Wilson at Syracuse added their voices to those calling for a clearer separation of the tasks of philosophy from those of science. Philosophy's continued low repute in the minds of many scientists inspired Brown to inquire into the future prospects for philosophy. He worried that many scientists regarded philosophy departments as "a luxury rather than as a necessity." His response was an attempt to demonstrate that philosophers and scientists inhabited different spheres of inquiry. Science, Brown wrote, dealt with "those questions the answer to which we can be content to take at second hand." Philosophers dealt with "those questions the answer to which each man must give for himself." Philosophers properly address the great questions of the meaning of life and thereby seek to clarify issues, to point out possibilities, and to recall the significant responses of the past in order to assist the individual in arriving at his own answers. Science, Brown felt, led inevitably to philosophy because it raised "great questions" of meaning and of understanding. But however much it might draw on the sciences, philosophy rightly conceived is more than a science or aggregation of the sciences. It is an individual, and yet unified, conception of the whole.[23]

George Wilson was also sensitive to the charge that philosophy had been superseded by science. He felt that "the typically scientific mind" saw philosophy as "merely the custodian of left-over problems." If that was true, then philosophy would ultimately be "unable to maintain its right to be taken seriously." Not surprisingly, Wilson did not believe that philosophy had fallen so low. Science, he alleged, despite its undeniable strengths, had "discovered that it is not all-conquering. At every step questions emerge that science has no way of handling." Although these questions are beyond the range of science, they are neither avoidable nor insoluble; many, in fact, "carry with them the major values of life." The questions are "impervious to scientific treatment." They are, instead, in the realm of philosophy.[24]

Wilson argued that these "extra-scientific" questions pertain to "the nature of the real." We need to know what constitutes the real and how we are a part of it. Philosophy, Wilson wrote, is "the ever-renewed attempt to satisfy this human need." Where science is "the study of processes," philosophy is "the study of reality as such." Implicit in this study of reality is the question of values. Science can assist us in securing or testing values, but when we ask "what a given value is for us, we ask a strictly philosophical question." Since reality is experienced as value and value is strictly personal, then "our universe is throughout and distinctly personal." Values can be shared and thus become a "joint product." Nature, in this scheme, is "secondary and instrumental, a tool . . . nothing more," whereas values ultimately suggest "a possible destiny for human beings that is particularly satisfying." For Wilson it was as a theory of value that "philosophy makes a permanent place for itself. It definitely transcends the sciences, and can never be superseded by them."[25]

The only way to preserve philosophy's role as a theory of value was to maintain scrupulously its separation from science. "Philosophy's characteristic problems must receive characteristic solutions, such as are all but meaningless to science in its more exacting moods." Wilson hoped that the reigning "rigidity of the scientific attitude" would soon be relaxed and that scientists would soon feel freer "to turn over to philosophy the troublesome questions that grow out of his studies, yet prove refactory to scientific treatment." When that happened, then science and philosophy each would be free "to pursue its task unmolested by the other, yet each in a way implying, supplementing, completing the other."[26]

Will Durant and Paul Schilpp both thought that American philosophy had abandoned vital tasks in the pursuit of science and specialization. Durant traced philosophy's contemporary failure to "the sudden uprising of the sciences" which had stolen its "ancient spacious realms." He lamented that "all the real and crucial problems" had escaped from philosophy, leaving nothing but "the arid deserts of metaphysics, and the childish puzzles of epistemology, and the academic disputes of an ethics that has lost all influence on mankind." Although science bore major responsibility for the fall of philosophy, Durant acknowledged that science and philosophy require a close relationship even as they pursue their separate courses. The sciences, according to him, are "the windows through which philosophy sees the world." Science is "the analytical description of parts; philosophy is the synthetic interpretation of a part in terms of its place and value for the whole." Philosophy, truly conceived, is more than highly generalized scientific knowledge; it is "wisdom." "It implies the difficult and elevated vision in which mere knowledge is lifted up into a total view that orders and clarifies the confusion of desire." Just as philosophy needs science to provide the knowledge gained by "honest observation and research," science requires philosophy to avoid becoming "decadent and dishonest, isolated from the flow of human growth." Without philosophy, science is "destructive and devastating."[27] Durant's arguments here clearly reflect his desire for a more broadly based philosophy with wider public appeal.

Schilpp, like Durant, was sensitive to the charge that philosophy was unscientific. He knew that many philosophers "would find life hard if our critics were to call either us or our speculations 'unscientific'. " That fear, Schilpp thought, had contributed to the tendency of American philosophers to ignore the questions of "practical or cultural values." He deplored the fact that much recent American philosophy had been "so extremely objective in its interest and output that there is little or no relation discernible between it and the great practical affairs of mankind." Schilpp admitted that "detailed philosophical discussion on technically minute problems" was necessary, but he urged philosophers not to "neglect the human element in our philosophizings." This more broadly conceived philosophy would synthesize the results of the sciences and social sciences, build "a theory of the universe," and, ultimately, "construct a plan for the direction of further human evolution."[28]

Although these philosophers were critics of the identification of philosophy with science and of narrow specialized studies, they nonetheless reveal the pervasive influence of science upon American philosophy. They all acknowledged the achievements of science and its power to gain knowledge of the physical world. They were even prepared to admit that science had properly stripped philosophy of some of its former fields. What they refused to accept, however, was the implication that philosophy no longer had a central role to play or that it was limited to certain barren academic disputes. For them philosophy was a matter of synthesis and integration, of conceiving the world as a whole and of understanding our place in it, of elaborating values as guides to action. However much knowledge science might provide, the task of the philosopher was to seek after wisdom and understanding. In that task, he would be unscientific in the best sense.

Morris Cohen was far more sympathetic to the claims of science than the philosophers just discussed, but he, too, sought to preserve for philosophy its own special tasks. Cohen laid out his mature views in *Reason and Nature*, published in 1931 but containing significant portions that had first been published between 1911 and 1927. In the preface Cohen noted the widespread contemporary "dissatisfaction with the arid state of present-day technical philosophy." He granted the value of some studies as a healthy reaction against "the older romantic fashion" of building individual and unique philosophical systems. Still, professional concerns were, Cohen thought, the principal motive for the specialized studies. "As teachers of philosophy see their colleagues gaining prestige through contributions in special technical fields, they are tempted to take the position: 'We too are specialists. We too have a definite technical field of our own'."[29]

Cohen did not advocate returning to the romantic mode of philosophy, as recently embodied in the work of James, Bergson, Croce, and Spengler. His sense of the "solid theoretic achievements" of science barred any "naive and unquestioning hope" in a new romanticism. He acknowledged, with James, that "philosophy is primarily a vision and all great philosophers have something in common with poets and prophets," but philosophy must be more than "a poetic image or prophecy. It must, like science be also vitally concerned with reasoned or logically demonstrable truth." The serious philosopher, according to Cohen, would apply to his vision a critical judgment, rigorous "logical rules of evidence," and "arduous scientific technique" so as to ensure "order and consistency." Cohen's notion of philosophy, then, merged the romantic and the scientific: "Philosophy can hope to be genuinely fruitful only by being more scientifically critical or cautious than the recent romantic efforts, and at the same time more daring and substantial than those microscopic philosophies which lose sight of the macrocosm."[30]

In relying on the sciences to bring order and consistency to philosophic vision, Cohen emphasized "their method rather than their results." The method of science, he felt, was more permanent than any particular result, for "the life of science is in exploration and in the weighing of evidence." There were some dangers in relying on science. Too great a reliance on scientific results merely creates "a new set of priests called scientists." Too much emphasis on "rigorous scientific evidence" could narrow the philosopher's perspective and lead to a neglect of nonscientific problems. Despite the potential problems, Cohen remained convinced that "greater regard for the rational methods of natural science must be joined with a more serious concern with the great historic traditions in philosophy." Cohen urged his colleagues to avoid "simple magical formulae" in their philosophizing. In its "maturer period," philosophy must, "like science and rational industry, depend upon more modest and workmanlike efforts, though it can never abandon the search for comprehensive vision."[31]

Science, as Cohen described it in *Reason and Nature,* is a method designed "to cure speculative excesses." The scientist exercises his method by applying logic to assumptions, "mathematically deducing their various consequences," and testing each against "such experimental facts as can be generally established." This method is not something mysterious; it is simply "a systematic effort to eliminate the poison of error from our common knowledge." Science begins with "the facts of common sense," but it then employs "the rigours of scientific research to attain purer and wider truth." In establishing conclusions based on evidence and proof, "science aims at knowledge that is certain." A key to the success of science is its self-correcting nature. Science, Cohen wrote, could be "challenged only by some other system which is factually more inclusive and, through the demand for proof, logically more coherent. But such a system would simply be science improved."[32]

Cohen argued that science had been applied to philosophy in one of three ways. Philosophers have "tried to build a world-view either (a) on the results,

(b) on the presuppositions, or (c) on the method of science." Many philosophers, he noted, tried to take "the generally accepted results of the various sciences and to weave them together in a picture of reality." There were, however, serious difficulties with this approach. It was difficult "for anyone but a specialist to know what *are* the results of any one special science" and more popular accounts were unreliable. More importantly, "a synthesis of the results of science is not necessarily scientific." The philosopher who took this approach to incorporating science into his thought faced a dilemma: "Either scientific philosophy makes no attempt to fill the gaps in our scientific knowledge or else it must do so by methods which the sciences themselves will not use, so that our result cannot claim to be scientific even though elements of our picture may be borrowed from the sciences." A way out of this dilemma was the second approach: "to view philosophy not as a synthesis of the results of science but as a dialectic argument concerning its presuppositions." This was the method of Kant. Though it had been significant in the development of philosophy, Cohen noted "two insuperable logical objections to it." He pointed out that as a result of modern mathematics and physics it was no longer possible to accept the idea that we have "a priori knowledge of nature." In addition, it was a logical fallacy to hold that any theory "that explains how knowledge is possible, is thereby demonstrated to be true."[33] The failure of the first two means of incorporating science into philosophy left only the third—scientific method.

Cohen wanted to go beyond the widely held view "that philosophy can be scientific only by applying scientific methods to its own subject matter which is distinct from the subject matter of the other sciences." He acknowledged that the application of scientific methods to philosophy's special problems had brought "great gains" to the field. But, Cohen argued, philosophers should not concentrate on their special subjects to the exclusion of the subject matter of the special sciences. Philosophy must also embrace the subject matter of the natural and social sciences if it is to respond to the "interest in the cosmos which has at all times been the heart of philosophic endeavour." This approach is more difficult, but the problems are not impossible. "Philosophy, seeking the most comprehensive vision, cannot ignore the insight gained by the sciences, but must go forward to envisage their synthesis." A certain amount of speculation, he argued, was necessary for the growth of science and philosophic speculation had often nurtured science. Furthermore, the dangers of unchecked speculation could be curbed by "a rigorously logical analysis of fundamental concepts and assumptions." The recent work of philosophers like Peirce, Frege, Whitehead, and Russell had established grounds for proof in areas "which science is not yet in a position to attack directly." In that regard "philosophy is continuous with science in method." The task of the philosopher in applying this method is to "go back to ever more rigorous analysis of the elements or rudiments of our knowledge, to examine the ideals which guide scientific effort, and to anticipate where possible what science *may* conquer in the future."[34]

Cohen's views thus stand between those of the philosophers who would restore philosophy to the grand manner by clearly separating it from science and the position of John Dewey, who would have philosophy adopt the methods of science in dealing with significant social and moral issues. Like the critics of a more scientific philosophy, Cohen believed that narrow, technical specialization was largely barren of significant results, however important it might be as a counter to romantic effusions or as a tool for professional advancement. But if he could not go as far as Dewey in celebrating and employing the methods of science, neither would he eliminate the influence of science properly conceived and properly used in philosophical inquiry. Rigorous and logical philosophical analysis could help ground scientific work, could properly examine and criticize the ideals of science, and ultimately could shape the direction of science. Although their relationship was close, philosophy and science remained separate, if often intertwined, modes of inquiry.

C. I. Lewis displayed little of this anxiety over the role of science in understanding the world or over the relationship of science to philosophy. In *Mind and the World-Order*, his important 1929 effort to develop a theory of knowledge, Lewis treated science and philosophy as complementary ways of knowing. Philosophy, he argued, is important for everybody because it deals with our responsibility for our own lives, with ends, not means. Philosophy, unlike science, cannot "add to the sum total of phenomena with which men are acquainted." A philosopher's, or anyone's, philosophizing reflects upon "what is already familiar." For Lewis, the "distinctively philosophic enterprise" was "bringing to clear consciousness and expressing coherently the principles which are implicitly intended in our dealing with the familiar." Philosophers ought not to "go adventuring beyond space and time," but neither should they become scientists focused on phenomenal facts. With regard to such facts, philosophers can do no more than "wait upon the progress of the special sciences." Lewis acknowledged that many of the most important questions of "the nature of life and mind" are questions of a "mixed sort" mingling metaphysics and science. Resolving such questions successfully requires additional data from the sciences, but since these problems "also turn upon questions of the fundamental criteria of classification and principles of interpretation," they are also "truly philosophic." Both science and philosophy, then, are necessary for any satisfactory interpretation of the world.[35]

The task of philosophers was to develop the fundamental concepts and classifications that make the empirical study of nature possible. These concepts antedate and are necessary for any scientific investigation; "their origin is social and historical and represents some enduring human interest." They are never simply derived from empirical inquiries, but rather arise out of important human needs and interests. Lewis did not reserve the delineation of these concepts solely for the philosophers. Scientific experts in particular fields may develop appropriate concepts, but they are never the scientist's exclusively, since "they are to be resolved as much by criticism and reflection as by empirical investigation." Similarly, the philosophers have a right to speculate about "undetermined scientific fact." Lewis here wanted to distinguish between the speculative and reflective elements of inquiry based on differences of method in resolving problems. Metaphysics deals only in the reflective elements of the problem of the real and not in scientific speculative and empirical investigations. The metaphysical problems of a special science form the philosophy of that science. "The problems of philosophy proper" are "those problems of initial principle and criteria which are common to all the sciences and to the general business of life." Thus, scientists who reflect on the fundamental concepts of their discipline are philosophizing, while metaphysicians who speculate on undetermined facts are in some measure scientists. While Lewis clearly felt that one individual in his various guises may mix roles, he also felt it was possible, indeed useful, to keep clearly in mind the different tasks of philosophy and science.[36]

Metaphysicians ought to remain strictly within the reflective mode seeking "to determine the nature of the real." Their chief task is to "*define* 'reality'", not to triangulate the universe." They should do this by dealing with the familiar, by formulating principles "already immanent in intelligent practice." Lewis's metaphysics was a metaphysics of this world, not of something transcendent or "strangely unfamiliar." The problem of metaphysics for Lewis was "the problem of the categories" attacked through "clear and cogent self-consciousness." The categories provide the basis for understanding the real, either in general or in particular contexts. They provide the framework through which experience is understood and interpreted: "Metaphysics is concerned to reveal just that set of major classifications of phenomena, and just those precise criteria of valid understanding, by which the whole array of given experience may be set in order and each item (ideally) assigned its intelligible and unambiguous place." These classifications, concepts, or categories are a priori in the sense that they are not simply derivative of experience. "The criteria of interpretation are of the mind; they are imposed upon the given by our active attitude." The task of the metaphysician, then, is to wrestle with "the problem of the categories; the formation of the criteria of reality, in its various types."[37]

In a passage reminiscent of Peirce, Lewis argued that successful definition of the real and exploration of empirical phenomena on the basis of that definition is an infinitely extended process. "The total picture of reality can be drawn only when the last experience of the last man, and the final facts of science, are summed up." That grand cosmological task is not exclusively philosophical, but must instead "be a coöperative enterprise, and presumably one that is always incomplete."[38] Our intermediate definitions and empirical findings enable us to operate in this world, to develop new and more precise definitions, which in turn foster new empirical discoveries. Through the cooperative enterprise of science and philosophy we gain fuller understanding and knowledge of the world, even if the ultimate goal remains elusive.

Lewis's a priori categories are not exclusively the product of reason nor are they "made in Plato's heaven in utter independence of the world we live in." They are, instead, the product of our reflection on experience and the development of concepts "which survive the test of practice." Because they are tested in practice, the categories become social phenomena which may help or hinder cooperation. As social beings, we tend to preserve those categories which foster cooperation, and they then become the basis of "our common understanding and our common world." Lewis did not assume agreement on the categories; such agreement arose only out of shared experience and critical discussion to hone the categories in the interest of cooperation. The categories are "almost as much a social product as is language, and in something like the same sense." The only thing which must be "antecedently assumed" is "the *possibility* of agreement."[39] Pragmatic considerations will ensure the survival of useful categories, and as we cooperate in discovering and interpreting the world, our separate interpretations will converge toward a common understanding, toward agreement, whether in general or in the more restricted world of the special sciences.

Lewis identified two elements of knowledge: "the concept, which is the product of the activity of thought, and the sensuously given, which is independent of such activity." It is the concept which creates the a priori, while "empirical truth, or knowledge of the objective, arises through conceptual interpretation of the given." Empirical objects are never simply "momentarily given," but are the products of interpretation based upon some concept. Applying a concept to the given is "essentially predictive and only partially verified." Our actual experience of the given can never exhaust the predictive pattern of interpretation which "constitutes the real object," and hence "all empirical knowledge is probable only." Lewis denied any metaphysical assumption of preestablished harmony between categories and the given and believed instead that "any conceivable experience will be such that it can be subsumed under concepts, and also such that predictive judgments which are genuinely probable will hold of it." Although Lewis focused on the necessity of interpretation using a priori categories, he also insisted on the reality of the given. The given may be "an excised element or abstraction," but it is not "unreal." For Lewis, there was no denying that the given was "an identifiable constituent in experience."[40]

Drawing upon both Peirce and Royce, Lewis developed the interplay of given and concept into the theory of a "community of meaning." His "community of meaning" was based on his attempt to "isolate" the "objective and impersonal" element of knowledge. To do so, he defined the pure concept as "that meaning which must be common to two minds when they understand each other by the use of a substantive or its equivalent." He believed that this kind of objectivity was "a fundamental assumption of science or of any other intellectual enterprise." Without some such objectivity, there is little point to reflection or discussion and no possibility of truth: "There must be meanings which are common to minds when they coöperate in scientific or even in merely practical endeavors. Otherwise the coöperation is illusory."[41]

Lewis acknowledged the difficulties in establishing what he also called the "community of knowledge." Among other difficulties was the psychological one of different feelings. Although there is no possibility of verifying a "community between minds" regarding feelings about experience, Lewis asserted that it was "fantastic" to assume that there was no such community. Whatever the difficulties in this regard, he felt that it was "obvious that common meanings do transcend such individual differences of perception and imagery." Common meanings will fail and our knowledge will be truly different and impossible of communication only if we fail to define our concepts "in the same or equivalent fashion" or fail to "apply the same substantives and adjectives to the same objects." For Lewis, the "only practical and applicable criteria of common knowledge" were that "we should share common definitions of the terms we use, and that we should apply these terms identically to what is presented."[42]

Lewis identified two means of verifying the community of meaning, though he conceded that neither is absolutely conclusive or complete. The two methods, "neither of which depends on any supposed community of feeling or imagery" are: to define the terms; or through behavior, to "exhibit their denotation." The method of denotation is "less conclusive," since one can never be certain that the examples offered are exhaustive and all-inclusive. It is also dependent upon the person receiving the meaning isolating "correctly just that totality of properties which is common to the things indicated." These "shortcomings" mean that the method of denotation is usually restricted to "conveying the meaning of a *word* where the *concept* itself is already something shared." In contrast, "the method of definition specifies a meaning directly." This method relies upon relating one concept to another and so on through the whole complex of relations. Although such a process can usually ensure "common meaning," it is necessarily incomplete. Nonetheless, agreement on common meanings allows us to get on with understanding the world and living in it.[43]

Lewis separated sensation and imagery, which are "essentially individual" and lacking in shareable common meaning, from "the concept, which is the common, shareable and expressible meaning." The pattern of conceptual relationships must be "identical and shared by all who really possess ideas in common and are capable of conveying them to one another." He conceded that this "conceptual pattern of relations" was an abstraction, but it was a necessary one if "we are to discover the basis of our common understanding of that reality which we all know." Just as the process of coming to knowledge begins with the unshareable images and the shareable concepts, so the analysis of meaning is fated to end at the same point. We are left with "the logical, shareable meaning of further conceptual relations, and the direct, non-shareable meaning of reference to some complex of sense-qualities." Thus, in our relation with the given, there remains both the unique individual experience and the common interpretation or meaning arising out of a shared conceptual a priori.[44]

Lewis acknowledged that his notion of the concept represented an ideal. For him, "the concept is a definitive structure of meanings, which is what *would verify* completely the coincidence of two minds when they understand each other by the use of language." His view "does *not* require coincidence of imagery or sensory apprehension," nor does it require that in every case there be a perfect meeting of the minds. Misunderstanding concepts, like misunderstanding language, is entirely possible. He accepted the fact that "both community of meaning and genuine understanding of reality are projected ideals more truly than realized actualities." We use these concepts as necessary and recognize that they are approximations which may be improved through practice. Despite their flaws, it is these "concepts, as precisely such ideal abstractions, which must be implicitly present in our practice, which constitute the element of interpretation which underlies our common understanding of our common world."[45]

Conceptions, for Lewis, were not idle abstractions; they made knowledge possible. Knowledge, in turn, lies behind possible action, and, since conceptions and knowledge can be shared, it is possible to speak of a "community of action." The existence of these common meanings and of the community of action is best revealed in the "tremendous achievement" of humans through history. Two factors increase the likelihood of the possibility of common concepts: "first, by the fact that we are creatures fundamentally alike, having in the large the same needs and interests and powers of discrimination and relation; and second, that we are confronted by a common reality, mediated to us in sense-experience which is comparable." These two factors mean that we can overcome the diversity of sense-experience as we abstract and reflect on our experiences through communally developed concepts: "Our common world is very largely a social achievement—an achievement in which we triumph over a good deal of diversity in sense experience." However the initial meeting of two minds arises, their joint conceptualization, if useful, is spread throughout the human community by "the exigencies of common life, the need of coöperation, the tendency to imitation in behavior, and the enormously developed institution of human education."[46]

Lewis argued that we generally understand one another because "a common reality is presented to us." However, to put it thus is to "reverse the order of knowledge. We have a common reality because—or in so far as—we are able to identify, each in his own experience, those systems of orderly relation indicated by behavior, and particularly by that part of behavior which serves the ends of coöperation." There may be individual differences in how we respond to the given and in how we frame the concept, but because we are intelligent creatures we can make reasonable adjustments for these differences and realize that we are responding to the environment comparably. The result is that "the 'common reality' projected by such understanding of each other is, to an extent not usually remarked, a social achievement." This common reality arises between humans, and not with other creatures, because as humans we share a certain "like-mindedness": "the possession of like needs and of like modes of behavior in satisfying them, second, the possession of common concepts, represented in behavior by discrimination and relation, and third, the capacity . . . of transcending our individual limitations of discrimination by indirect methods," by using our intelligence. Because our common reality arises out of our like-mindedness and "reflects our common categories," it is "implausible to assume this fundamental community to be simply ready-made and miraculous." It is far more likely that "the sharing of a common 'reality' is, in some part, the aim and the result of social coöperation, not an initial social datum, prerequisite to common knowledge."[47]

Shared concepts, arising out of our communal effort to impose order on the chaos of the given experience, eventually become, according to Lewis, the a priori truth which shapes our future understandings and behavior. Concepts, what the mind brings to experience, are necessary to make sense of the world, but until they become fixed modes of interpretation, it is impossible to assign meaning to given experience. A priori truth thus is based in the concepts and develops in two ways: first, there is the a priori truth typified by mathematics, which "represents the elaboration of concepts in the abstract, without reference to any particular application to experience"; and second, there is the a priori truth applied to the given, which represents "the predetermined principles of interpretation, the criteria of our distinguishing and relating, of classification, and hence the criteria of reality of any sort." Both of these ways of fixing the truth, either independent of or in advance of experience, represents "the explication or elaboration of the concept itself." The a priori, then, is simply "*definitive or analytic in its nature.*"[48]

Lewis's a priori is not something transcendent. It arises out of our everyday attempts to make sense of the world we inhabit. It is "a truth about our own interpretative attitude" and thus "imposes no limitation upon the future possibilities of experience." The a priori "represents the contribution of the mind itself to knowledge," but Lewis does not require that "this mind be universal, absolute, or a reality of a higher order than the object of its knowledge." His a priori is "knowable simply through the reflective and critical formulation of our own principles of classification and interpretation." This means that even though the a priori "may be known in advance to hold good for all experience," it also has alternatives. As we reflect critically upon our experience and behavior, we may reformulate the concepts with which we address reality. The process of reformulation may give rise to a new a priori, which would guide future action. It is not that the old a priori was false, but that it is abandoned in favor of a new, more appropriate and workable one. The alteration of the a priori comes as a result of pragmatic considerations. Building on our fundamental likenesses, the human community through cooperation develops categories that reflect the changing needs of that community. Just as we modify our behavior to meet our needs, so too, we modify the categories which shape our behavior.[49]

The alterability of the a priori on pragmatic grounds has particular application in the sciences. Both general and scientific "concepts and principles of interpretation are subject to historical alteration and in terms of them there may be 'new truth'." This does not mean that the new truth contradicts the old truth. New tools of inquiry, new empirical discoveries may compel an alteration of the categories of analysis, but "when this happens *the truth remains unaltered and new truth and old truth do not contradict.* Categories and concepts do not literally change; they are simply given up and replaced by new ones." Arguing along lines later developed by Thomas Kuhn, Lewis pointed out that the Copernican revolution was a good example of the phenomena by which new technologies and new empirical data force a reinterpretation. The new Copernican truth did not falsify the old Ptolemaic truth but replaced it, because for some purposes the Copernican truth worked better. The pragmatic element, for Lewis, meant that concepts and categories are responsive to changing human needs, and since they are products of the mind, they can be altered to accommodate new experience or new data. The choice between conceptual schemes is the pragmatic one of determining what works better in serving particular human needs and interests. These changes in interpretation produce new truth "whose newness represents the creative power of human thought and the ruling consideration of human purpose." In the interpretation which he offered here, Lewis maintained the absoluteness of both the abstract concepts and of brute experience. "It is between these two, in the choice of conceptual system for application and in the assigning of sensuous denotation to the abstract concept, that there is a pragmatic element in truth and knowledge." Our unceasing efforts to understand and control nature are thus played out in "this middle ground of trial and error, of expanding experience and the continual shift and modification of conception in our effort to cope with it."[50]

The relationship of the a priori categories and the given experience as outlined by Lewis gave rise to the problem of the probability of knowledge. If even simple statements about empirical fact imply some absolute a priori category, and if verification can only be partial with complete verification remaining unalterably out of reach, then *"all interpretation of particulars and all knowledge of objects is probable only,* however high the degree of its probability." Lewis conceded that "knowledge—the knowledge of empirical particulars at least—never *is* completely verified."[51] In part, the problem is resolved by the existence in knowledge of the a priori element, which is certain. "The determination of the criteria of reality, in its various categories, and of principles of interpretation, antecedent to particular experience, is purely analytic" and is, thus, certain truth. These categories, though useful and necessary, function on a very high level, and most of us are forced to rely on "more lowly knowledge of probabilities based on generalities which have their known exceptions." If we did not, "we should most of us be dead within the week." Even in the more exacting realms of science, the probability of knowledge lends a certain appeal to the enterprise: "There is just about enough chance that our trusted generalizations may be false to make the pursuit of science pleasantly exciting. What a dull business life would be if *everything* we ventured to act upon should turn out true!"[52]

Lewis introduced two considerations to help overcome the difficulty of the probability of knowledge. First, he pointed out that even when "a 'law' having a high degree of probability" is abandoned, it may remain useful and valid in many cases: "the practical use made of laws which are superseded may, and often does, stand as still justified." Second, he argued that pragmatic considerations determined how and to what extent probable justifications can serve as the basis for practical action. Lewis did not require that the probable be true in the majority of cases or that there be no limiting exceptions. Rather, "reflection will reveal that what is requisite to its justification as a practical attitude is that action in accordance with probabilities must *in general* be more successful than action which ignores them." This argument requires, as Lewis acknowledged, that "the world be such that probabilities *in general* are justified by the future—that the world is 'orderly'."[53]

In taking up the notion of an orderly world and in attempting to justify it, Lewis accepted the idea that our conception of this order can itself never be certain. There was always the possibility of mistakes, but what was necessary for empirical knowledge to be valid was the genuine probability of connections between the sensuous experience of the given and the concepts which interpret it. "In general, there must be the possibility of arguing from past to future; not with certainty, but with probability." It follows that "it is reality, not experience, which must be orderly." As we collectively construct our common reality "what we do is to look for *some* order of a certain general type and, if we do not find that, to look for some *other*." According to Lewis, it is not necessary to develop some sense of total order; "not order 'through and through' but *some* order is what is requisite to intelligibility." This limited sense of order then becomes a "regulative principle" which directs our search for more comprehensive conceptions of order: "A certain minimal order is prescribed a priori in the recognition of the real. It is a regulative maxim of reason to seek further uniformities which may be stated in principles finally of maximal comprehensiveness and simplicity. But there neither is nor can be any prescription of the specific type of uniformity or correlation which is demanded in this interest of intelligibility."[54]

Lewis's conceptual pragmatism was an attempt to develop a theory of knowledge based on the cooperative community of humans and on their particular like-minded qualities and pragmatic self-interest. He began with the likelihood that our common responses to the given and the communal development of ideas enable us to understand our world and to shape it in our own interests. The concepts which arise out of experience eventually give rise to a priori categories, which in turn direct our future interactions with and interpretations of the given. Knowledge becomes a process in which absolute a priori categories are developed only to be abandoned or altered as the result of new experience and of the pragmatic effort to make sense of that experience. Truth, for Lewis, is only probable, but that probability allows us to deal with the day-to-day world, to expand the boundaries of science, and to order our reality. Our sense of order may be only probable, but it is not capricious. It is worked out cooperatively through pragmatic experience which continually seeks a closer fit between the experienced given and the conceived order, whether we are talking about common experience or science. Whatever changes await us, "the mind will always be capable of discovering that order which is requisite to knowledge, because a mind such as ours, set down in any chaos that can be conjured up, would proceed to elicit significance by abstraction, analysis and organization, to introduce order by conceptual classification and categorial delimitation of the real, and would, through learning from accumulated experience, anticipate the future in ways which increasingly satisfy its practical intent."[55]

Throughout the 1920s, John Dewey, like Lewis, refused to be pushed to either extreme in the debate between science and philosophy. Following his effort to bring about reconstruction in philosophy, Dewey's major works of the decade, *Experience and Nature* (1925) and *The Quest for Certainty* (1929), sought to understand the split between science and philosophy and to comprehend its implications for philosophy. Building on themes developed earlier, he continued to insist that scientific method was a key to any philosophic achievement. Knowing was a process, not a static assemblage of facts, and the scientific method of hypothesis, test, and validation offered the surest results. The purpose of knowing was control, particularly control over human nature and over social and cultural problems which had proven resistant to previous efforts.[56]

Dewey traced the triumph of science and the break between science and philosophy to the scientific revolution of the seventeenth century. The methods of science gave certain knowledge in the realm of nature. The scientists originally found it difficult to carry out their studies, and partly in defense created specialized and technical disciplines set apart from the broader concerns of religion or philosophy. As Dewey observed, "'Science', meaning physical knowledge, became a kind of sanctuary. A religious atmosphere, not to say an idolatrous one, was created. 'Science' was set apart; its findings were supposed to have a privileged relation to the real." Philosophers tried to maintain "a superior form of knowledge" by taking "an invidious and so to say malicious attitude toward the conclusions of natural science." Before long, the rivalry between competing claims of knowledge became "converted in effect into a rivalry between the spiritual values guaranteed by the older philosophic tradition and the conclusions of natural knowledge." The separation of philosophy and science had, by the early twentieth century, produced "a genuine cultural crisis." Dewey urged philosophers to confront the crisis directly, rather than continuing the futile exercise of trying to reconcile the realities of science with the ultimate and the ideal.[57]

The method of science, rather than the results of the particular sciences, had the most serious implications for philosophy. Science, or "systematized knowledge, exists in practice for the sake of stimulating, guiding and checking further inquiries." Practically speaking, "knowledge is an affair of *making* sure, not of grasping antecedently given sureties." The method of science starts with a hypothesis, with an opinion. Opinion, as Dewey wished to use it, is more than an "unwarranted surmise"; it is "an occasion of new observations, an instigator of research, an indispensable organ in deliberate discovery."[58] From that beginning, experimental inquiry exhibits three key traits. First, all experimentation, Dewey wrote, "involves *overt* doing, the making of definite changes in the environment or in our relation to it." Second, inquiry is not random, but is focused on meeting the needs of a particular problem. Third, "the outcome of directed activity is the construction of a new empirical situation in which the objects are differently related to one another, and such that the *consequences* of directed operations form the objects that have the property of being *known*." Certainty is no longer a property of "fixed objects with fixed characters." With science, "the quest for certainty becomes the search for methods of control; that is, regulation of conditions of change with respect to their consequences."[59]

The methods of science could and should be applied in philosophy, but some philosophers, Dewey felt, used science inappropriately. It was a mistake simply to borrow "from various sources the conclusions of special analyses, particularly of some ruling science of the day" and to insert them unaltered into philosophy. The problem with using the results of science in this fashion is that "these results are not employed to reveal new subject-matters and illuminate old ones of gross experience." Such a procedure tends to generate "artificial problems" rather than to solve real ones. If the empirical method does not guarantee success, it does increase the probability that the problems it addresses are significant and that the provisional solutions it develops are directly related to experience and not artificial. Philosophers who adopt the empirical method procure "for philosophic reflection something of that cooperative tendency toward consensus which marks inquiry in the natural sciences."[60] In addition, they are no longer setting themselves up as rivals to the sciences in claiming a more ultimate knowledge than that of the scientists.

If philosophers could not successfully compete with scientists at their own game, then what was their proper role in the modern world? Philosophers who abandoned their "guardianship of fixed realities, values and ideals, would find a new career." They could turn their attention to uncovering the meaning of science " in terms of the great human uses to which it may be put, its meaning in the service of possibilities of secure value." Dewey believed that "the search for values to be secured and shared by all, because buttressed in the foundations of social life" would be a "vocation of greater vitality" than the traditional "search for absolute and immutable reality." Philosophy so conceived would be no rival of science. Rather, it would serve the crucial function as "a liaison officer between the conclusions of science and the modes of social and personal action through which attainable possibilities are projected and striven for." In an age of "over-specialization and division of interests" philosophy could thus serve as "a generalized medium of intercommunication, of mutual criticism through all-around translation from one separated region of experience into another."[61]

This reconceived philosophy would have a role to play as a critic, with "a wide field of criticism before it." Its "critical mind would be directed against the domination exercised by prejudice, narrow interest, routine custom and the authority which issues from institutions." But this critical function would only be a prelude to "the creative work of the imagination" in discovering new possibilities inherent in the results of science and in proposing ways in which they might be employed to alleviate the ills of mankind. If the "ideal of a complete integration of knowledge" was no longer tenable, Dewey still felt "the need for integration of the specialized results of science." Philosophy, he believed, "should contribute to the satisfaction of the need." This need was not, however, "intrinsic to science itself." Rather, "the direction of action in large social fields" required some "unification of scientific conclusions." All too often, dogmatism, prejudice and ignorance still determined action in these fields. The new office of philosophy, as Dewey envisioned it, would overcome obstructions, criticize destructive habits, direct attention to present needs, and "interpret the conclusions of science with respect to their consequences for our beliefs about purposes and values in all phases of life."[62] Philosophy so conceived would take the best from the new science and from the older tradition of philosophy. It would bring together the knowledge and control made possible through scientific method with the heritage of value and tradition that has arisen out of human needs.

In Dewey's mature view, philosophy was to adopt the method of science without actually becoming a specialized science. The empirical method of hypothesis, test, and validation developed in the sciences offered the surest knowledge of the world and of knowledge responsive to rapid change. Dewey repeatedly urged philosophers to adopt the empirical method in their own studies. Their studies, however, were not properly the narrow inquiries of a specialized science. Human and social needs and the values arising out of them were the central objects of philosophical inquiry. The scientist was little concerned with these larger issues, whereas they were the key issues for the philosopher. Philosophers were to bring the empirical method to bear upon them and in that fashion serve as a "liaison officer" between the knowledge of the physical world discovered by science and the values and needs of human beings living and dying in that world. Philosophers, thus, were to take up the methods of the sciences without abandoning the broader outlook and interests which had long characterized their study.

The major works of C. I. Lewis and John Dewey from the 1920s suggest a resolution of the tension between science and philosophy that had characterized the preceding decades. Both men saw the two approaches to knowledge as complementary and cooperative, and as necessary to understand the given and to exercise some control over our futures. For both men, in varying ways, the needs and values of the community pragmatically shaped our response to the given and our construction of an ordered reality. Dewey of course put more emphasis on the practical aspects of active social reconstruction, but that concept was at least implicit in Lewis's thought. Science and philosophy were cooperative partners in the pragmatic construction of an ordered reality capable of directing our day-to-day lives.

Not all philosophers were as sanguine about the cooperative endeavor of science and philosophy as Dewey and Lewis. Some, like Creighton, Durant, and Schilpp sought to continue in the traditional manner, emphasizing vision and viewing philosophy as providing some individualized glimpse into the ultimately real. Others, like Lovejoy, pursued their technical and specialized inquiries in logic, epistemology, or history, with little reference to the broader cultural or philosophical implications. Significantly, the practitioners of a wide variety of philosophical outlooks and practices found relatively secure homes in the profession and in the universities. Increasingly, the profession viewed each philosopher as a specialist of one sort or another—as a logician, epistemologist, metaphysician, or historian. The discipline had largely abandoned the generalist outlook and approach of the moral philosopher and had replaced it with the image of an academic specialist under the broad umbrella of "philosopher."

If, as Bruce Kuklick has argued, philosophy had superseded theology in the nineteenth century, then science was superseding philosophy in the twentieth.[63] Just as philosophy did not totally supplant theology, so science by 1930 had not totally replaced philosophy. But the values and methods of science had become so much a part of philosophy that the discipline had been largely transformed over the previous seventy years. The generalist had been replaced by the specialist, the moralist by the academic professional. Where one generalist had worn the many hats of the moral philosopher, there was now a department of diverse specialized professionals. We have seen the struggle which accompanied this transformation; there remains only some assessment of the achievements and the costs.

N I N E

Conclusion

In 1930 Macmillan published two volumes of essays, *Contemporary American Philosophy*, by thirty-four prominent philosophers. The contributors summarized their philosophical positions and the processes by which they had achieved their mature views. Almost without exception, these thirty-three men and one woman (Mary Whiton Calkins) testified to the impact science had had on the development of their thought. It is not surprising that some philosophers celebrated the liberating and enriching influence of science, but even most of those who thought the rise of science had been deleterious acknowledged its power and appeal. Like it or not, science was ubiquitous, and philosophers had been forced to come to terms with it.

For some of those who had begun their study of philosophy around the turn of the century, science had opened new and stimulating vistas. W. P. Montague recalled that "science was discovering most exciting things." As a result, philosophy must now "acquaint itself with the new truths and exploit whatever speculative possibilities they contained." Montague and his colleagues among the new realists had consciously set out to "introduce into philosophy the two methods that had been so profitably employed in science: the method of cooperative work and the method of isolating problems and tackling them one by one." E. B. McGilvary, like Montague, remained convinced that "if ever we are to have an even partially satisfactory philosophy, we shall get it only by the use of scientific methods." The philosopher's task, as McGilvary saw it, was to integrate the interpretations of the special sciences. He hoped to contribute some small part to the solution of problems and perhaps, to the "ultimate reckoning," if there be such a thing. McGilvary recommended keeping philosophy within "very narrow limits," for no one person could "attempt a wholesale integration." This change in philosophical practice would require different and more scientific training. McGilvary regretted his own inadequate training in "the higher mathematics and in mathematical physics," for he believed "the metaphysics of the next generation . . . will be in the hands of those who have a command of a knowledge of mathematical physics." Both Montague and McGilvary would have been sympathetic to J. E. Boodin's comment that "in the main, twentieth-century science has furnished the content of my philosophy."[1]

Even those who were more restrained in their enthusiasm for science still recognized the significant ways in which it had altered their thinking. C. J. Ducasse, for example, rejected the notion that philosophy was simply a more generalized science. For him, the essential difference between science and philosophy lay in "subject-matter": "The subject-matter which philosophy alone studies, and which seems to me its only proper subject-matter, is values." But if philosophy's subject matter was radically different from that of science, Ducasse believed that philosophy "in respect of method . . . is, or rather should be, like science." Both philosophers and scientists seek knowledge, and there is "only one trustworthy road to knowledge in whatever field, the road, namely, called Scientific Method." Like Ducasse, George P. Adams acknowledged the seductiveness of science, but he retained his conviction that philosophy had tasks which set it apart from both science and from "practical life." Because philosophy is "the desire for, and the love of, knowledge," philosophers are understandably tempted by scientific methods. Philosophy, however, is not fundamentally concerned with objective facts and description, but with "the desire to reach intellectual clarity with respect to just those meanings and values whose nature seems to preclude them from the domain of what can be known and understood." Philosophy is not science, but neither is it art or religion, poetry or life. Adams conceived philosophy as an inquiry into "meanings embedded within experience which require reflection and theory for their apprehension and clarification."[2] Ducasse more than Adams accepted scientific methods in philosophy, but both men acknowledged that the rise of science had posed new problems and paradoxes for philosophy. For them, these problems and difficulties allowed no easy solution; they would neither make philosophy more scientific nor deny the influence of science.

The philosophers who reflected on their recent past in *Contemporary American Philosophy* also included several men who felt that the influence of science had been profoundly destructive of philosophy. Most graphically,

Wilbur M. Urban spoke of suffering the "evil fortune" of having begun his philosophical study during "the most unphilosophical atmosphere the world has ever seen—that period of scientific positivism that began about 1850 and lasted on into the twentieth century." As a student in "the anti-metaphysical atmosphere" of the late 1890s, Urban had felt "it to be almost a sacred duty to suppress all the spiritual initiatives, all the natural metaphysics of the human soul, and the intellectual and moral scars left by these inhibitions will probably never be completely removed." Not all philosophers opposed to the influence of science bore such obvious wounds. Some, like Hartley B. Alexander, seem to have developed their philosophies with little concern for the rise of science. Alexander celebrated philosophy as "the Great Art" whose touchstone was "aesthetic understanding." Philosophy properly begins in "wonder" at "the miracle which each man knows himself to be and knows his world to be." The philosopher ultimately discovers truth in the parable that is each person's existence.[3] For Urban and Alexander, science was something to be overcome or to be ignored in the pursuit of more elemental truth.

In testifying to the impact of science on their thought, these philosophers reflected the diversity within the profession in 1930. Despite the pressures of science, the leaders in the field had developed their own individual visions of philosophy. If most felt the influence of science, only a few recalled trying to transform philosophy into a science. Nonetheless, the impact was clear. Science had affected both the development of their ideas and the intellectual and social matrix within which they worked.

These philosophers represented an aging generation. Most of them had been educated in the late nineteenth century and had begun to write and teach no later than the first decade of the twentieth century. Their views of philosophy, of science, and of the idea of community had been shaped by the debates discussed in the preceding chapters. Although several of them, such as John Dewey, Arthur O. Lovejoy, and R. W. Sellars, would remain active into the 1950s, mainstream American philosophy was on the verge of a major shift inspired by new developments in continental and English philosophy.

Logical positivism was the first of the European movements to have a significant impact on American philosophy. It grew out of the work of a group of scientists and philosophers in Vienna who wanted to combine an empiricism modelled on that of Ernst Mach with a greater understanding and sensitivity to mathematics, logic, and theoretical physics. Scientists were key figures in the Vienna Circle, and scientific and mathematical concerns dominated their philosophical thinking. Scientist-philosophers such as Moritz Schlick, Rudolf Carnap, and Herbert Feigl and mathematicians such as Kurt Gödel believed that "all knowledge could be accounted for, without resort to metaphysics, from the perspective of the scientific world-view." Unlike Mach, who they believed had underestimated the role of mathematics and logic in science, the logical positivists wanted "to depict knowledge in a way that did full justice to its empirical and logical components."[4]

The impact of logical positivism began to be felt in the United States in the 1930s, first through essays describing and advocating the new approach and later in the decade through the direct influence of emigres such as Carnap, Feigl, and Hans Reichenbach. In 1936, for example, two reports on logical positivism appeared in the *Journal of Philosophy*. Hans Reichenbach, a Berlin associate of the Vienna Circle, argued that what characterized the group was not a "philosophical 'system'," but a community of working methods—an agreement to treat philosophical problems as scientific problems whose answers are capable of soliciting universal assent." He was confident that this "common working program" distinguished the group from "philosophical sects" and made "possible progress in research." Ernest Nagel, a young American philosopher, reported on his impressions and appraisals of the developments in Europe and England. He noted the positivists' impatience with philosophical systems and their "preoccupation . . . with philosophy as *analysis . . .* with *clarifying* its meaning and implications." In his visits with the logical positivists he found a combination of "green pastures for intellectual analysis" and "a terribly serious adventure" which aimed "to make as clear as possible what it is we really know."[5]

After World War II logical positivism in the United States merged with the analytic and linguistic philosophy originating at Oxford and Cambridge. The movement was diverse, and, as Richard Bernstein has noted, defies "any attempt to state precise criteria or common underlying presuppositions." Still, he argues that central to their project was "a dominant concern with language and a commitment to the belief that the investigation of linguistic issues is the best way of clarifying, resolving, and dissolving philosophic perplexities."[6] Even though the analytic philosophers' commitment to a technical, rigorous, and scientifically oriented philosophy was shared by at least some American philosophers of preceding generations, the work of Peirce, Dewey, James, and the others tended to be viewed as "insufficiently rigorous," as something to be overcome, if not largely ignored. Thus, a native, American tradition based in pragmatism was eclipsed by these European philosophies in the years following the war.[7]

If the "linguistic turn" in philosophy largely ignored the philosophers of the classic period of American philosophy, the more recent "pragmatic turn" has again brought them under serious and sustained consideration. Central to this reevaluation of the pragmatists have been the themes discussed here—the fallibility of knowledge, even scientific knowledge, and the importance of community in establishing warranted belief. What James Kloppenberg has described as the victory of uncertainty has become even more evident at the end of the twentieth century, and contemporary philosophers have rediscovered the pragmatists as historical participants in the continuing discourse regarding the proper role and task of philosophy.[8]

The pragmatic turn of recent philosophy has had wide ramifications, and the implications of the renaissance of the pragmatists are still being worked out. Without writing another volume, I can not explore the many ways in which the pragmatic conceptions of science and of community are developed in contemporary philosophy. Instead, by looking briefly at selected recent works of Richard Bernstein, Hilary Putnam, and Richard Rorty, I want to suggest the diverse ways in which these philosophers have found some of the pragmatic conceptions explored in previous chapters relevant to contemporary philosophical thought.

For example, Richard Bernstein in *Praxis and Action* examined philosophies of human activity as developed in Marxism, existentialism, pragmatism, and analytic philosophy. He devoted the third part of his study to Peirce and Dewey: Peirce because he "most systematically and rigorously developed a logical understanding of the nature of action and conduct," and Dewey for his focus on "the social implications of the pragmatic understanding of action."[9] He found in the work of both men concepts essential to the contemporary discussion of praxis and action.

Peirce's theory of knowledge is central to Bernstein's reading of his thought. Bernstein noted that throughout his career Peirce "refined and modified" a "view of inquiry as a self-corrective process which has no absolute beginning or end points and in which any claim is subject to further rational criticism, although we cannot question all claims at once." Any claims to knowledge, for Peirce, are legitimized by "the norms and rules of inquiry itself," although these rules are themselves subject to rational criticism. All knowledge, thus, is fallible, for "every knowledge claim is part of a system of signs that is open to further interpretation and has consequences that are to be publicly tested and confirmed." All inquiry, as well as all claims to knowledge based on it, is social and involves the notion of community.[10]

Bernstein argued that the "conception of rationality as self-controlled conduct" lies at "the heart of Peirce's philosophy." Man is not only a knower and inquirer; he can also "control his habits." We can thus shape and modify our conduct under appropriate conditions. Bernstein found that at the center of this idea of self-control is Peirce's "commitment to the growth of concrete reasonableness as the *summum bonum.*" Despite problems with Peirce's theory of the self, Bernstein found his notion of the growth of concrete reasonableness to be grounds for hope in providing a warrant for rational action. We can aid this process by striving to establish a "free, open, self-critical community of inquirers" modelled on Peirce's ideal and by adhering to Peirce's cardinal rule: "Do not block the road to inquiry!" Bernstein concluded that "Peirce's theory of inquiry stands as one of the great attempts to show how the classic dichotomies between though and action, or theory and *praxis* can be united in a theory of a community of inquirers committed to continuous, rational, self-critical activity."[11]

In addition to Peirce, Bernstein also took inspiration from the work of John Dewey. While he found striking differences between the two pragmatists, Bernstein also discerned "a convergence of point of view." Peirce emphasized logic, based his conception of inquiry on his knowledge of and participation in the sciences of his day, and was skeptical of involving philosophical or scientific inquiry in contemporary social and political issues. Dewey, on the other hand, had little of Peirce's intimate knowledge of the sciences, "lacked Peirce's creative logical genius," and "advocated a conception of philosophy in which it would become a form of social criticism." Bernstein believes that their rival conceptions of pragmatism are, when put together, fruitful. If "Peirce supplied the intellectual backbone to pragmatism," it was Dewey who "perceived the ways in which Peirce's ideal of a self-critical community of inquirers had important consequences for education, social reconstruction, and a revitalization of democracy." Central to the philosophy of both men was "the theory of inquiry as a continuous self-corrective process."[12]

Dewey's primary goal, in Bernstein's view, was "to bring the problems and procedures of our moral and social life into closer harmony with the dramatic advances made in experimental scientific inquiry." One way to get at Dewey's approach to philosophy is to examine his metaphors and analogies. Bernstein found Dewey abandoning the post-Cartesian metaphor of "the fixed 'mental eye' " in favor of the "esthetic analogy of the craftsman or artist involved in doing and making." Dewey pictured the craftsman creating his art through long experience of "tried and tested procedures," rather than in conformity to some ideal. The art of experimental knowing is thus a process of "conscious directed manipulation of objects and situations." We reconstruct our world through "continuous interaction" with it.[13]

Bernstein argued that we have important lessons to relearn from the pragmatists' emphasis "on inquiry as a self-corrective rational process, their insistence on fallibilism, and their general suspicion of ontological, epistemological, and even linguistic dichotomies." Most significant for this study is Bernstein's contention that following the pragmatists means abandoning the attempt to delineate sharply between science and philosophy. Dewey and Peirce have taught us that we "can recognize the differences" between science and philosophy "without reifying the dichotomies and that the relation of philosophy and science is and ought to be dialectical." While all philosophic claims are subject to modification as a result of scientific inquiry, philosophy is not limited to responding to the developments of science. Philosophers have "the perennially important task of clarifying what we know and what we do not know, of articulating the present landscape of human knowledge and providing us with a way of 'knowing our way about'."[14]

Bernstein also underlined the importance of the theme of a community of inquiry in pragmatic and contemporary thought. Peirce and Dewey were sensitive to the nature and importance of scientific inquiry. Pragmatism celebrated the "'experimental spirit' of science" and viewed it as "inquiry, as a perpetual, critical, and self-corrective process." It envisioned the individual as a "craftsman" whose practice and activity were "informed by reason and intelligence" in setting about reconstructing the world. This reconceptualization of the individual had a central social feature, for it took place in a community of inquiry. The pragmatist idea of community, Bernstein concluded, has important implications for us today. "If such a community is to be approximated, then it requires that we develop in ourselves and others those critical habits and modes of rational conduct by which we can advance concrete reasonableness." If we take the pragmatists seriously, we will purge "ourselves of the quest for absolute certainty in our intellectual and moral lives." And that, Bernstein believes, will unblock the road to inquiry and enable us to "secure and warrant our knowledge claims."[15]

Bernstein pointed to several important features of the recent recovery of pragmatism, features which suggest the continuing relevance of the turn-of-the-century philosophers' attempt to come to terms with science. His emphasis on the fallibility of inquiry, including scientific inquiry, his argument that belief can, nonetheless, be warranted, and his stress on the centrality of community all recall major features of the pragmatic voice in the turn-of-the-century debates. What seemed a striking departure from philosophic practice nearly a century ago, Bernstein treated as commonplace today. In his more recent volume, *Beyond Objectivism and Relativism*, Bernstein took up the implications of "postempiricist philosophy and history of science" to show how radically our conceptions of rationality and of inquiry have been modified by such developments as Peirce's notion of fallibilism and Thomas Kuhn's theory of incommensurability. Throughout the book, Bernstein returned to a "major theme": "the reclamation and clarification of the interrelated concepts and experiences of dialogue, debate, conversation, and communication." Peirce and Dewey are among those whose ideas are reclaimed. Bernstein did not engage in sustained analysis of the pragmatists in this volume, for his focus is on his contemporary colleagues in their collective search to establish a dialogical community in which traditional dichotomies can be overcome and belief and knowledge can be warranted, if not grounded. Peirce, in particular, is treated as the originator of the development of post-Cartesian philosophy with its emphasis on the fallibility of knowledge and the importance of the community to the assessment of the results of inquiry.[16]

Bernstein concluded that, despite the significant differences marking the thought of Hans-Georg Gadamer, Jürgen Habermas, Hannah Arendt, and Richard Rorty, there is a central focus on the themes of "dialogue, conversation, undistorted communication, communal judgment, and the type of rational wooing that can take place when individuals confront each other as equals and participants." He saw them all seeking "some common ground to reconcile differences through debate, conversation, and dialogue." Bernstein did not minimize the difficulties in attaining meaningful dialogue, but he interpreted these contemporary philosophers as each "attempting to foster and nurture those forms of communal life" in which such a conversation or dialogue can take place. We will get beyond the dichotomies of objectivism and relativism only if we "dedicate ourselves to the practical task of furthering the type of solidarity, participation, and mutual recognition that is founded in dialogical communities."[17]

For Bernstein, Peirce and to a lesser extent Dewey represent the beginnings of significant chains of argumentation. Peirce's challenge to the Cartesian framework for knowledge, his emphasis on communal inquiry, and his arguments on behalf of fallibilism have given rise to a body of thought that has sought to come to terms with uncertainty and to overcome increasingly sterile dichotomies. Dewey remains important for Bernstein because, more clearly than Peirce, he thought it imperative that philosophy and philosophers be deeply engaged in interaction with and reconstruction of the social and political communities of which they are members. For Dewey, as for Bernstein, it is not enough to reconstruct philosophy or science; we have an obligation to be engaged in our world and to attempt to make it a better place through the exercise of rational intelligence. In the dialogue that will reshape our world, Peirce and Dewey remain significant historical participants.

Like Bernstein, Hilary Putnam, in *Reason, Truth, and History,* sought to "break the strangle hold which a number of dichotomies appear to have on the thinking of both philosophers and laymen." Among the dichotomies he attacked are those between objective and subjective, between fact and value, and between "ahistorical unchanging canons of rationality" and "cultural relativism." He argued that these distinctions, while they may be culturally based, are no longer fruitful ways of viewing the world or of our interaction with it. The poles of these dichotomies are arbitrary and false; we can no longer draw such sharp and neat distinctions. His characterization of the fact-value distinction as "hopelessly fuzzy" could apply to the other dichotomies as well. His project here recalls John Dewey's earlier efforts to overcome these and similar dualisms. Both wanted to reject traditional dichotomies while enabling people to have a rational basis for making choices and for constructing the world in which they live. If Dewey's metaphor is that of the craftsman, Putnam's embraces a more reciprocal relationship between us and the world: "The mind and the world jointly make up the mind and the world."[18]

Putnam's Carus lectures, *The Many Faces of Realism*, draw even more clearly on the pragmatists, although not uncritically. At various points Putnam credited James, Dewey, and Peirce with raising relevant points and suggested that the pragmatists may have something new to tell us. Perhaps his clearest reliance on pragmatism in this volume is in his discussion of the importance of the community in establishing the value of equality. Here he drew on Peirce's notions as filtered through the work of Apel and Habermas. He agreed with them that "the notion of a warranted or justified statement involves an implicit reference to a community." A "fully *justified* statement" is one that "can withstand tests and withstand criticism." These considerations led him to conclude that "*if I am a rational person in the sense of having the aim of making statements which are true humanly speaking, i.e., which can withstand rational criticism now and in the future, then I am committed to the idea of a possible community of inquirers.*" And like Peirce, he thinks that this community will have to be infinitely extended if every inquiry is to be subject to criticism and revision. For the community to be truly effective, it must be one in which all members are free to develop hypotheses, to have them taken seriously, and to have their criticisms heard and considered. It must be a community which "respects the principles of intellectual freedom and equality." Otherwise, Peirce's "method of authority" will intrude and undermine the search for truth. Although Putnam disagreed with Apel and Habermas that a universal ethic can be drawn from the conceptualization of communal warrantability, he believed that their arguments "*do* show that our values of equality, intellectual freedom, and rationality, are deeply interconnected: and, consequently, that we have "a rich and multifaceted idea of the good" whose parts are interdependent.[19]

Like Bernstein, then, Putnam treated the pragmatists as participants in the contemporary debate on the nature of science and rationality and on the centrality of community. As Putnam said of James, "if we allow that William

James might have had something 'new' to say—something new to *us*, not just new to his own time," and if James and his successors have not completely worked out a new more appropriate program for philosophy, then "there is still something new, something *unfinished and important* to say about reality and truth."[20] Putnam, in part by looking back at his pragmatic predecessors, engaged in the dialogue and contributes to this unfinished communal project.

The dialogue is not restricted to American philosophers, as Putnam's references to Habermas and Apel suggest. For example, Karl-Otto Apel has played a major role in the rediscovery of Peirce and the other pragmatists by continental philosophers. But his own encounter with Peirce has been one of discovery. He began by wanting to present Peirce to a German audience through an edition of Peirce's writings, but as he "entered more deeply into Peirce's philosophy, this historical conception receded into the background." As he thought through and beyond Peirce, Apel came to realize that Peirce had become "important for me primarily as an ally in the systematic undertaking of a 'transformation of (transcendental) philosophy'." Peirce is not Apel's only historical ally; Joseph Royce's conception of an interpretive community has helped Apel to overcome several of the shortcomings of Peirce's philosophy.[21] Both of the Americans, as Apel sees them, are signifiant not only as historical figures, but also as philosophers with contemporary relevance.

Apel's reliance on Peirce and Royce as allies in his proposed transformation of transcendental philosophy is clearest in his essay "Scientism or Transcendental Hermeneutics?" Apel wanted to develop an alternative to scientism, which he defined as the reduction of "the human subject of science to an object of science. For scientism, a pragmatically orientated philosophy of science is a social science of science as behaviour." Where scientism requires the "behavioristic reduction of the subject of science," Apel proposed to substitute a "transcendental hermeneutics" in which "the subject of cognition not only experiences what is other than himself—as a world that is describable and explicable externally—but also experience himself in reflexive contemplation and in the other." This alternative, Apel argued, must situate itself in the "objective idealist tradition of the hermeneutic human sciences." It is at this point that the work of Peirce and Royce becomes especially relevant.[22]

For all of the contemporary philosophers discussed above, the recovery of pragmatism has facilitated their reconceptualization of knowledge as warranted belief achieved through communal consensus. Bernstein, Putnam, and Apel, each in his own way, wants philosophy and philosophers to get beyond the twentieth-century hope of grounding our knowledge of the world in something certain, whether that be the methods of science as advocated by Lovejoy or the analysis of language developed in analytic philosophy. If their post-Cartesian, postanalytic project becomes a reality, philosophy and philosophic practice will undoubtedly be transformed. However, there is still a measure of the traditional hope in their project; it is just that they now believe that we will have to settle for knowledge that is less certain than philosophers had sought for most of this century. The consensus of the competent community, after all, does provide a kind of provisional certainty within specified contexts and the means for understanding the ways in which today's consensus may be transformed into tomorrow's. The task of the philosopher remains what it has been for some time, to provide a rational basis for understanding what we can know and how we can know it in the light of contemporary science.

Richard Rorty has been advocating a more radical transformation of philosophy. He has argued that it is time to accept the end of philosophy as it has traditionally been conceived and to have philosophers participate in the conversation of the West as simply another voice. He wants to free philosophers from the task of trying to discover a "permanent framework for inquiry" and from the "notion that philosophy can explain what science leaves unexplained." Philosophers, Rorty urges, should abandon epistemology for edification; they should "help their readers, or society as a whole, break free from outworn vocabularies and attitudes, rather than to provide 'grounding' for the institutions and customs of the present."[23] Although his goal is quite different from those of the philosophers already discussed, Rorty does share one characteristic with them: a rediscovery of the pragmatists, particularly James and Dewey.

James is one of Rorty's heroes on the margins of mainstream philosophy, but it is John Dewey who, along with Heidegger and Wittgenstein, provides him with the model of edification he urges upon his colleagues. He finds Dewey, Heidegger, and Wittgenstein valuable mentors because each in his own way overcame his early commitment to making philosophy foundational and to developing a representational theory of knowledge. As these philosophers matured, Rorty sees them abandoning this mainstream goal of philosophers to make their later work "therapeutic rather than constructive, edifying rather than systematic, designed to make the reader question his own motives for philosophizing rather than to supply him with a new philosophical program." All three wanted to "set aside" the representational theory of knowledge and to abandon epistemology and metaphysics as the characteristic disciplines of philosophy. Their vision of philosophy is revolutionary, in the Kuhnian sense, for it would mean new vocabularies, new paradigms, new philosophies incommensurate with the Kantian task of grounding knowledge.[24]

In his presidential address to the American Philosophical Association, Rorty celebrated the attempts of James and Dewey to overcome the "Kantian epistemological tradition." In that effort, he believes, they also broke with Peirce, whom Rorty sees as "the most Kantian of thinkers." Rorty found James and Dewey especially valuable because they wrote "in a spirit of social hope." They wanted to liberate civilization by "giving up the notion of 'grounding' our culture, our moral lives, our politics, our religious beliefs, upon 'philosophical bases'." But unlike Nietzsche and Heidegger, they "did not make the mistake of turning against the community which takes the natural scientist as its moral hero—the community of secular intellectuals." Rorty recognized that James and Dewey were not simply prophets, that they did have significant things to say about the traditional problems of philosophy, but he also believes that they did not offer new theories to replace the old; James and Dewey thought we could and must get along without such theories.[25]

In his interpretation of pragmatism without Peirce, Rorty focuses on three characteristics of James's and Dewey's thought. First, their pragmatism is "simply anti-essentialism when applied to notions like 'truth', 'knowledge', 'language', 'morality', and similar objects of philosophical theorizing." Second, Rorty characterizes them as holding that there is "no epistemological difference between truth about what ought to be and truth about what is, nor any metaphysical difference between facts and values, nor any methodological difference between morality and science." This implies that "the pattern of all inquiry—scientific as well as moral—is deliberation concerning the relative attractions of various concrete alternatives." Third, Rorty describes pragmatists as holding "the doctrine that there are no constraints on inquiry save conversational ones—no wholesale constraints derived from the nature of the objects, or of the mind, or of language, but only those retail constraints provided by the remarks of our fellow-inquirers."[26]

It is in this third characterization of pragmatism that Rorty discovers the social hope which typifies the thought of James and Dewey. This characterization makes clear, he believes, our necessity to choose between "accepting the contingent character of starting-points, and attempting to evade this contingency." There have been many attempts to evade it, from the Platonic to the Christian and the Kantian, but Rorty believes that accepting the contingency instead of seeking certainty gives us "a renewed sense of community." The pragmatists envisioned a community that was "*ours* rather than *nature's*, *shaped* rather than *found*, one among many which men have made." And in a image more Roycean than anything else, Rorty declares that "what matters is our loyalty to other human beings clinging together against the dark, not our hope of getting things right."[22]

Rorty's pragmatism-without-Peirce stresses those themes in James and Dewey that support his goal of getting beyond philosophy as an epistemological project. But even here, his account of Dewey's pragmatism ignores that strain in Dewey which sought to develop a pragmatic metaphysics. As R. W. Sleeper has argued, "What Rorty is missing is Dewey's sense of metaphysics as more a matter of perspective gained than a matter of 'categories' or 'first principles'. Rorty fails to see how both metaphysics *and* epistemology can be valuable instruments for coping with our environment once they have been thoroughly 'naturalized' and positioned once more in the biological and cultural matrices from which they have been removed by the 'tradition'." Dewey, according to Sleeper, tried "to work out a metaphysics of *existence* on the basis of the successes of inquiry already in practice. It would *not* be a 'first philosophy' in anything like the traditional sense. It would not be a metaphysics that dictates to the sciences, but one that learns from them."[28] In this view, Dewey's goal was to pragmatize the traditional task of philosophy—explaining what and how we know—but not to abandon the task as impossible or not worth pursuing.

Rorty, in replying to Sleeper, has acknowledged that his reading of Dewey was based not on a close reading of Dewey's work, but on his discovery that many of the things he wanted to say about the state of philosophy had their origins in Dewey. In his view, developments in analytic philosophy have led us back to Dewey and James, or at least to a particular strain in Dewey and James. He granted that Dewey believed that philosophy had a "constructive task—that its job is not merely to criticize the tradition which runs from Plato to Kant but to put something in its place which will play the same role." But Rorty, of course, did not "think that contemporary culture requires anything to play that role," nor did he believe that Dewey was successful in his attempts to fill that role. Analytic philosophy and Kuhnian history of science, Rorty argued, have made Dewey's faith in scientific method outmoded. Dewey may have suffered from an "inferiority complex" about "laboratory scientists," but we are no longer under the same delusion. Dewey's notions of "scientific method" need to be overcome through the "kind of criticism of contemporary social science found in Habermas and Foucault." Ultimately, Rorty acknowledged that his critics can find in Dewey ideas that point away from the notion of philosophy as edification, but he wanted to "adapt pragmatism to a changed intellectual environment by emphasizing the differences rather than the similarities with the philosophical tradition." This means, for Rorty, substituting for the traditional conception of philosophy "the notion of a seamless web of culture, within which the traditional divisions between art, science, and philosophy have become, if not untenable dualisms, at least impediments to thought." He remained convinced that there are "lots of pointers in the direction of this way of doing things to be found in Dewey."[29]

This exchange on the implications of Dewey's pragmatism suggests an important characteristic of the contemporary revival of pragmatic thought: it is not a single conception of pragmatism that is being rediscovered, but several varieties suited to the needs of contemporary discourse and inquiry. If Lovejoy could find thirteen pragmatisms in 1908, the number has certainly multiplied with these recent interpretations and variations.[30] The important point for this study is not whether Bernstein, Putnam, Apel, and Rorty are fully justified in their respective interpretations of the pragmatists, but rather that they have found Peirce, James, or Dewey significant to their own philosophical projects. Whatever their particular interpretations of pragmatism, these contemporary philosophers, and others, have again included Peirce, James, Dewey, and even Royce, as participants in the community of discourse regarding the characteristics of science, the possibility and nature of knowledge, and the importance of community itself. By once again taking pragmatism seriously, contemporary philosophers have, in some measure, fulfilled Peirce's hope that the community of inquiry investigating these questions will be indefinitely extended. They have also returned American philosophy to its own tradition without chauvinism.

The pragmatic turn in contemporary philosophy has reanimated debates which flourished at the turn of the century. It is not simply the same debate, however, for as Rorty reminds us, the new discussion of these issues is filtered through the lenses of logical positivism, analytical philosophy, and Kuhnian history and philosophy of science. Nor would I want to claim that we have made progress toward a fuller understanding of the task and role of philosophy vis-à-vis science. That, contemporary philosophers seem to agree, is the wrong approach. Our science and our philosophy are not better, only different. They ask different questions, speak in a different vocabulary, devise different answers to the questions, and seek the best judgment of those in a position to judge, rather than universal certainties. But the discourse has not changed so radically that the pragmatists no longer have anything to say; rather, it has changed in ways that make their ideas once again relevant even as they are reinterpreted. The contemporary relevance of the pragmatists suggests that the community of philosophical discourse has a strong historical component, that it is possible in some circumstances to translate the ideas of previous generations into meaningful statements for the present. A key element of the pragmatic test was the future value of an idea. By their own test, the work of the pragmatists has succeeded. It remains to be seen what the future will bring for the neopragmatism of contemporary philosophy.

Science and scientific values transformed philosophy at the end of the nineteenth and beginning of the twentieth century, but not exactly in the way the advocates of the transformation had hoped. Philosophy did not become a science, nor has it become one since. However, the scientific, professional, and specialized milieu which has dominated academic and intellectual life for much of the last one hundred years fostered an alteration in philosophical thought and practice as philosophers sought to retain their central role in education and culture. Although the whole range of philosophical views could still be found in the 1920s and even today, the prevailing scientism has encouraged an emphasis on logic and epistemology. Both were thought to be more susceptible to scientific treatment, and hence were particularly appealing to those who would have philosophers more closely emulate the scientists. These tendencies were enhanced after 1930 when logical positivism and, later, analytic philosophy were taken up by American philosophers. The recent pragmatic and hermeneutic turn against constructing a philosophy rooted in a scientistic conception of reason and knowledge seems to go against the dominant characteristic of philosophy in this century. However, it is based in part on a post-Kuhnian conception of science, so that philosophers are still transforming their discipline in light of science. Only now fallibility, warrantability, and communities of interpretation dominate the discussions instead of positivism, foundationalism, and the search for certainty.[31]

The rise of science a century ago did more than reshape the model of philosophical inquiry. It also altered the practice of philosophy. At the beginning of this period the philosopher was typically a generalist, often a moral philosopher, who provided students in a small college with a grounding in ethics and perhaps some introduction to the history of philosophy. In the intervening years, philosophers followed the lead of their colleagues in the sciences and social sciences in creating a professionalized and specialized academic discipline. Although philosophy's defensive organization at the turn of the century set it apart, the impetus was similar to that of the other disciplines. The philosophers, like their colleagues, were motivated by the desire to establish clear and recognized boundaries of authority, to secure control over the training, hiring, and retention of their associates and successors, and to establish a permanent niche in the emerging research universities. As J. E. Boodin bluntly put it, "the chief end of academic philosophy is to furnish a living for professors of philosophy."[32]

The shift to a professional, specialized academic discipline meant that philosophers increasingly abandoned the moral philosopher's audience of the broadly educated intellectual elite. The philosophers of the early twentieth century more and more spoke only to each other. Professional standards, specialized journals, and more scientific methods meant that the philosophers' audience had shifted primarily to their philosophical peers. There were, of course, notable exceptions in this period, and the process was by no means completed by the 1920s. Yet it is clear that by 1930 the subject matter and methods of academic philosophy were well on their way to becoming as esoteric and as unfathomable to the educated public as nuclear physics or molecular biology.

The boundaries of philosophic discourse had shifted quite dramatically in seventy years. The vocabulary was no longer that of traditional ethics, metaphysics, and religion, but of logic and science. The metaphors were changing from those of positivism and certainty to those of relativity and uncertainty. Philosophers no longer built systems; they analyzed logical or linquistic problems. Philosophers less frequently sought the understanding and approval of the broader intellectual community, and increasingly focused their efforts on achieving a consensus of those competent to judge particular results. In doing so, they conformed to a model of discourse and community developed by Peirce, which was rooted in his understanding of scientific method and practice. Versions of Peirce's community have recently become common, but in the early twentieth century it represented a significant departure in the way philosophers conceived of their discipline. Clearly, not all philosophers thought of philosophy in Peircean terms, but his model, or some variation on it, became a powerful ideal for those who sought to appropriate the values and methods of science.

Some philosophers in the period, most notably John Dewey, resisted the deleterious effects of specialization even as they worked to integrate the knowledge gained by specialized and scientific inquiry into a wider framework of understanding. Dewey's stature and his vision of philosophy as a vital link between science and the problems of society ensured him a respectful hearing, but his efforts as a "liaison officer" grew outmoded in succeeding decades as the values of professionalization and specialization triumphed in academic philosophy. More recently, Dewey's criticisms of dichotomies and the quest for certainty have been revived by philosophers such as Bernstein and Rorty, who are exploring the limitations of the scientistic philosophy which has dominated for so long.

Many of these changes in philosophy at the turn of the century were unavoidable; philosophers could not wholly escape the influence of science, nor did they want to. The philosophers had to adapt in some fashion if they were to preserve a place for themselves in the new universities and in modern thought. But the changes were not simply an effort to preserve jobs; they went deeper and were more fundamental. One clearly senses the intellectual excitement which science fostered and the enthusiasm with which these men and women pursued new avenues of inquiry. Although individual vision remained important, a higher premium was placed on cooperative inquiry and on securing results amenable to communal assent. If philosophy did not become a science, more and more of its practitioners counted themselves as members of a community of the competent, whose consensus represented the furthest progress of the discipline.

In becoming a professional, specialized academic discipline some things were lost. Individual vision was often subordinated to the consensus of the competent. Grand metaphyscial theories and systems were replaced by narrower inquiries in logic, epistemology, and linguistic analysis. For some, an emphasis on values gave way to the requirements of scientific rigor. The audience for philosophical works was no longer the educated elite but the much narrower circle of one's philosophical colleagues. Perhaps these changes were inevitable, given the changing intellectual and cultural matrix of the time, but they left philosophy somewhat diminished. Some of the more humanistic characteristics of philosophy had been sacrificed to the methodological techniques and assured results of science. At least part of the recent pragmatic and hermeneutic turn of philosophy has been a reaction against the scientific impulses and an effort to recapture some of the humanistic side of philosophy, to rejoin what Rorty has called the "conversation of the west."[33]

Philosophy emerged from its transformation and crisis of confidence considerably reduced from its standing as queen of the sciences, but enjoying new authority and legitimacy as an academic discipline. In responding to the challenge of science, philosophers had not wholly transformed their discipline into a science; the goal was unattainable in any case given the disparate inquiries properly considered philosophical. They had, however, transformed philosophy into an academic discipline more cognizant of the values and methods of modern science, more professional in its standards for training, teaching, and publishing, more specialized in the type of inquiries pursued by individual philosophers, and more established in the intellectual and institutional context of the research university. In the period that followed, from the 1930s to the 1970s, the already established tendencies toward a scientific, specialized philosophy were enhanced by logical positivism and analytic philosophy, which dominated the major philosophical centers after World War II.

The pragmatic and hermeneutic turn of the last fifteen years has brought to the fore once again the debates that animated philosophical discussion some eighty years ago. Some of the neopragmatists, such as Putnam and Apel, have found in Peirce the philosophical origins of a conception of science and philosophy that recognizes the fallibility of knowledge and yet provides a basis for warrantability in the consensus of the scientific and philosophical community. Peirce's notions are especially valuable because they are consistent with a post-Kuhnian understanding of the history and philosophy of science. Peirce's ideas hold the promise of a fruitful accommodation between science and philosophy that has been the hope of so many in this century. But if the revival of Peirce's conceptions seems to continue the project of linking philosophy to modern science, the ideas of other pragmatists, particularly James and Dewey, have been taken up as astute criticism of the attempt to make philosophy into a science. Richard Rorty and Richard Bernstein have both found in James and Dewey support for their contention that philosophy is more than a science, that it has a broader humanistic and hermeneutic role to play. They build on James's and Dewey's criticisms of the reduction of philosophy to science to support their own efforts to reconceive philosophy as an active participant in social reconstruction or as a partner in the conversation of the West. Thus, the transformation of philosophy that took place between 1860 and 1930 began a process which has not yet been completed. The pragmatists continue to be participants in the discussion.

Chapter 1

1. William James to H. N. Gardiner, November 14, 1901, in *The Letters of William James,* ed. Henry James (Boston: Atlantic Monthly Press, 1920), 2:164; Charles Sanders Peirce, "What Pragmatism Is," in *The Collected Papers of Charles Sanders Peirce,* ed. Charles Hartshorne and Paul Weiss (Cambridge: Harvard Univ. Press, 1934), 5.413. (Citations to the *Collected Papers* will follow the usual convention of volume number followed by paragraph number.)

2. Daniel Walker Howe, *The Unitarian Conscience: Harvard Moral Philosophy, 1805–1861* (Cambridge: Harvard Univ. Press, 1970), pp. 2–3. Howe's book is a comprehensive study of Unitarian moral philosophy at Harvard. Elizabeth Flower and Murray G. Murphey examine Scottish realism and moral philosophy at other universities in *A History of Philosophy in America,* 2 vols. (New York: G. P. Putnam's Sons, Capricorn Books, 1977), 1:203–361. Bruce Kuklick sees nineteenth-century "collegiate philosophy" gaining in importance compared to theology and moving from "Scottish realism to a full-fledged idealism," in *Churchmen and Philosophers: From Jonathan Edwards to John Dewey* (New Haven: Yale Univ. Press, 1985), pp. 128–45.

3. George H. Daniels, *American Science in the Age of Jackson* (New York: Columbia Univ. Press, 1968), pp. 32–35; Robert V. Bruce, *The Launching of Modern American Science, 1846–1876* (New York: Alfred A. Knopf, 1987), p. 4. See also, Nathan Reingold, "Definitions and Speculations: The Professionalization of Science in America in the Nineteenth Century," in *The Pursuit of Knowledge in the Early American Republic: American Scientific and Learned Societies from Colonial Times to the Civil War,* ed. Alexandra Oleson and Sanborn C. Brown (Baltimore: Johns Hopkins Univ. Press, 1976), pp. 33–69.

4. Roger L. Geiger, *To Advance Knowledge: The Growth of American Research Universities, 1900–1940* (New York: Oxford Univ. Press, 1986), p. 9; Laurence R. Veysey, *The Emergence*

of the American University (Chicago: Univ. of Chicago Press, 1965; Phoenix Books, 1970), p. 174; David A. Hollinger, "Inquiry and Uplift: Late Nineteenth-Century American Academics and the Moral Efficacy of Scientific Practice," in The Authority of Experts: Studies in History and Theory, ed. Thomas L. Haskell (Bloomington: Indiana Univ. Press, 1984), p. 153; See also, Bruce, Launching of Modern American Science, pp. 326–28.

5. Bruce, Launching of Modern American Science, pp. 75–93; Reingold, "Definitions and Speculations," pp. 33–55; Geiger, To Advance Knowledge, pp. 20–30. See also, John Higham, "The Matrix of Specialization," and Edward Shils, "The Order of Learning in the United States: The Ascendancy of the University," both in The Organization of Knowledge in Modern America, 1860–1920, ed. Alexandra Oleson and John Voss (Baltimore: Johns Hopkins Univ. Press, 1979), pp. 3–18, 19–47.

6. On the culture of professionalism, see Burton J. Bledstein, The Culture of Professionalism: The Middle Class and the Development of Higher Education in America (New York: W. W. Norton, 1976). On the characteristics of academic disciplines, see Geiger, To Advance Knowledge, pp. 20–30; and Laurence Veysey, "The Plural Organized Worlds of the Humanities," Dorothy Ross, "The Development of the Social Sciences," and Daniel Kevles, "The Physics, Mathematics, and Chemistry Communities: A Comparative Analysis," all in The Organization of Knowledge, pp. 51–106, 107–38, 139–72. Good studies of individual disciplines include Thomas L. Haskell, The Emergence of Professional Social Science: The American Social Science Association and the Nineteenth-Century Crisis of Authority (Urbana: Univ. of Illinois Press, 1977); Mary O. Furner, Advocacy and Objectivity: A Crisis in the Professionalization of American Social Science, 1865–1905 (Lexington: Univ. Press of Kentucky, 1975); Daniel J. Kevles, The Physicists: The History of a Scientific Community in Modern America (New York: Alfred A. Knopf, 1977); Bruce Kuklick, The Rise of American Philosophy: Cambridge, Massachusetts, 1860–1930 (New Haven: Yale Univ. Press, 1977); W. Bruce Fye, The Development of American Physiology: Scientific Medicine in the Nineteenth Century (Baltimore: Johns Hopkins Univ. Press, 1987); and Robert C. Bannister, Sociology and Scientism: The American Quest for Objectivity, 1880–1940 (Chapel Hill: Univ. of North Carolina Press, 1987).

7. See Geiger, To Advance Knowledge, pp. 20–24; Haskell, Emergence of Professional Social Science, pp. 65–68, 88–90, 234–40; Ross, "Development of the Social Sciences," pp. 107–8, 113–21; and Magali Sarfatti Larson, "The Production of Expertise and the Constitution of Expert Power," in The Authority of Experts, pp. 56–57. On the somewhat different pattern in the humanities, see Veysey, "Plural Organized Worlds of the Humanities," pp. 51–58.

8. On the appeal of science and on the conflicting views of science and scientism in the other disciplines, see Ross, "Development of the Social Sciences," pp. 125–30; Richard Hofstadter, The Progressive Historians: Turner, Beard, Parrington (New York: Random House, Vintage Books, 1970), p. 37; and Hollinger, "Inquiry and Uplift," pp. 143–45.

9. Veysey, Emergence of the American University, pp. 173–79; Geiger, To Advance Knowledge, pp. 9–10, 22–30; Ross, "Development of the Social Sciences," pp. 125–30; and James Turner, Without God, Without Creed: The Origins of Unbelief in America (Baltimore: Johns Hopkins Univ. Press, 1985), pp. 123–24, 137–38, 189–90. Robert Bruce suggests that by the 1870s the American public began to have some misgivings about science; Launching of Modern American Science, pp. 353–56.

10. In addition to the work of Hollinger, Haskell, and Larson cited above, see David A. Hollinger, "Historians and the Discourse of Intellectuals," *In the American Province: Studies in the History and Historiography of Ideas* (Bloomington: Indiana Univ. Press, 1985), pp. 130–51; Thomas Bender, "The Cultures of Intellectual Life: The City and the Professions," in *New Directions in American Intellectual History*, ed. John Higham and Paul K. Conkin (Baltimore: Johns Hopkins Univ. Press, 1979), pp. 181–95; Thomas L. Haskell, "Professionalism *versus* Capitalism: R. H. Tawney, Emile Durkheim, and C. S. Peirce on the Disinterestedness of Professional Communities," in *The Authority of Experts*, pp. 202–12; Richard Rorty, "Pragmatism, Relativism, and Irrationalism," in *Consequences of Pragmatism (Essays: 1972–80)* (Minneapolis: Univ. of Minnesota Press, 1982), pp. 160–75; Hilary Putnam, *The Many Faces of Realism: The Paul Carus Lectures* (LaSalle, Ill.: Open Court, 1987); Karl-Otto Apel, "Scientism or Transcendental Hermeneutics? On the Question of the Subject of the Interpretation of Signs in the Semiotics of Pragmatism," in *Towards a Transformation of Philosophy*, trans. Glyn Adey and David Frisby (London: Routledge and Kegan Paul, 1980), pp. 93–135; and Stanley Fish, *Is There a Text in this Class? The Authority of Interpretive Communities* (Cambridge: Harvard Univ. Press, 1980).

11. Hollinger, "Historians and the Discourse of Intellectuals," pp. 132, 141, 148.

12. Richard Rorty, "Overcoming the Tradition: Heidegger and Dewey," in *Consequences of Pragmatism*, p. 41.

13. David E. Leary, "Telling Likely Stories: The Rhetoric of the New Psychology, 1880–1920," *Journal of the History of the Behavioral Sciences* 23 (1987):320, 326. See also, Dominick LaCapra, "Rhetoric and History," in *History and Criticism* (Ithaca: Cornell Univ. Press, 1985), pp. 15–44.

14. Larson, "Production of Expertise," p. 56.

15. James Kloppenberg has recently examined the influence of James and Dewey in undermining the possibility of certain truth. His *Uncertain Victory* deals at length with James's and Dewey's critiques of science and scientific certainty along lines that will be developed below. Peirce's community of inquiry, with its ideal of convergence on truth in some indefinite future, is antithetical to Kloppenberg's emphasis on uncertainty. Although there are some striking parallels between Kloppenberg's discussion of James and Dewey and mine, our arguments were developed separately. Kloppenberg's emphasis on the philosophic challenge to uncertainty as a prelude to social democracy and progressivism takes his study in different directions from mine. James T. Kloppenberg, *Uncertain Victory: Social Democracy and Progressivism in European and American Thought, 1870–1920* (New York: Oxford Univ. Press, 1986), pp. 98, 113–14.

16. Richard Rorty, *Philosophy and the Mirror of Nature* (Princeton: Princeton Univ. Press, 1979).

17. Putnam, *The Many Faces of Realism*, pp. 80–86; Apel, "Scientism or Transcendental Hermeneutics?" pp. 101–27.

18. Richard J. Bernstein, *Praxis and Action: Contemporary Philosophies of Human Activity* (Philadelphia: Univ. of Pennsylvania Press, 1971), pp. 165–229.

Chapter 2
1. Chauncey Wright to Mrs. J. P. Lesley, February 12, 1860, in *The Letters of Chauncey Wright, With Some Account of His Life*, ed. James Bradley Thayer (Cambridge: Press of John Wilson and Son, 1878), p. 43.

2. George H. Daniels, *American Science in the Age of Jackson* (New York: Columbia Univ. Press, 1968), p. 65.

3. On McCosh, see J. David Hoeveler, Jr., *James McCosh and the Scottish Intellectual Tradition: From Glasgow to Princeton* (Princeton: Princeton Univ. Press, 1981), pp. 180–211, 313, 320–21.

4. Ibid., p. 228; Bruce Kuklick, *Churchmen and Philosophers: From Jonathan Edwards to John Dewey* (New Haven: Yale Univ. Press, 1985), p. 144; Daniel Walker Howe, *The Unitarian Conscience: Harvard Moral Philosophy, 1805–1861* (Cambridge: Harvard Univ. Press, 1970), pp. 2–3.

5. On the rise of academic professionalization in the nineteenth century, see Nathan Reingold, "Definitions and Speculations: The Professionalization of Science in America in the Nineteenth Century," and Sally Gregory Kohlstedt, "Savants and Professionals: The American Association for the Advancement of Science, 1848–1860," both in *The Pursuit of Knowledge in the Early American Republic: American Scientific and Learned Societies from Colonial Times to the Civil War,* ed. Alexandra Oleson and Sanborn C. Brown (Baltimore: Johns Hopkins Univ. Press, 1976), pp. 33–69, 299–325; Robert A. McCaughey, "The Transformation of American Academic Life: Harvard University 1821–1892," *Perspectives in American History* 8 (1974):239–332; and Burton J. Bledstein, *The Culture of Professionalism: The Middle Class and the Development of Higher Education in America* (New York: W. W. Norton, 1976).

6. For biographical information on Wright, see Edward H. Madden, *Chauncey Wright and the Foundations of Pragmatism* (Seattle: Univ. of Washington Press, 1963); for Peirce, see Murray G. Murphey, *The Development of Peirce's Philosophy* (Cambridge: Harvard Univ. Press, 1961); and for James, see Ralph Barton Perry, *The Thought and Character of William James,* 2 vols. (Boston: Little, Brown, and Company, 1935); Howard M. Feinstein, *Becoming William James* (Ithaca: Cornell Univ. Press, 1984); Gerald E. Myers, *William James: His Life and Thought* (New Haven: Yale Univ. Press, 1986); and Daniel W. Bjork, *William James: The Center of His Vision* (New York: Columbia Univ. Press, 1988).

7. Perry, *Thought and Character of William James* 1:169–216; Feinstein, *Becoming William James,* pp. 103–68; Myers, *William James,* pp. 15–40.

8. Murphey, *Development of Peirce's Philosophy,* pp. 12–13.

9. Madden, *Chauncey Wright,* pp. 10–14; Perry, *Thought and Character of William James* 1:520–21, 534–35; Murphey, *Development of Peirce's Philosophy,* pp. 97–98.

10. Daniels, *American Science,* pp. 34–36. On Harvard, see McCaughey, *Transformation of American Academic Life,* pp. 263–64, 266–67; and Ronald Story, *The Forging of an Aristocracy: Harvard and the Boston Upper Class, 1800–1870* (Middletown, Conn.: Wesleyan Univ. Press, 1980), pp. 57–61, 214n.2.

11. Madden, *Chauncey Wright,* pp. 5–6; Murphey, *Development of Peirce's Philosophy,* pp. 17–18.

12. Murphey, *Development of Peirce's Philosophy,* pp. 18–19.

13. See Feinstein, *Becoming William James,* on James's choice of a career, especially pp. 103–222, 316–47; Charles W. Eliot is quoted in Feinstein, p. 155. Daniel Bjork has suggested that James saw a specialized professional career as a means of separating himself from his "vocationless" father; Bjork, *William James,* pp. 48–49, 70, 182.

14. Feinstein, *Becoming William James,* p. 147.

15. Madden, *Chauncey Wright*, pp. 10–11.

16. Charles Sanders Peirce, "Preface," in *The Collected Papers of Charles Sanders Peirce*, ed. Charles Hartshorne and Paul Weiss (Cambridge: Harvard Univ. Press, 1934), 5.12. On the Metaphysical Club, see Philip P. Wiener, *Evolution and the Founders of Pragmatism* (1949; reprint, New York: Harper and Row, Harper Torchbooks, 1965), pp. 18–30; and Max H. Fisch, "Was There a Metaphysical Club in Cambridge?" in *Studies in the Philosophy of Charles Sanders Peirce*, 2d ser., ed. Edward C. Moore and Richard S. Robin (Amherst: Univ. of Massachusetts Press, 1964), pp. 3–32. (Citations to the *Collected Papers* will follow the usual convention of volume number followed by paragraph number.)

17. William James, "The Ph.D. Octopus," in *Memories and Studies* (1911; reprint, New York: Greenwood Press, 1968), pp. 329–47; William James to Henry Bowditch, January 24, 1869, in *The Letters of William James*, ed. Henry James (Boston: Atlantic Monthly Press, 1920), 1:149.

18. Madden, *Chauncey Wright*, pp. 7–8, 21, 27.

19. E. W. Gurney to James B. Thayer, in *Letters of Chauncey Wright*, pp. 212–13; Henry W. Holland to James B. Thayer, in *Letters of Chauncey Wright*, p. 214; Madden, *Chauncey Wright*, pp. 24–27.

20. Quoted in Madden, *Chauncey Wright*, p. 16.

21 Murphey, *Development of Peirce's Philosophy*, pp. 18–19, 97–105; Max H. Fisch, "Peirce as Scientist, Mathematician, Historian, Logician, and Philosopher," in *Proceedings of the C. S. Peirce Bicentennial International Congress*, ed. Kenneth L. Ketner et al., Texas Tech University Graduate Studies, no. 23 (Lubbock: Texas Tech Press, 1981), pp. 13–19.

22. Fisch, "Peirce as Scientist," p. 14.

23. For the range of Peirce's early writings, see the list of articles and essays in *Writings of Charles S. Peirce: A Chronological Edition*, vol. 1, *1857–1866*, ed. Max H. Fisch et al. (Bloomington: Indiana Univ. Press, 1982), pp. 569–77.

24. Murphey, *Development of Peirce's Philosophy*, p. 19.

25. William James to Daniel Coit Gilman, November 25, 1875, in *Studies in the Philosophy of Charles Sanders Peirce*, ed. Philip P. Wiener and Frederic H. Young (Cambridge: Harvard Univ. Press, 1952), p. 363. See also, Max H. Fisch and Jackson I. Cope, "Peirce at the Johns Hopkins Univeristy," in *Studies in the Philosophy of Charles Sanders Peirce*, pp. 277–311.

26. Fisch and Cope, "Peirce at Johns Hopkins," pp. 287–92; Murphey, *Development of Peirce's Philosophy*, pp. 104–5; Christine Ladd-Franklin, "Charles Peirce at The Johns Hopkins," *Journal of Philosophy* 13(1916):716; Joseph Jastrow, "Charles Peirce as a Teacher," *Journal of Philosophy*13(1916):725.

27. Peirce is quoted in Murphey, *Development of Peirce's Philosophy*, p. 292. See also, Fisch and Cope, "Peirce at Johns Hopkins," pp. 294–302, 309; Murphey, pp. 291–93.

28. Charles S. Peirce, "A Detailed Classification of the Sciences," in *Collected Papers*, 1.236.

29. In addition to Feinstein, *Becoming William James*, see Daniel J. Wilson, "Neurasthenia and Vocational Crisis in Post–Civil War America," *Psychohistory Review* 12(1984):31–38; Myers, *William James*, pp. 19–21; and Bjork, *William James*, pp. 48–49, 182.

30.William James to his parents, May 3–10, 1865, in Perry, *Thought and Character* of William James, 1:219; William James, The Varieties of Religious Experience, in The Works of William James (Cambridge: Harvard Univ. Press, 1985), pp. 134–35; William James to Henry James, August 24, 1872, in Letters of William James, 1:167; Perry, 1:335.

31. Chauncey Wright to F. E. Abbot, February 10, 1869, in Letters of Chauncey Wright, p. 140.

32. Chauncey Wright, "The Philosophy of Herbert Spencer," in Philosophical Discussions (1877; reprint, New York: Burt Franklin, 1971), p. 48; Chauncey Wright, "McCosh on Tyndall," in Philosophical Discussions, p. 375.

33. Wright, "Philosophy of Herbert Spencer," p. 51.

34. Ibid., p. 49.

35. Chauncey Wright, "German Darwinism," in Philosophical Discussions, pp. 403–5; see also, Wright, "Philosophy of Herbert Spencer," p. 47.

36. Chauncey Wright, "Mill on Comte," Nation 2(1866):21; Chauncey Wright to F. E. Abbot, July 9, 1867, in Letters of Chauncey Wright, p. 113.

37. Chauncey Wright to F. E. Abbot, August 13, 1867, in Letters of Chauncey Wright, p. 113.

38. E. W. Gurney quoted in Letters of Chauncey Wright, p. 380; Perry, Thought and Character of William James, 1:521, 525.

39. Madden argues that "The Will to Believe" was directed as much at Wright as at its explicit targets, William K. Clifford and Thomas Huxley. Madden, Chauncey Wright, pp. 43–50.

40. Wright, "Philosophy of Herbert Spencer," p. 47.

41. Chauncey Wright, "The Genesis of Species," in Philosophical Discussions, pp. 131–32; Wright, "Philosophy of Herbert Spencer," p. 46.

42. Chauncey Wright, "Evolution of Self-Consciousness," in Philosophical Discussions, pp. 205–6; Chauncey Wright, "A Fragment on Cause and Effect," in Philosophical Discussions, p. 408.

43. Wright, "Philosophy of Herbert Spencer," p. 74; Chauncey Wright, "Evolution by Natural Selection," in Philosophical Discussions, p. 170; Chauncey Wright to Mrs. J. P. Lesley, March 22, 1870, in Letters of Chauncey Wright, p. 177.

44. Chauncey Wright to Grace Norton, August 12, 1874, in Letters of Chauncey Wright, p. 289; Chauncey Wright, "Books Relating to the Theory of Evolution," in Philosophical Discussions, pp. 395–96.

45. Chauncey Wright to Grace Norton, October 16, 1870, in Letters of Chauncey Wright, p. 203; Chauncey Wright, "Lewes's Problems of Life and Mind," in Philosophical Discussions, p. 367.

46. Wright, "Evolution of Self-Consciousness," p. 203; Chauncey Wright to Grace Norton, August 22, 1875, in Letters of Chauncey Wright, p. 348; Chauncey Wright to C. E. Norton, July 24, 1866, in Letters of Chauncey Wright, p. 87.

47. Chauncey Wright, "The Life and Works of Bishop Berkeley," Nation 13(1871):60; Wright, "Evolution of Self-Consciousness," p. 249; Chauncey Wright to F. E. Abbot, February 10, 1869, in Letters of Chauncey Wright, p. 141.

48. Wright, "Evolution by Natural Selection," p. 196.

49. Charles Sanders Peirce, "Lecture 1: Early Nominalism and Realism," in Writings of Charles S. Peirce: A Chronological Edition, vol. 2, 1867–1871, ed. Edward C. Moore (Bloomington: Indiana Univ. Press, 1984), p. 314. On Peirce and evolution, see Wiener, Evolution and the Founders of Pragmatism, pp. 70–96.

50. Wiener, *Evolution and the Founders of Pragmatism*, pp. 76–77.

51. Charles S. Peirce, "Preface," in *Collected Papers*, 1.3.

52. Charles S. Peirce, "Reply to the Necessitarians," in *Collected Papers*, 6.604 (Peirce's emphasis).

53. Charles S. Peirce, "Private Thoughts, principally on the conduct of life," in *Writings of Peirce*, 1:9; Charles S. Peirce, "[A Treatise on Metaphysics]," in *Writings of Peirce*, 1:52.

54. Charles S. Peirce, "Lecture XI," in *Writings of Peirce*, 1:490; Charles S. Peirce, "[Critique of Positivism]," in *Writings of Peirce*, 2:127.

55. Charles S. Peirce, "Some Consequences of Four Incapacities," in *Writings of Peirce*, 2:212; Charles S. Peirce, "Potentia ex Impotentia," in *Writings of Peirce*, 2:189–90.

56. Peirce, "Potentia ex Impotentia," p. 188.

57. Peirce, "Lecture I," p. 315.

58. Charles S. Peirce, "Whewell," in *Writings of Peirce*, 2:339.

59. Peirce, "Some Consequences of Four Incapacities," p. 212; Charles S. Peirce, "How to Make Our Ideas Clear," in *Writings of Charles S. Peirce: A Chronological Edition*, vol. 3, *1872–1878*, ed. Christian J. W. Kloesel (Bloomington: Indiana Univ. Press, 1986), p. 273; Peirce, "Lecture I," p. 313.

60. Peirce, "Some Consequences of Four Incapacities," p. 239; Charles S. Peirce, "The Fixation of Belief," in *Writings of Peirce*, 3:253–54; see also Murphey, *Development of Peirce's Philosophy*, pp. 140–42; and Bruce Kuklick, *The Rise of American Philosophy: Cambridge, Massachusetts, 1860–1930* (New Haven: Yale Univ. Press, 1977), pp. 114–17.

61. Peirce, "Some Consequences of Four Incapacities," pp. 212–13.

62. William James, "The Mood of Science and the Mood of Faith," *Nation* 19 (1874):437.

63. William James, "The Teaching of Philosophy in Our Colleges," in *Essays in Philosophy, The Works of William James* (Cambridge: Harvard Univ. Press, 1978), pp. 178–79.

64. Perry, *Thought and Character of William James*, 2:30.

65. James, "Teaching of Philosophy," p. 4; William James, "The Sentiment of Rationality," in *Essays in Philosophy*, pp. 56–57.

66. William James, "The Sentiment of Rationality," in *The Will to Believe and Other Essays in Popular Philosophy, The Works of William James* (Cambridge: Harvard Univ. Press, 1979), pp. 77–78.

67. James, "The Sentiment of Rationality," in *The Will to Believe*, pp. 79, 79n, 78, 79n.

Chapter 3

1. G. Stanley Hall, "College Instruction in Philosophy," *Nation* 23 (1876):180.

2. William James, "The Teaching of Philosophy in Our Colleges," in *Essays in Philosophy, The Works of William James* (Cambridge: Harvard Univ. Press, 1978), pp. 3–5.

3. Ibid, pp. 5–6.

4. G. Stanley Hall, "Philosophy in the United States," *Mind* 4 (1879):89–91, 95–97.

5. Ibid, pp. 99–105.

6. On the development of professionalization in higher education and the impact on academic careers in late nineteenth-century America, see: Bruce Kuklick, *The Rise of American Philosophy: Cambridge, Massachusetts, 1860–1930* (New Haven: Yale Univ. Press, 1977); Laurence R. Veysey, *The Emergence of the American University* (Chicago: Univ. of Chicago Press, 1965; Phoenix Books, 1970), pp. 317–24; Burton J. Bledstein, *The Culture of Professionalism: The Middle Class and the Development of Higher Education in America* (New York: W. W. Norton, 1976), pp. 159–78; Laurence Veysey, "The Plural Organized Worlds of the Humanities," and Dorothy Ross, "The Development of the Social Sciences," both in *The Organization of Knowledge in Modern America, 1860–1920,* ed. Alexandra Oleson and John Voss (Baltimore: Johns Hopkins Univ. Press, 1979), pp. 51–106, 107–38; Daniel J. Wilson, "Neurasthenia and Vocational Crisis in Post–Civic War America," *Psychohistory Review* 12 (1984):31–38; and Edward Shils, "The Order of Learning in the United States from 1865 to 1920; The Ascendancy of the Universities," *Minerva* 16(1978):160–83.

7. Dorothy Ross, *G. Stanley Hall: The Psychologist as Prophet* (Chicago: Univ. of Chicago Press, 1972), pp. 22–26, 29–30; John M. O'Donnell, *The Origins of Behaviorism: American Psychology, 1870–1920* (New York: New York Univ. Press, 1985), pp. 110–11. On Mark Hopkins, see Herbert W. Schneider, *A History of American Philosophy* (New York: Columbia Univ. Press, 1946), pp. 243–45.

8. Ross, *G. Stanley Hall,* pp. 30–42; G. Stanley Hall, *Life and Confessions of a Psychologist* (New York: D. Appleton and Company, 1927), p. 196.

9. Ross, *G. Stanley Hall,* pp. 50–55, 59–61; O'Donnell, *Origins of Behaviorism,* pp. 111–12; Hall, *Life and Confessions,* pp. 199–203.

10. Ross, *G. Stanley Hall,* pp. 62–64, 68–80; O'Donnell, *Origins of Behaviorism,* pp. 112–13.

11. Max H. Fisch and Jackson I. Cope, "Peirce at the Johns Hopkins University," in *Studies in the Philosophy of Charles Sanders Peirce,* ed. Philip P. Wiener and Frederic H. Young (Cambridge: Harvard Univ. Press, 1952), pp. 280–86; Ross, *G. Stanley Hall,* pp. 81–83, 103–6, 134–39; O'Donnell, *Origins of Behaviorism,* pp. 117–19; Hall, *Life and Confessions,* pp. 225–26.

12. John Clendenning, *The Life and Thought of Josiah Royce* (Madison: Univ. of Wisconsin Press, 1985), pp. 26–27, 45–47, 51–59; *The Letters of Josiah Royce,* ed. John Clendenning (Chicago: Univ. of Chicago Press, 1970), pp. 13–16.

13. *Letters of Josiah Royce,* pp. 16–19, 52; Clendenning, *Life and Thought,* pp. 68–81.

14. Josiah Royce to Daniel Coit Gilman, September 16, 1878, in *Letters of Josiah Royce,* p. 60; Clendenning, *Life and Thought,* pp. 82–87, 94–95.

15. Josiah Royce to William James, January 8, 1880, in *Letters of Josiah Royce,* p. 77; Josiah Royce to William James, August 28, 1881, in *Letters of Josiah Royce,* pp. 100–101.

16. William James to Josiah Royce, April 23, 1882, in Ralph Barton Perry, *The Thought and Character of William James,* 2 vols. (Boston: Little, Brown and Company, 1935), 1:794–96; Clendenning, *Life and Thought,* pp. 109–10, 122.

17. *Letters of Josiah Royce,* pp. 21–23, 28; Clendenning, *Life and Thought,* pp. 122–23, 138, 160, 191, 198.

18. Quoted in Perry, *Thought and Character of William James,* 1:779–80.

19. William James and George Sylvester Morris were both willing advisors, helpful

in advancing the careers of their students and proteges. Not all professors, however, were as helpful. G. Stanley Hall, though he had benefited from the advice and support of both James and Morris, was a reluctant and unwilling mentor to younger scholars. Dorothy Ross notes that at Johns Hopkins, Hall blocked opportunities for two of his students, James McKeen Cattell and John Dewey, to stay at the university. She concludes that while Hall might have still been "insecure in his position," he also seems to have felt "safer without strong intellectual challengers around him and set about to eliminate them." Ross, *G. Stanley Hall*, pp. 144–47.

20. George Dykhuizen, *The Life and Mind of John Dewey* (Carbondale: Southern Illinois Univ. Press, 1973), pp. 6–10; Neil Coughlan, *Young John Dewey: An Essary in American Intellectual History* (Chicago: Univ. of Chicago Press, 1975), pp. 4–8.

21. Dykhuizen, *Life and Mind of John Dewey*, pp. 14–16; Coughlan, *Young John Dewey*, pp. 11–16; Bruce Kuklick, *Churchmen and Philosophers: From Jonathan Edwards to John Dewey* (New Haven: Yale Univ. Press, 1985), p. 231.

22. John Dewey, "From Absolutism to Experimentalism," in *Contemporary American Philosophy: Personal Statements*, ed. George P. Adams and William Pepperell Montague (New York: Macmillan Company, 1930), 2:14–15; Dykhuizen, *Life and Mind of John Dewey*, pp. 16–26.

23. Dewey, "From the Absolutism to Experimentalism," p. 16; Dykhuizen, *Life and Mind of John Dewey*, pp. 26–27.

24. Dewey, "From Absolutism to Experimentalism," pp. 18–19; Dewey's view of Peirce is quoted in Dykhuizen, *Life and Mind of John Dewey*, p. 31.

25. Dykhuizen, *Life and Mind of John Dewey,*pp. 30–31; Coughlan, *Young John Dewey*, pp. 39–40.

26. Dykhuizen, *Life and Mind of John Dewey*, pp. 39–43; Coughlan, *Young John Dewey*, p. 54. Coughlan discusses the difficulties Morris had in securing an academic appointment in the 1870s. His difficulties paralleled those of Hall and Royce and may have made Morris more sympathetic to the plight of young scholars in the 1880s, when he was in a position to help. Coughlan, pp. 18–32.

27. Dykhuizen, *Life and Mind of John Dewey*, pp. 44–47, 57–63.

28. Hall, "Philosophy in the United States," pp. 99–100.

29. *Encyclopedia of Philosophy*, s.v. "Philosophical Journals" and "Carus, Paul."

30. [Jacob Gould Schurman], "Prefatory Note," *Philosophical Review* 1 (1892):1, 4–5.

31. Some contemporaries recognized that philosophy was changing along the lines suggested above. See especially, Josiah Royce, "Present Ideals of American University Life," *Scribner's Magazine* 10 (1891):385; A. C. Armstrong, "Philosophy in the United States," *Educational Review* 10 (1895):1–11; and A. C. Armstrong, "Philosophy in American Colleges," *Educational Review* 13 (1897):10–22.

Chapter 4

1. See, for example, Elizabeth Flower and Murray G. Murphey, *A History of Philosophy in America*, 2 vols. (New York: G. P. Putnam's Sons, Capricorn Books, 1977), 1:215–69; and Theodore Dwight Bozeman, *Protestants in an Age of Science: The Baconian Ideal and Antebellum American Religious Thought* (Chapel Hill: Univ. of North Carolina Press, 1977).

2. For a discussion of the current debate, see chapter 9.

3. There are some striking parallels and also some significant differences between the ideas of Peirce and James and the theory of scientific revolutions developed by Thomas Kuhn. See Thomas Kuhn, _The Structure of Scientific Revolutions,_ 2d ed., enlarged, in _International Encyclopedia of Unified Science,_ vol. 2, no. 2 (Chicago: Univ. of Chicago Press, 1970). On the current debate regarding community, see chapter 9.

4. James is quoted in Gay Wilson Allen, _William James: A Biography_ (New York: Viking Press, 1967), p. 286. On James's pursuit of a middle way, see also Gerald E. Myers, _William James: His Life and Thought_ (New Haven: Yale Univ. Press, 1986), pp. 447–49, 464; Flower and Murphey, _A History of Philosophy in America,_ 2:635–39, 684; and Mark R. Schwehn, "Making The World: William James and the Life of the Mind," _Harvard Library Bulletin_ 30 (1982):434–35.

5. William James, "Is Life Worth Living?" in _The Will to Believe and Other Essays in Popular Philosophy, The Works of William James_ (Cambridge: Harvard Univ. Press, 1979), pp. 49–50; William James, "What Psychical Research Has Accomplished," in _The Will to Believe,_ pp. 241, 239; William James, _Talks to Teachers on Psychology and to Students on Some of Life's Ideals, The Works of William James_ (Cambridge: Harvard Univ. Press, 1983), pp. 15–16.

6. William James, "The Hidden Self," in _Essays in Psychology, The Works of William James_ (Cambridge: Harvard Univ. Press, 1983), p. 247; William James, _The Principles of Psychology, The Works of William James_ (Cambridge: Harvard Univ. Press, 1981), 2:1230–31; William James, "A Plea for Psychology as a Natural Science," in _Essays in Psychology,_ p. 271. Cf., William James, "Are We Automata?" in _Essays in Psychology,_ pp. 59–60.

7. James, _Talks to Teachers,_ p. 79.

8. James, _Principles of Psychology,_ 1:191.

9. Ibid., 1:6. See also, ibid., 1:141. James's efforts to create a natural science of psychology are placed in the context of the period by Gerald E. Myers, "Introduction: The Intellectual Context," and by Rand B. Evans, "Introduction: The Historical Context," both in James, _Principles of Psychology,_ 1:xi–xl, xli–lxviii.

10. James, "A Plea for Psychology as a Natural Science," p. 271.

11. James, "The Hidden Self," pp. 247–48. See also James, "Is Life Worth Living?" pp. 49–50; and James, _Principles of Psychology,_ 1:19, 2:1232–33. Compare James with Kuhn, _Structure of Scientific Revolutions,_ pp. 52–53, 57, 84–85. Daniel W. Bjork discusses James's emphasis on the margins and the fringe in _William James: The Center of His Vision_ (New York: Columbia Univ. Press, 1988), pp. 213–18.

12. Myers, _William James,_ pp. 290–91; James, _Principles of Psychology,_ 2:1260.

13. James, _Principles of Psychology,_ 2:1232–33.

14. James, "What Psychical Research Has Accomplished," pp. 223–24; see also, William James to Thomas Davidson, February 1, 1885, in _The Letters of William James,_ ed. Henry James (Boston: Atlantic Monthly Press, 1920), 1:249–50. Gerald Myers views James's interest in psychical phenomena as an extension of his interest in abnormal psychology, in _William James,_ pp. 369–86. Daniel W. Bjork discusses the impact of James's participation in psychical research on his standing as a scientist in _The Compromised Scientist: William James in the Development of American Psychology_ (New York: Columbia Univ. Press, 1983), pp. 145–62. See also, Bjork, _William James,_ pp. 207–27.

15. William James to Thomas Davidson, February 1, 1885, in _Letters of William_

James, 1:250. For a recent view of James's psychical research that also emphasizes his cautious, middle-of-the-road approach to this subject, see Robert A. McDermott, "Introduction," in William James, *Essays in Psychical Research, The Works of William James* (Cambridge: Harvard Univ. Press, 1986), pp. xiii–xiv, xix, xxxi–xxxiii.

16. James, *Principles of Psychology*, 2:1236n; James, "Is Life Worth Living?" pp. 49–50. See also, James, "Are We Automata?" pp. 59–60; William James, "Reflex Action and Theism," in *The Will to Believe*, pp. 104-5; and Myers, *William James*, pp. 463–65.

17. James, *Principles of Psychology*, 2:1179; James, "Preface," in *The Will to Believe*, p. 7. See also, Bjork, *William James*, pp. 114–15.

18. John Dewey, "The New Psychology," in *The Early Works, 1882–1898*, vol. 1, *1882–1888* (Carbondale: Southern Illinois Univ. Press, 1969), pp. 53, 56. See also, Neil Coughlan, *Young John Dewey: An Essay in American Intellectual History* (Chicago: Univ. of Chicago Press, 1975), p. 80.

19. John Dewey, "The Obligation to Knowledge of God," in *The Early Works, 1882–1898*, 1:62.

20. John Dewey, "Psychology as Philosophic Method," in *The Early Works, 1882–1898*, 1:144, 148–49, 152.

21. Ibid., pp. 156–57. See also, Coughlan, *Young John Dewey*, pp. 62–63; and Bruce Kuklick, *Churchmen and Philosophers: From Jonathan Edwards to John Dewey* (New Haven: Yale Univ. Press, 1985), p. 239.

22. Dewey, "Psychology as Philosophic Method," pp. 157–58. See also, John Dewey, *Psychology*, in *The Early Works, 1882–1898*, vol. 2, *1887* (Carbondale: Southern Illinois Univ. Press, 1967), pp. 76–77, 201–2.

23. Dewey, "Psychology as Philosophic Method," pp. 158–59. See also, Dewey, *Psychology*, pp. 9–10.

24. Kuklick, *Churchmen and Philosophers*, p. 239.

25. John Dewey, "Ethics and Physical Science," in *The Early Works, 1882–1898*, 1:206–9.

26. Ibid., pp. 209–10, 225.

27. On the influence of Peirce, see, S. Morris Eames, "Introduction," in John Dewey, *The Early Works, 1882–1898*, vol. 3, *1889–1892* (Carbondale: Southern Illinois Univ. Press, 1969), pp. x–xi; Morton White, *Science and Sentiment in America: Philosophical Thought from Jonathan Edwards to John Dewey* (New York: Oxford Univ. Press, 1972), pp. 274–75; and R. W. Sleeper, who argues that Dewey rejected the formalism of Peirce's logic while being attracted to the psychological aspects of Peirce's theory, in *The Necessity of Pragmatism: John Dewey's Conception of Philosophy* (New Haven: Yale Univ. Press, 1986), pp. 47–50.

28. John Dewey, "The Present Position of Logical Theory," in *The Early Works, 1882–1898*, 3:126; John Dewey, "Is Logic a Dualistic Science?" in *The Early Works, 1882–1898*, 3:75.

29. Dewey, "Is Logic a Dualistic Science?" pp. 81–82.

30. John Dewey, "The Logic of Verification," in *The Early Works, 1882–1898*, 3:88–89; Dewey, "Is Logic a Dualistic Science?" p. 80.

31. John Dewey, "Reconstruction," in *The Early Works, 1882–1898*, vol. 4, *1893–1894* (Carbondale: Southern Illinois Univ. Press, 1971), pp. 102–3.

32. John Dewey, "Introduction to Philosophy: Syllabus of Course 5, Philosophical

Department," in *The Early Works, 1882–1898*, 3:211; John Dewey, "The Significance of the Problem of Knowledge," *The Early Works, 1882–1898,* vol. 5, *1895–1898* (Carbondale: Southern Illinois Univ. Press, 1972), p. 14.

33. Dewey, "Introduction to Philosophy," p. 229; Dewey, "Significance of the Problem of Knowledge," pp. 21–22; see also, Kuklick, *Churchmen and Philosophers,* pp. 240, 246–47.

34. Charles Sanders Peirce, "The Marriage of Religion and Science," in *The Collected Papers of Charles Sanders Peirce,* ed. Charles Hartshorne and Paul Weiss (Cambridge: Harvard Univ. Press, 1935), 6.428. (Citations to the *Collected Papers* will follow the usual convention of volume number followed by paragraph number.)

35. Charles Sanders Pierce, "Lessons from the History of Science," in *Collected Papers,* 1.44, 99. See also, Francis E. Reilly, *Charles Peirce's Theory of Scientific Method* (New York: Fordham Univ. Press, 1970), pp. 9–14.

36. Charles Sanders Peirce, "The Backward State of Metaphysics," in *Collected Papers,* 6.3.

37. Peirce, "Lessons from the History of Science," 1.109, 120–21. See also, Reilly, *Charles Peirce's Theory of Scientific Method,* pp. 25–38.

38. Peirce's formulations, like those of James, prefigure some of the ideas of Thomas Kuhn. Kuhn, *Structure of Scientific Revolutions,* pp. 170–71, 206–7.

39. Peirce, "Backward State of Metaphysics," 6.2; Charles Sanders Peirce, "Vitally Important Topics," in *Collected Papers,* 1.620.

40. Peirce, "Vitally Important Topics," 1.645; Charles Sanders Peirce, "Preface," in *Collected Papers,* 1.7; Charles Sanders Peirce to William James, December 26, 1897, in Ralph Barton Perry, *The Thought and Character of William James* (Boston: Little, Brown and Company, 1935), 2:419.

41. Charles Sanders Peirce, "Josiah Royce, *The World and the Individual,*" in *Collected Papers of Charles Sanders Peirce,* ed. Arthur W. Burks (Cambridge: Harvard Univ. Press, 1958), 8.109.

42. Ibid., 8.118.

43. Murray G. Murphey, *The Development of Peirce's Philosophy* (Cambridge: Harvard Univ. Press, 1961), p. 294. See also, Timothy Shanahan, "The First Moment of Scientific Inquiry: C. S. Peirce on the Logic of Abduction," *Transactions of the Charles S. Peirce Society* 22 (1986):462–65.

Chapter 5

1. Joseph Jastrow, "The Reconstruction of Psychology," *Psychological Review* 34 (1927):170.

2. R. Steven Turner, "Helmholtz, Sensory Physiology, and the Disciplinary Development of German Psychology," in *The Problematic Science: Psychology in Nineteenth-Century Thought,* ed. William R. Woodward and Mitchell G. Ash (New York: Praeger Publishers, 1982), pp. 148–50. See also, Mitchell G. Ash, "Reflections on Psychology in History," in *The Problematic Science,* pp. 361–62.

3. William James to Charles W. Eliot, December 2, 1875, in Ralph Barton Perry, *The Thought and Character of William James* (Boston: Little, Brown, and Company, 1935), 2:10–11; William James, "The Teaching of Philosophy in Our Colleges," in *Essays in Philosophy, The Works of William James* (Cambridge: Harvard Univ. Press, 1978), p. 6; Gerald E. Myers, *William James: His Life and Thought* (New Haven: Yale Univ. Press, 1986), pp. 485n.11, 486n.12; Howard M. Feinstein, *Becoming William*

James (Ithaca: Cornell Univ. Press, 1984), pp. 332–40; John M. O'Donnell, *The Origins of Behaviorism: American Psychology, 1870–1920* (New York: New York Univ. Press, 1985), p. 99.

4. Dorothy Ross, *G. Stanley Hall: The Psychologist as Prophet* (Chicago: Univ. of Chicago Press, 1972), pp. 59, 72–73; O'Donnell, *Origins of Behaviorism,* pp. 111–19(quotation on p. 117).

5. Lorraine J. Daston, "The Theory of the Will versus the Science of the Mind," in *The Problematic Science,* pp. 89–90; Ross, *G. Stanley Hall,* pp. 66–67, 72–73; O'Donnell, *Origins of Behaviorism,* pp. 7–9; David E. Leary, "Telling Likely Stories: The Rhetoric of the New Psychology, 1880–1920," *Journal of the History of the Behavioral Sciences* 23 (1987):316–20.

6. O'Donnell, *Origins of Behaviorism,* p. 7.

7. William James quoted in Perry, *Thought and Character of William James,* 2:28–31; Myers, *William James,* p. 9.

8. Neil Coughlan, *Young John Dewey: An Essay in American Intellectual History* (Chicago: Univ. of Chicago Press, 1975), pp. 39, 48.

9. John Dewey, "The New Psychology," in *The Early Works, 1882–1898,* vol. 1, *1882–1888* (Carbondale: Southern Illinois Univ. Press, 1969), pp. 52–53, 55.

10. Ibid., pp. 56–58, 60.

11. Ibid., p. 60.

12. John Dewey, "The Psychological Standpoint," in *The Early Works, 1882–1898,* 1:123; John Dewey, "Psychology as Philosophic Method," in *The Early Works, 1882–1898,* 1:144, 158–59.

13. George Dykhuizen, *The Life and Mind of John Dewey* (Carbondale: Southern Illinois Univ. Press, 1973), p. 54; Herbert W. Schneider, "Introduction to Dewey's *Psychology,*" in John Dewey, *Psychology, The Early Works, 1882–1898,* vol. 2, *1887* (Carbondale: Southern Illinois Univ. Press, 1967), pp. vii–viii.

14. Dewey, *Psychology,* pp. 3–4.

15. Ibid., pp. 7–10.

16. Ibid., pp. 11–16.

17. Ibid., pp. 16, 41–42.

18. Ibid., pp. 212, 215, 295–96, 299, 357, 362.

19. Morris quoted in Dykhuizen, *Life and Mind of John Dewey,* pp. 54–55; G. Stanley Hall, "Review of John Dewey, *Psychology,*" *American Journal of Psychology* 1 (1887):158; William James quoted in Perry, *Thought and Character of William James,* 2:516.

20. William James, *The Principles of Psychology, The Works of William James* (Cambridge: Harvard Univ. Press, 1981), 1:5. On the writing of *The Principles,* see Perry, *Thought and Character of William James,* 2:34–50; and "The Text of *The Principles of Psychology:* I. The History," in James, *The Principles of Psychology,* 3:1532–64.

21. William James to Henry Holt, May 9, 1890, in William James, *The Letters of William James,* ed. Henry James (Boston: Atlantic Monthly Press, 1920), 1:293–94; William James to Alice H. G. James, May 24, 1890, in *Letters of William James,* 1:295; William James to Henry James, June 4, 1890, in *Letters of William James,* 1:296.

22. William James to Henry Holt, November 22, 1878, in Perry, *Thought and Character of William James,* 2:35; James, *Principles of Psychology,* 1:6–7.

23. James, *Principles of Psychology,* 1:15–21.

24. Ibid., 1:27, 110, 126.

25. Thomas H. Huxley quoted in ibid., 1:135.

26. Ibid., 1:140–41. See also, William James, "Are We Automata?" in *Essays in Psychology, The Works of William James* (Cambridge: Harvard Univ. Press, 1983) pp. 38–61.

27. James, *Principles of Psychology*, 1:181–82.

28. Mark R. Shwehn, "Making the World: William James and the Life of the Mind," *Harvard Library Bulletin* 30 (1982):426–27, 454. For a similar argument, see Daniel W. Bjork, *William James: The Center of His Vision* (New York: Columbia Univ. Press, 1988), pp. 148–49, 167–68, 173.

29. James, *Principles of Psychology*, 1:185, 191. David Leary has drawn attention to the role of rhetoric in establishing the new psychology in "Telling Likely Stories," pp. 320–22.

30. James, *Principles of Psychology*, 1:191–92.

31. Ibid., p. 193.

32. Daniel W. Bjork discusses James's relations with his psychological contemporaries and their attitudes towards James's view of the science, in *The Compromised Scientist: William James in the Development of American Psychology* (New York: Columbia Univ. Press, 1983), pp. 9–13, 163–74, and passim.

33. William James to Hugo Münsterberg, quoted in *Letters of William James*, 1:301; William James to Theodore Flournoy, September 19, 1892, in *Letters of William James*, 1:325; Bjork makes a similar point in *William James*, p. 173.

34. G. Stanley Hall, "Review of William James, *The Principles of Psychology*," *American Journal of Psychology* 3(1891):589, 591; William Dean Howells quoted in Perry, *Thought and Character of William James*, 2:109–10.

35. [Charles S. Peirce], "James's Psychology," *Nation* 53(1891):15; George Trumbull Ladd, "Psychology as So-Called 'Natural Science'," *Philosophical Review* 1(1892):24, 38. On the reception of *The Principles*, see Perry, *Thought and Character of William James*, 2:91–111, and Gerald E. Myers, "Introduction: The Intellectual Context," in James, *Principles of Psychology*, 1:xxxvi–xxxviii.

36. Ladd, "Psychology as So-Called 'Natural Science'," pp. 50–52.

37. William James, "A Plea for Psychology as a 'Natural Science'," in *Essays in Psychology*, pp. 270–71, 275–77. See also, William James to Henry Holt, May 9, 1890, and William James to Henry James, June 4, 1890, both in *Letters of William James*, 1:293–94, 296.

38. Jastrow, "Reconstruction," p. 170.

Chapter 6

1. Joseph Jastrow, "The Reconstruction of Psychology," *Psychological Review* 34(1927):170.

2. John M. O'Donnell, *The Origins of Behaviorism: American Psychology, 1870–1920* (New York: New York Univ. Press, 1985), p. 9. See also, Thomas M. Camfield, "The Professionalization of American Psychology, 1870–1917," *Journal of the History of the Behavioral Sciences* 9(1973):66; and David E. Leary, "Telling Likely Stories: The Rhetoric of the New Psychology, 1870–1920," *Journal of the History of the Behavioral Sciences* 23(1987):320, 322, 325.

3. R. Steven Turner, "Helmholtz, Sensory Physiology, and the Disciplinary Devel-

opment of German Psychology," in *The Problematic Science: Psychology in Nineteenth-Century Thought,* ed. William R. Woodward and Mitchell G. Ash (New York: Praeger Publishers, 1982), p. 150; Mitchell G. Ash, "Reflections on Psychology in History," in *The Problematic Science,* pp. 361–62; O'Donnell, *Origins of Behaviorism,* pp. 25–51.

4. On the dispute between James and Hall, see Ralph Barton Perry, *The Thought and Character of William James* (Boston: Little, Brown, and Company, 1935), 2:3–24; and Gerald E. Myers, *William James: His Life and Thought* (New Haven: Yale Univ. Press, 1986), pp. 6, 486n.12. On the establishment of psychological laboratories generally, see Camfield, "Professionalization of American Psychology," pp. 67–68.

5. O'Donnell, *Origins of Behaviorism,* pp. 7–8.

6. Camfield, "Professionalization of American Psychology," p. 67; O'Donnell, *Origin of Behaviorism,* p. 144.

7. O'Donnell, *Origins of Behaviorism,* pp. 154–58.

8. Daniel W. Bjork, *The Compromised Scientist: William James in the Development of American Psychology* (New York: Columbia Univ. Press, 1983); O'Donnell, *Origins of Behaviorism,* p. 131; Camfield, "Professionalization of American Psychology," pp. 66–68; Leary, "Telling Likely Stories," pp. 316, 325–26.

9. H. N. Gardiner, "The First Twenty-Five Years of the American Philosophical Association," *Philosophical Review* 35(1926):147.

10. William James to Hugo Münsterberg, February 21, 1892, in Perry, *Thought and Character of William James,* 2: 139. See also, Bruce Kuklick, *The Rise of American Philosophy: Cambridge, Massachusetts, 1860–1930* (New Haven: Yale Univ. Press, 1977), pp. 186–87.

11. James quoted in Perry, *Thought and Character of William James,* 2:115; William James to George Holmes Howison, April 2, 1894, in ibid., 2:116.

12. William James to Theodore Flournoy, September 19, 1892, in *The Letters of William James,* ed. Henry James (Boston: Atlantic Monthly Press, 1920), 1:325. See also, James to Howison, April 2, 1894, in *Thought and Character of William James,* 2:116–17.

13. [Jacob Gould Schurman], "Prefatory Note," *Philosophical Review* 1 (1892):1, 4–7.

14. J. Mark Baldwin, "Psychology, Past and Present," *Psychological Review* 1(1894):372–74, 389.

15. George Trumbull Ladd, "President's Address Before the New York Meeting of the American Psychological Association," *Psychological Review* 1 (1894):15, 17–18.

16. J. McKeen Cattell, "Address of the President Before the American Psychological Association, 1895," *Psychological Review* 3(1896):148.

17. A. C. Armstrong, Jr., "Philosophy in the United States," *Educational Review* 11(1895):9–10; A. C. Armstrong, Jr., "Philosophy in American Colleges," *Educational Review* 13(1897):14–16, 22.

18. John Dewey, "'Consciousness' and Experience, [Psychology and Philosophic Method]," *The Middle Works, 1899–1924,* vol. 1, *1899–1901* (Carbondale: Southern Illinois Univ. Press, 1976), pp. 115–16.

19. Ibid., pp. 125–26, 128.

20. Ibid., p. 129. See also, John Dewey, "Psychology and Social Practice," *The Middle Works, 1899–1924,* 1:150.

21. Camfield, "Professionalization of American Psychology," pp. 67–68.

22. Gardiner, "First Twenty-Five Years," pp. 145–47.

23. Ibid., pp. 149, 154. See also, Laurence Veysey, "The Plural Organized Worlds of the Humanities," in *The Organization of Knowledge in Modern America, 1860–1920*, ed. Alexandra Oleson and John Voss (Baltimore: Johns Hopkins Univ. Press, 1979), pp. 79–80; and Daniel J. Wilson, "Professionalization and Organized Discussion in the American Philosophical Association, 1900–1922," *Journal of the History of Philosophy* 17(1979):53–69.

24. J. E. Creighton, "The Purposes of a Philosophical Association," *Philosophical Review* 11(1902):220, 226–27.

25. Ibid., pp. 230, 232–34.

26. Ibid., pp. 235–37.

27. Camfield, "Professionalization of American Psychology," pp. 70–71, 73. See also, Leary, "Telling Likely Stories," pp. 325–26.

28. "Notes and News," *Journal of Philosophy, Psychology, and Scientific Methods* 1(1904):27.

29. Edward F. Buchner, "A Quarter Century of Psychology in America: 1878–1903," *American Journal of Psychology* 14(1903):405, 410–11.

30. Frank Thilly, "Psychology, Natural Science, and Philosophy," *Philosophical Review* 15(1906):130.

31. Ibid., p. 131.

32. Ibid., pp. 132–33, 138–39, 141. For a similar view, see J. MacBride Sterrett, "The Proper Affiliation of Psychology—with Philosophy or with the Natural Sciences?" *Psychological Review* 16(1909):86–90, 106.

33. Robert M. Yerkes, "Psychology in its Relations to Biology," *Journal of Philosophy, Psychology, and Scientific Methods* 7(1910):113–16.

34. Ibid., pp. 117–20.

35. Ibid., pp. 120–21.

36. On Yerkes's career, see O'Donnell, *Origins of Behaviorism*, pp. 191–200.

37. Christian A. Ruckmich, "The History and Status of Psychology in the United States," *American Journal of Psychology* 23 (1912):522–24.

38. O'Donnell, *Origins of Behaviorism*, pp. 203, 208, 240–43. Certain types of psychology and philosophy have continued to share affinities, though the relationship is often more complex than it first appears. See, for example, Laurence D. Smith, *Behaviorism and Logical Positivism: A Reassessment of the Alliance* (Stanford: Stanford Univ. Press, 1986).

39. J. E. Creighton, "The Standpoint of Psychology," *Philosophical Review* 23(1914):174–75; George H. Sabine, "Philosophical and Scientific Specialization," *Philosophical Review* 26(1917):24, 18.

40. John Dewey, "Psychological Doctrine and Philosophical Teaching," *The Middle Works, 1899–1924*, vol. 7, *1912–1914* (Carbondale: Southern Illinois Univ. Press, 1979), pp. 47–50.

41. Ibid., pp. 50, 52–54.

42. Ibid., p. 55.

Chapter 7

Portions of this chapter are taken from "Professionalization and Organized Discussion in the American Philosophical Association, 1900–1922," *Journal of the*

History of Philosophy 17(1979):53–69, and from "Science and the Crisis of Confidence in American Philosophy, 1870–1930," *Transactions of the Charles S. Peirce Society* 23 (1987):235–62.

1. Richard Hofstadter, *The Progressive Historians: Turner, Beard, Parrington* (New York: Random House, Vintage Books, 1970), p. 37; David A. Hollinger, "Inquiry and Uplift: Late Nineteenth-Century Academics and the Moral Efficacy of Scientific Practice," in *The Authority of Experts: Studies in History and Theory,* ed. Thomas L. Haskell (Bloomington: Indiana Univ. Press, 1984), pp. 144–45.

2. Charles W. Eliot, "Address of President C. W. Eliot," *Popular Science Monthly* 12(1878):473; Edmund J. James, "The Function of the State University," *Science,* n.s., 22(1905):615.

3. R. S. Woodward, "The Progress of Science," *Science,* n.s., 14(1901):311–12; R. S. Woodward, "Academic Ideals," *Science,* n.s., 21 (1905):45; Charles S. Minot, "The Problem of Consciousness in its Biological Aspects," *Science,* n.s., 16(1902):8–9; Ira Remsen, "Scientific Investigation and Progress," *Science,* n.s., 19(1904):9; Laurence R. Veysey, *The Emergence of the American University* (Chicago: Univ. of Chicago Press, 1965; Phoenix Books, 1970), p. 174. See also, Roger L. Geiger, *To Advance Knowledge: The Growth of American Research Universities, 1900–1940* (New York: Oxford Univ. Press, 1986), p. 9.

4. Thomas L. Haskell, *The Emergence of Professional Social Science: The American Social Science Association and the Nineteenth-Century Crisis of Authority* (Urbana: Univ. of Illinois Press, 1977), p. 65. See also, Magali Sarfatti Larson, "The Production of Expertise and the Constitution of Expert Power," in *The Authority of Experts,* pp. 51, 56; Thomas Bender, "The Erosion of Public Culture: Cities, Discourses, and Professional Disciplines," in *The Authority of Experts,* pp. 97–98, 101; and, Geiger, *To Advance Knowledge,* pp. 20–30.

5. Bruce Kuklick, *The Rise of American Philosophy: Cambridge, Massachusetts, 1860–1930* (New Haven: Yale Univ. Press, 1977), p. xxii; Haskell, *Emergence of Professional Social Science,* p. 73. See also, Laurence R. Veysey, "The Plural Organized Worlds of the Humanities," and Dorothy Ross, "The Development of the Social Sciences," both in *The Organization of Knowledge in Modern America, 1860–1920,* ed. Alexandra Oleson and John Voss (Baltimore: Johns Hopkins Univ. Press, 1979), pp. 51–106, 107–38.

6. H. N. Gardiner, "The First Twenty-Five Years of the American Philosophical Association," *Philosophical Review* 35 (1926):145–58; Mary O. Furner, *Advocacy and Objectivity: A Crisis in the Professionalization of American Social Science* (Lexington: Univ. Press of Kentucky, 1975), pp. 4–6, 278–79; Gladys Bryson, "The Emergence of the Social Sciences from Moral Philosophy," *International Journal of Ethics* 42(1931–32):304–23; Geiger, *To Advance Knowledge,* pp. 20–21, 27.

7. On the important role of a journal for academic professional organizations, see Geiger, *To Advance Knowledge,* pp. 22–24. The formation of the national board of the American Philosophical Association is described in Maurice Mandelbaum, "The Reorganization of the American Philosophical Association (c. 1965–1970)" (paper prepared for the American Philosophical Association, April 1977).

8. Charles S. Peirce to William James, March 9, 1909, in Ralph Barton Perry, *The Thought and Character of William James* (Boston: Little, Brown, and Company, 1935), 2:438.

9. Charles Sanders Peirce, "Why Study Logic?" in *The Collected Papers of Charles*

Sanders Peirce, ed. Charles Hartshorne and Paul Weiss (Cambridge: Harvard Univ. Press, 1932), 2.162; Charles Sanders Peirce, "Josiah Royce, *The World and the Individual,*" in *Collected Papers of Charles Sanders Peirce,* ed. Arthur W. Burks (Cambridge: Harvard Univ. Press, 1958), 8.118.

10. Charles Sanders Peirce, "Karl Pearson, *The Grammer of Science,*" *Collected Papers,* 8.136.

11. Charles Sanders Peirce, "Scientific Method," in *Collected Papers,* 7.50, 7.54.

12. Ibid., 7.51, 7.87.

13. Charles Sanders Peirce, "What Pragmatism Is," in *Collected Papers,* 5.413.

14. Charles Sanders Peirce, "Preface," in *Collected Papers,* 5.13. See also, Charles Sanders Peirce, "The Ethics of Terminology," in *Collected Papers,* 2.223.

15. Peirce, "What Pragmatism Is," 5.143. See also, Charles Sanders Peirce, "J. M. Baldwin, *Dictionary of Philosophy and Psychology,* Vol. 2," in *Collected Papers,* 8.169; and Charles S. Peirce to William James, October 3, 1904, in Perry, *Thought and Character of William James,* 2:432. David Leary has emphasized the way in which a new technical rhetoric helped give rise to the new psychology at the turn of the century, in "Telling Likely Stories: The Rhetoric of the New Psychology, 1870–1920," *Journal of the History of the Behavioral Sciences* 23(1987):315–31.

16. Peirce, "What Pragmatism Is," 5.414.

17. Charles Sanders Peirce, "Laboratory and Seminary Philosophies," in *Collected Papers,* 1.127.

18. John Dewey, *The Educational Situation,* in *The Middle Works, 1899–1924,* vol. 1, *1899–1901* (Carbondale: Southern Illinois Univ. Press, 1976), pp. 303–5, 310.

19. John Dewey, "Logical Conditions of a Scientific Treatment of Morality," in *The Middle Works, 1899–1924,* vol. 3, *1903–1906* (Carbondale: Southern Illinois Univ. Press, 1977), p. 3; John Dewey, "Science as Subject-Matter and as Method," in *The Middle Works, 1899–1924,* vol. 6, *1910–1911* (Carbondale: Southern Illinois Univ. Press, 1978), pp. 125, 127.

20. Dewey, "Logical Conditions of a Scientific Treatment of Morality," pp. 19, 38–39. See also, Darrell Ruckes, "Introduction" to John Dewey, *The Middle Works,* 3:xiii.

21. John Dewey, "The Evolutionary Method as Applied to Morality," in *The Middle Works, 1899–1924,* vol. 2, *1902–1903* (Carbondale: Southern Illinois Univ. Press, 1976), p. 19; John Dewey, "Philosophy and American National Life," in *The Middle Works,* 3:77.

22. F. J. E. Woodbridge, "The Problem of Metaphysics," *Philosophical Review* 12(1903):370–71.

23. William James, *The Varieties of Religious Experience, The Works of William James* (Cambridge: Harvard Univ. Press, 1985), pp. 104–5; William James, *Pragmatism, The Works of William James* (Cambridge: Harvard Univ. Press, 1975), p. 93. Daniel W. Bjork expands on these themes in *William James: The Center of His Vision* (New York: Columbia Univ. Press, 1988).

24. J. E. Creighton, "The Purposes of a Philosophical Association," *Philosophical Review* 11(1902):224, 237.

25. Charles S. Peirce, "Lecture I: Early Nominalism and Realism," in *Writings of Charles S. Peirce: A Chronological Edition,* vol. 2, *1867–1871,* ed. Edward C. Moore (Bloomington: Indiana Univ. Press, 1984), p. 313; Charles S. Peirce, "Some Consequences of Four Incapacities," in *Writings,* 2:212.

26. D. S. Miller, "The Conditions of Greatest Progress in American Philosophy," *Journal of Philosophy* 3(1906):72; Christine Ladd-Franklin, "Epistemology for the Logician," in *Bericht über den III Internationalen Kongres für Philosophie zu Heidelberg* (Heidelberg: Carl Winter's Universitätsbuchhandlung, 1909):665–66. See also, Karl Schmidt, "Concerning a Philosophical Platform," *Journal of Philosophy* 6(1909):679.

27. For a fuller treatment of these organized discussions, see Daniel J. Wilson, "Professionalization and Organized Discussion in the American Philosophical Association," pp. 57–58, 60–65.

28. William James to H. N. Gardiner, November 14, 1901, in *The Letters of William James,* ed. Henry James (Boston: Atlantic Monthly Press, 1920), 2:164; Perry, *Thought and Characters of William James,* 2:700; William James to Theodore Flournoy, August 9, 1908, in *Letters of William James,* 2:311.

29. George R. Dodson, "The Function of Philosophy as an Academic Discipline," *Journal of Philosophy* 5(1908):454; J. E. Creighton, "The Idea of a Philosophical Platform," *Journal of Philosophy* 6(1909):141–43. See also, Norman Kemp Smith, "How Far is Agreement Possible in Philosophy?" *Journal of Philosophy* 9(1912):701–11.

30. Morris R. Cohen, "The Conception of Philosophy in Recent Discussion," *Journal of Philosophy* 7(1910):402–3.

31. Ibid., pp. 401–2, 404–6.

32. Ibid., pp. 405–7, 409–10.

33. Josiah Royce, "On Definitions and Debates," *Journal of Philosophy* 9(1912):85, 99.

34. Harry T. Costello, *Josiah Royce's Seminar, 1913–1914: As Recorded in the Notebooks of Harry T. Costello,* ed. Grover Smith (New Brunswick, NJ: Rutgers Univ. Press, 1963), pp. 1–3.

35. Ibid., pp. 8–10, 13, 21–35, 39–44, 51–56, 87–91, 149–59.

36. On the writing of *The Problem of Christianity* and its place in Royce's thought, see John Clendenning, *The Life and Thought of Josiah Royce* (Madison: Univ. of Wisconsin Press, 1985), pp. 361–62, 366–75; and Kuklick, *Rise of American Philosophy,* pp. 385–400.

37. Josiah Royce, *The Problem of Christianity,* 2 vols. (New York: Macmillan, 1913), 2:59–61, 67–69, 82–85, 88.

38. Ibid., pp. 115–16, 140, 142, 148–50.

39. Ibid., pp. 211–17.

40. Ibid., pp. 227–32.

41. Ibid., pp. 249–52.

42. Ibid., pp. 254–57. Clendenning recounts an episode which may account for some of Royce's disillusionment with the community of philosophers and with their lack of charity toward one another's interpretations. In 1912 Royce had engaged in a public controversy with Arthur O. Lovejoy, regarding comments Lovejoy had made about idealists in a review of Ralph Barton Perry's *Present Philosophical Tendencies.* Clendenning, *Life and Thought of Josiah Royce,* pp. 364–66.

43. Royce, *Problem of Christianity,* 2:260–73.

44. Ibid., pp. 284–86.

45. The Committee on Discussion, "The American Philosophical Association," *Journal of Philosophy* 9(1912):615–16. Members of this committee were A. O. Love-

joy, D. S. Miller, W. P. Montague, E. G. Spaulding, Frank Thilly, and F. J. E. Woodbridge.

46. James B. Pratt, "The Twelfth Annual Meeting of the American Philosophical Association," *Journal of Philosophy* 10(1913):91–92.

47. Kemp Smith, "How Far is Agreement Possible in Philosophy?" pp. 701–5; Karl Schmidt, "Agreement," *Journal of Philosophy* 9(1912):715–17; Pratt, "Twelfth Annual Meeting," pp. 92–93.

48. Pratt, "Twelfth Annual Meeting," pp. 93–94.

49. H. C. Brown, "The Thirteenth Annual Meeting of the American Philosophical Association," *Journal of Philosophy* 11(1914):57–58; A. O. Lovejoy and E. G. Spaulding, "Topic for Discussion at the 1916 Meeting of the American Philosophical Association," *Journal of Philosophy* 13(1916):573–81; Albert G. A. Balz, "The Sixteenth Annual Meeting of the American Philosophical Association," *Journal of Philosophy* 14(1917):201–2, 214–16.

50. Arthur O. Lovejoy, "On Some Conditions of Progress in Philosophical Inquiry," *Philosophical Review* 26(1917):126–30.

51. Ibid., pp. 132–33, 144.

52. Ibid., pp. 144, 148–50, 154–63.

53. Ernest Albee, Charles Bakewell, and others, "Progress in Philosophical Inquiry and Mr. Lovejoy's Presidential Address," *Philosophical Review* 26(1917):315–16, 320–21, 329–31.

54. Arthur O. Lovejoy, "Progress in Philosophical Inquiry," *Philosophical Review* 26(1917):538, 543–44.

55. John Dewey, "The Problem of Truth," in *The Middle Works*, 6:28–31.

56. Ibid., pp. 51–52, 57.

57. John Dewey, "The Need for a Recovery of Philosophy," in *The Middle Works, 1899–1924,* vol. 10, *1916–1917* (Carbondale: Southern Illinois Univ. Press, 1980), p. 46.

58. John Dewey, *Democracy and Education,* in *The Middle Works, 1899–1924,* vol. 9, *1916* (Carbondale: Southern Illinois Univ. Press, 1980), pp. 227, 231, 233, 236.

59. Ibid., pp. 333–34.

60. Ibid., pp. 334–35.

61. Ibid., p. 336.

62. Ibid., p. 339.

Chapter 8

1. Carol S. Gruber, *Mars and Minerva: World War I and the Uses of the Higher Learning in America* (Baton Rouge: Louisiana State Univ. Press, 1975), pp. 46, 52, 70–71, 79–80; Bruce Kuklick, *The Rise of American Philosophy: Cambridge, Massachusetts, 1860–1930* (New Haven: Yale Univ. Press, 1977), pp. 435–47.

2. Daniel J. Wilson, *Arthur O. Lovejoy and the Quest for Intelligibility* (Chapel Hill: Univ. of North Carolina Press, 1980), pp. 122–23.

3. Kuklick, *Rise of American Philosophy,* pp. 439–43; Josiah Royce to E. B. Poulton, July 6, 1915, in *The Letters of Josiah Royce,* ed. John Clendenning (Chicago: Univ. of Chicago Press, 1970), p. 632; Gruber, *Mars and Minerva,* pp. 62–65; John Clendenning, *The Life and Thought of Josiah Royce* (Madison: Univ. of Wisconsin Press, 1985), pp. 389–90.

4. John Dewey, "In a Time of National Hesitation," in *The Middle Works, 1899–1924,* vol. 10, *1916–1917* (Carbondale: Southern Illinois Univ. Press, 1980), pp. 257, 259; George Dykhuizen, *The Life and Mind of John Dewey* (Carbondale: Southern Illinois Univ. Press, 1973), pp. 153–59.

5. Gruber, *Mars and Minerva,* p. 95. See also, David O. Levine, *The American College and the Culture of Aspiration, 1915–1940* (Ithaca: Cornell Univ. Press, 1986), pp. 23–32.

6. Wilson, *Arthur O. Lovejoy,* pp. 124–28; Kuklick, *Rise of American Philosophy,* pp. 443–44; Dykhuizen, *Life and Mind of John Dewey,* p. 159.

7. Kuklick, *Rise of American Philosophy,* p. 476.

8. Clarence Irving Lewis, "German Idealism and its War Critics," in *Collected Papers of Clarence Irving Lewis,* ed. John D. Goheen and John L. Mothershead, Jr. (Stanford: Stanford Univ. Press, 1970), p. 65.

9. C. I. Lewis, "Autobiography," in *The Philosophy of C. I. Lewis,* ed. Paul Arthur Schilpp, Library of Living Philosophers, vol. 13 (LaSalle, Ill.: Open Court, 1968), p. 17; Kuklick, *Rise of American Philosophy,* pp. 560–62.

10. Wilson, *Arthur O. Lovejoy,* pp. 103–13, 139. For Lovejoy's writings in philosophy and the history of ideas in this period, see Daniel J. Wilson, *Arthur O. Lovejoy: An Annotated Bibliography* (New York: Garland Publishing, 1982), pp. 48–59.

11. Herbert W. Schneider, "The Twenty-Fourth Annual Meeting of the Eastern Division of the American Philosophical Association," *Journal of Philosophy* 22(1925):43–44.

12. Ibid., p. 44.

13. John Dewey, *Reconstruction in Philosophy,* in *The Middle Works, 1899–1924,* vol. 12, *1920* (Carbondale: Southern Illinois Univ. Press, 1982), p. 94.

14. Ibid., pp. 110, 114, 123.

15. Ibid., p. 103.

16. Ibid., pp. 133–35.

17. Ibid., pp. 149–51.

18. Ibid., pp. 151–52.

19. J. E. Creighton, "Philosophy as the Art of Affixing Labels," *Journal of Philosophy* 17(1920):226–27; J. E. Creighton, "The Form of Philosophical Intelligibility," *Journal of Philosophy* 19(1922):255.

20. Creighton, "Philosophy as the Art," p. 233; Creighton, "Form of Philosophical Intelligibility," pp. 258, 260–61. See also, J. E. Creighton, "The Form of Philosophical Objectivity," *Philosophical Review* 32(1923):262.

21. Harold C. Brown, "The Problem of Philosophy," *Journal of Philosophy* 17(1920):285.

22. Ibid., pp. 285–89, 299.

23. William A. Brown, "The Future of Philosophy as a University Study," *Journal of Philosophy* 18(1921):673, 677–80.

24. George A. Wilson, "Philosophy Over Against Science," *Philosophical Review,* 31(1922):257–58.

25. Ibid., pp. 258, 264–65.

26. Ibid., pp. 266–67.

27. Will Durant, "The Failure of Philosophy," *Harpers* 154(1926–27):80–81, 85–86.

28. Paul A. Schilpp, "American Neglect of a Philosophy of Culture," *Philosophical Review* 35(1926):434–38.

29. Morris R. Cohen, *Reason and Nature: An Essay on the Meaning of Scientific Method* (New York: Harcourt, Brace and Company, 1931), p. viii. On Cohen's view of specialized philosophy, see David A. Hollinger, *Morris R. Cohen and the Scientific Ideal* (Cambridge: MIT Press, 1975), pp. 51, 82.

30. Cohen, *Reason and Nature,* p. ix.

31. Ibid., pp. x, xiii.

32. Ibid., pp. 39–40, 79, 83, 87.

33. Ibid., pp. 147–48.

34. Ibid., pp. 149–50.

35. Clarence Irving Lewis, *Mind and the World Order: Outline of a Theory of Knowledge* (New York: Dover Publications, 1956), pp. 2–5.

36. Ibid., pp. 6–8.

37. Ibid., pp. 10–14.

38. Ibid., pp. 16–17.

39. Ibid., p. 21.

40. Ibid., pp. 37–38, 65–66.

41. Ibid., pp. 70–71.

42. Ibid., pp. 71–73, 75–76.

43. Ibid., pp. 78–79.

44. Ibid., pp. 80–81.

45. Ibid., p. 89.

46. Ibid., pp. 90–95.

47. Ibid., pp. 110–15.

48. Ibid., pp. 230–31.

49. Ibid., pp. 238–39.

50. Ibid., pp. 267–72. For a recent discussion of the issues involved in the question of a Copernican Revolution, see I. Bernard Cohen, *Revolution in Science* (Cambridge: Harvard Univ. Press, Belknap Press, 1985), pp. 105–25.

51. Lewis, *Mind and the World Order,* pp. 280–83.

52. Ibid., pp. 311, 334, 340.

53. Ibid., p. 343.

54. Ibid., pp. 346, 349, 352–53.

55. Ibid., p. 391.

56. John Dewey, *Experience and Nature,* in *The Later Works, 1925–1953,* vol. 1, *1925* (Carbondale: Southern Illinois Univ. Press, 1981), pp. 17, 34, 63, 123–24; John Dewey, *The Quest for Certainty,* in *The Later Works, 1925–1953,* vol. 4, *1929* (Carbondale: Southern Illinois Univ. Press, 1984), pp. 86, 249.

57. Dewey, *Quest for Certainty,* pp. 176–77, 22–23, 38.

58. Dewey, *Experience and Nature,* pp. 122–24.

59. Dewey, *Quest for Certainty,* pp. 69–70, 103.

60. Dewey, *Experience and Nature,* pp. 34, 37–38.

61. Dewey, *Quest for Certainty,* p. 248; Dewey, *Experience and Nature,* p. 306.

62. Dewey, *Quest for Certainty,* pp. 248–50.

63. Bruce Kuklick, *Churchmen and Philosophers: From Jonathan Edwards to John Dewey* (New Haven: Yale Univ. Press, 1985), pp. 119, 195, 197–98.

Chapter 9

1. William Pepperell Montague, "Confessions of an Animistic Materialist," in *Contemporary American Philosophy: Personal Statements,* ed. George P. Adams and William Pepperell Montague (New York: Macmillan Company, 1930), 2:143, 145; Evander Bradley McGilvary, "A Tentative Realistic Metaphysics," in *Contemporary American Philosophy,* 2:109–10, 132; John Elof Boodin, "Nature and Reason," in *Contemporary American Philosophy,* 1:142.

2. C. J. Ducasse, "Philosophical Liberalism," in *Contemporary American Philosophy,* 1:306–7, 309–10; George P. Adams, "Naturalism or Idealism," in *Contemporary American Philosophy,* 1:65–68.

3. Wilbur M. Urban, "Metaphysics and Value," in *Contemporary American Philosophy,* 2:357–58; Hartley Burr Alexander, "The Great Art Which is Philosophy," in *Contemporary American Philosophy,* 1:89–90, 93–94, 97–98.

4. Laurence D. Smith, *Behaviorism and Logical Positivism: A Reassessment of the Alliance* (Stanford: Stanford Univ. Press, 1986), p. 27; *Encyclopedia of Philosophy,* s.v. "Logical Positivism."

5. Hans Reichenbach, "Logistic Empiricism in Germany and the Present State of its Problems," *Journal of Philosophy* 33(1936):142; Ernest Nagel, "Impressions and Appraisals of Analytic Philosophy in Europe," *Journal of Philosophy* 33(1936):6, 9.

6. Richard J. Bernstein, *Praxis and Action: Contemporary Philosophies of Human Activity* (Philadelphia: Univ. of Pennsylvania Press, 1971), p. 250.

7. Richard Rorty, *Consequences of Pragmatism (Essays: 1972–1980)* (Minneapolis: Univ. of Minnesota Press, 1982), pp. xvii–xviii. For similar assessments of the dominance of analytic philosophy, see Richard Rorty, "Professionalized Philosophy and Transcendentalist Culture," in *Consequences of Pragmatism,* pp. 61–64; Richard Rorty, "Philosophy in America Today," in *Consequences of Pragmatism,* pp. 214–16; John E. Smith, "The New Need for a Recovery of Philosophy," *Proceedings and Addresses of the American Philosophical Association* 56(1982):7; John J. McDermott, "Appendix: The Renascence of Classical American Philosophy," in *Streams of Experience: Reflections on the History and Philosophy of American Culture* (Amherst: Univ. of Massachusetts Press, 1986), pp. 226–27. Not all observers agree that analytic philosophy has dominated American philosophy. Edward Pitts argues that philosophy in the 1970s was "more eclectic and diversified than ever before in its history." Edward L. Pitts, "The Profession of Philosophy in America" (Ph.D. diss., Pennsylvania State University, 1979), p. 178.

8. James T. Kloppenberg, *Uncertain Victory: Social Democracy and Progressivism in European and American Thought, 1870–1920* (New York: Oxford Univ. Press, 1986), p. 11. On the "linguistic turn," see the volume edited by Richard Rorty, *The Linguistic Turn: Recent Essays in Philosophical Method* (Chicago: Univ. of Chicago Press, 1967). On the pragmatic turn, see Rorty, *Consequences of Pragmatism,* pp. xvii–xviii; Richard Rorty, "Solidarity or Objectivity?" in *Post-Analytic Philosophy,* ed. John Rajchman and Cornel West (New York: Columbia Univ. Press, 1985), p. 5; and Ralph W. Sleeper, "Recent Developments in American Philosophy," *Revue Française D'Etudes Americaines* 34(1987):505–6.

9. Bernstein, *Praxis and Action,* pp. 1, 9.

10. Ibid., pp. 175–76.

11. Ibid., pp. 189, 196–99.

12. Ibid., pp. 200–2, 226.

13. Ibid., pp. 218–19.

14. Ibid., pp. 298–99.

15. Ibid., pp. 313–14.

16. Richard J. Bernstein, *Beyond Objectivism and Relativism: Science, Hermeneutics, and Praxis* (Philadelphia: Univ. of Pennsylvania Press, 1985), pp. xiv–xv, 12, 71, 78, 128, 178.

17. Ibid., pp. 223, 229, 231.

18. Hilary Putnam, *Reason, Truth and History* (Cambridge: Cambridge Univ. Press, 1981), pp. ix–xi, 128. On Dewey's efforts to overcome the fact-value dichotomy, see James Gouinlock, *John Dewey's Philosophy of Value* (New York: Humanities Press, 1972), pp. 206–32.

19. Hilary Putam, *The Many Faces of Realism: The Paul Carus Lectures* (LaSalle, Ill.: Open Court, 1987), pp. 53–56. On the need for mutual respect in the development of a community of philosophy, see Julius Moravcsik, "Communal Ties," *Proceedings and Addresses of the American Philosophical Association* 62, supplement (1988):221–23. This is Moravcsik's Presidential Address to the Pacific Division of the American Philosophical Association.

20. Putnam, *The Many Faces of Realism*, p. 17.

21. Karl-Otto Apel, *Charles S. Peirce: From Pragmatism to Pragmaticism*, trans. John Michael Krois (Amherst: Univ. of Massachusetts Press, 1981), pp. vii–xi.

22. Karl-Otto Apel, "Scientism or Transcendental Hermeneutics? On the Question of the Subject of the Interpretation of Signs in the Semiotics of Pragmatism," in *Towards a Tranformation of Philosophy*, trans. Glyn Adey and David Frisby (London: Routledge and Kegan Paul, 1980), pp. 97–101.

23. Richard Rorty, *Philosophy and the Mirror of Nature* (Princeton: Princeton Univ. Press, 1979), pp. 380, 12.

24. Ibid., pp. 5–6.

25. Richard Rorty, "Pragmatism, Relativism, and Irrationalism," in *Consequences of Pragmatism*, pp. 160–62.

26. Ibid., pp. 162–65.

27. Ibid., p. 166.

28. R. W. Sleeper, "Rorty's Pragmatism: Afloat in Neurath's Boat, But Why Adrift?" *Transactions of the Charles S. Peirce Society* 21(1985):15, 18.

29. Richard Rorty, "Comments on Sleeper and Edel," *Transactions of the Charles S. Peirce Society* 21(1985):39–40, 44, 47.

30. Arthur O. Lovejoy, "The Thirteen Pragmatisms," *Journal of Philosophy* 5(1908):5–12, 29–39; Sleeper, "Rorty's Pragmatism," p. 11.

31. See, for example, the essays included in *Post-Analytic Philosophy*.

32. Boodin, "Nature and Reason," p. 150.

33. Rorty, *Philosophy and the Mirror*, p. 394.

Index